In 1991, while still at college, Kora Reddy began to trade the markets by trial and error. After obtaining his engineering degree, Kora worked with Fortune 500 companies in the field of telecommunication software. In late 1990s he turned his attention to using proprietary mathematical modelling and analysis for short term trading. In the early 2000s he was instrumental in developing automated trading strategies for a proprietary hedge fund based out of London.

Kora is currently co-founder of an early stage quantitative trading portal (http://stocksiq.in) for analysing and backtesting of listed stocks on the Indian stock market.

HIGH PROFIT TRADING PATTERNS

Kora Reddy

VISION BOOKS

www.visionbooksindia.com

Dedicated to

My Mother

www.visionbooksindia.com

Disclaimer

The author and the publisher disclaim all legal or other responsibilities for any losses which investors may suffer by investing or trading using the methods described in this book. Readers are advised to seek professional guidance before making any specific investments. This book is meant purely for the purpose of investor and trader education.

First Published 2012
Reprinted 2014, 2015, 2020, 2021, 2022, 2023

ISBN 10: 81-7094-832-0
ISBN 13: 978-81-7094-832-2

A Vision Books Original

Published by
Vision Books Pvt. Ltd.
(Incorporating Orient Paperbacks and CARING imprints)
24 Feroze Gandhi Road, Lajpat Nagar 3
New Delhi-110024, India.
Phone: (+91-11) 2984 0821 / 22
e-mail: visionbooks@gmail.com

Printed at
Saurabh Printers
67A-68, Ecotech 1, Extn 1, Kasna, Greater Noida
Uttar Pradesh, India.

Contents

Preface 11

Acknowledgements 15

A Word of Caution 17

Introduction 19

Section 1
Trading Basics

1. Day Trading **25**
- What is Day Trading? 25
- Why Day Trade? 26
- Why Day Traders Lose Money 28

2. Nifty Futures **29**
- Origins of Futures 29
- What is Margin? 30
- Who Trades Futures? 30
- Basics of Nifty Futures 31
- Why Trade Nifty Futures? 32

3. Chart Types **34**
- Line Chart 34
- Bar Chart 35
- Candlestick Chart 36
- Point and Figure Charts 38

4. Entries and Exits **40**
- Types of Entry Orders 40
- Selecting Suitable Entry Orders 41
- Strategies Used in Exit 42
- Selecting a Suitable Exit Strategy 43

5. Market Structure **44**
- Technical Indicators 45
- Taylor Trading 46
- Elliott Waves 47
- Gann Angles 47
- How Can We Effectively Trade the Market's Next Move? 49

6. Price Patterns **50**
- Short-term Price Patterns 51
- Why No Volume? 52

Section 2
Price Patterns on Nifty

7. Moves from Open and Close **55**
- Data Sample 55
- Open-to-Close Observations 57

8. Multiple Day Action from Open and Close **62**
- How to Read the Tables 62
- Close-to-Close Patterns 64
- Open-to-Close Patterns 67
- Application 69

9. Day of the Week **70**
- Application 76

10. New High and New Low **78**
- 20-Day High / Low Patterns 79
- Application 80

11. Gaps and Laps **81**
- Definitions 81
- Gap Patterns 84
- Application 90

12. Range Expansion and Contraction **91**
- Contraction / Expansion 91
- NR / WS Patterns 91
- NR Open-to-Close Pattern 94
- WS Open-to-Close Pattern 95
- Application 96

13. NR4, NR7 & WS4, WS7 Days **97**
- Definitions 98
- Close-to-Close Observations 99
- Open-to-Close Observations 104
- Application 109

14. Opening Range Breakout **110**
- Some Concepts 110
- High / Low ORB 111
- Stretch ORB 114
- Range ORB 116
- Pivot Point Based ORB 117
- Conclusion 119

15. Inside Day **121**
- Definitions 121
- ID Patterns 122
- ID and High / Low as Entry Reference 124
- Application 127

16. Doji **128**
- Definition 128
- Application 138

17. Pivot Points **139**
- Calculation of Pivot Points 139
- Pivot Point Distributions 140
- Application 141

18. Tri- and Penta-Section **142**
- Observing Tri-section 142
- Penta-Section 143
- Application 145

19. Hook Days **147**
- Definitions 147
- Hook Observations 147

Section 3

Money and Risk Management

20. Pyramids and Day Dreams **151**
- How Long Does it Take to Make ₹ 10 Crore? 152
- Are We Being Realistic? 154

21. The Risk of Ruin **155**
- Consecutive Losers 156
- Some Calculations 156
- Our Example 157
- Conclusion 157

22. Drawdown: A Trader's Best Friend **158**
- Drawdown 158
- 24 Wild Swings 159
- You Win a Few, You Lose Many 160

23. Performance Summary **162**
- Backtesting 162
- Some Other Considerations 164
- Theory into Reality 166

24. Trading Rules **170**
- Rule # 1: Trading is a Business 170
- Rule # 2: Have a Trading Plan 170
- Rule # 3: Be Patient 171
- Rule # 4: Remain Consistent 172
- Rule # 5: Let Winners Run, Not the Losers 172
- Rule # 6: Never Average Down and Never Lie about Your Losses 174
- Rule # 7: Follow the Pattern, Not the Price 175
- Rule # 8: Use Stop Loss 175
- Rule # 9: Don't Be Obsessed by Minute-by-Minute Market Movements 177

- Rule # 10: Avoid Over-Reliance on Market Gurus 177
- Rule # 11: Maintain a Trading Log 178
- Rule # 12: Don't Think "This Market Stuff" is Easy 179
- And the Rule # 13: Live by the Rules 179

Section 4

High Profit Trading Secrets

25. Minute and Mega Market Clock **183**

- Weekly 183
- Intraday Characteristics 185
- Monthly Characteristics 187
- Yearly 189

26. Greed is Good **190**

- Buy and Hold Strategy 191
- Compounding 192
- Perfect Prediction 193

27. Pivot Point Trading Secrets **196**

- Pattern 1: Manic Monday 199
- Pattern 2: Momentum-Aided Manic Monday 201
- Pattern 3: Buy When There is a Blood on the Street 202
- Pattern 4: Buy When There is a Blood on the Street (Tuesday) 203
- Pattern 5: Buy When There is a Blood on the Street (Tuesday — Modified) 205
- Pattern 6: Buying "Monday" 206
- Pattern 7: Buying "Thursday" 207
- Pattern 8: Buying "Thursday" — Modified 208
- Pattern 9: "Dip Buyer's Advantage" Monday 209
- Pivot Patterns Combined 211

28. Gap Trading Secrets **225**

- Pattern 1:Turtle Short 225
- Pattern 2: Turtle Short on a Gap Up 226
- Pattern 3: Three Steps and a Stumble 227
- Pattern 4: Two Tumbles and a Jump 229
- Pattern 5: Three Tumbles and a Jump 230
- Pattern 6: Modified Three Tumbles and a Jump 231
- Pattern 7: Two Tumbles, and Another Tumble 232

- Pattern 8: Outside Day 233
- Pattern 9: Inside Day 235
- Pattern 10: Short Bias Doji 236
- Pattern 11: Buying Mondays and Fridays 237
- Pattern 12: Buying Mondays and Fridays — Modification 1 239
- Pattern 13: Buying Mondays and Fridays — Modification 2 240
- Gap Patterns Combined 242

29. Walk Forward **257**
- Pivot Points Combined 258
- Gap Trading Patterns Combined 259

30. Sayonara **263**
- The Next Step 263
- You Need This, Too 264

Afterword: Listening to Amartya Sen 265

Glossary 267

References 279

Index 281

Preface

I've loved mathematics all my life and adore the application of mathematics in real world. I studied engineering from NIT Warangal, and began observing the financial markets from 1991 while still at college. My first inclination was to study the price movements of stocks. Short-term price movements captured my imagination and I used to observe such movements on a regular basis. I also sought to understand the relationship between prices and their short-term patterns which, in turn, led me to study technical analysis.

I remember vividly the first time when I discovered that there was something called a moving average. I used to cut the stock prices section from the newspapers and judiciously keep the cuttings in a folder, just to calculate the various daily moving averages. I was filled with joy and spent weeks just calculating them. I would manually draw the various moving averages and try to figure out whether there existed any relationship between the moving averages and the future stock price. Soon I grew thirsty for more knowledge and began looking for additional indicators and trading books because I was convinced that they would make me more successful. Many weekends were spent reading books on technical analysis and trade magazines and my collection, which started in 1997, now stands at more than 1,000 books and magazines.

In the late 1990s I was fortunate to start working as a systems programmer in a hedge fund based out of London. During my stint of about five years there, I met one of the brightest hedge fund managers and quite a few technical analysis gurus and learnt from them some important aspects of market behaviour. That was the turning point for me and eventually I found myself involved in the financial markets. The markets offer me a never-ending challenge for combining the application of my true passions, mathematics and computers. Currently, I am a full time trader following some mechanical trading strategies with a systematic risk and optimisation approach aided by some of the short-term patterns that I have shared in this book.

For years I thought of writing an article for a trade magazine but felt that I couldn't write well enough. Sometimes I was also discouraged because of not finding the time needed to write, and at other times due to that mental block connected with the process of writing, editing, reviewing, rewriting, etc. With encouragement and support from my brother, I finally gained the courage, motivation and focus to begin writing a book. It took me more than two years to find a clear concept and framework for this book in a format that would work well for the full spectrum of traders, from novices to experts. I sincerely hope you will enjoy reading this book. And gain from it.

—●—

Why This Book

There are many tools available to traders today. Equally, many books have been written on market analysis and different trading methods. Most of these books feature very detailed concepts and excellent examples.

On the other hand, so far very few of books have been written taking Indian markets as a base. Additionally, very few books cover exactly when and how to trade. Most traders are anxious to know what and how to trade, and to know where to enter a trade. This book focuses on precisely such missing points and gives you details of profitable trading patterns derived from Nifty. Apart from the above, there are three motives for writing this book.

A well-known Chinese proverb says, "Give a man a fish and you feed him for a day. Teach a man to fish and you feed him for a lifetime." My goal is to provide you with the knowledge and a framework so that you can add what you learn in this book to whatever trading approach you are most comfortable using. I believe that an understanding of the patterns described in this book will give the trader a great edge, as well as reduce the stress arising from a hit and miss approach based on inadequate knowledge of market behaviour. The ability to look at the market and to have confidence in your trading decisions is worth its weight in gold.

In life everybody has goals — I must get an educational degree, I must get a job, I must marry, I must have children, I must have a house for myself, and so on. Soon these end up as a list of 50 or 100 must-have, must-do things. One such aim of mine was to write a book on a subject that I am passionate about, a book on trading. Last, but not the least, I can't deny that the possibility of fame and money from a successful book are attractive as well.

What You Will Learn from This Book

All said and done, market analysis is not some complex rocket science; all that is needed to make sense of the evolving price data is fairly simple knowledge and some experience. This book is about price patterns and the overall behaviour of the market. Some of the patterns aid you in understanding the market behaviour and will enable you to see the current market action and assess, with a high degree of reliability, what is likely to happen next.

This book is not meant to be a road-to-riches book or a no-risk type of book. You should be ready to put in serious effort, requiring both study and concentration. As you read through the book and study the examples and explanations, you will quickly realize the tremendous value of the information it contains.

As an engineer and a mathematician, I understand very well the power and the importance of statistics; hence I have provided elaborate statistical analysis with each pattern in this book.

There is an old adage which says that knowledge can be communicated but wisdom has to be self-taught. Hopefully, by the end of this book, you will have enough knowledge to evolve your own market wisdom for the next several years.

I have tried to write this book in a simple language. I did not want the readers to be overwhelmed by off-putting market jargon. I hope the reader will pardon me if at any place in this book I have veered away from that intent.

How to Use This Book

This book will immediately benefit the trading enthusiasts. Keep observing the market every day during and after studying the book, and you might find fresh examples of the trading patterns covered in this book in the on-going market action. The best results will come when the reader practices these patterns through actual trade execution. Experiment with the new concepts and add them slowly into your trading strategy. They will open up new tactics and build confidence before firing a trade. With more practice you will be able to find some additional patterns as well; the patterns are there, just waiting to be uncovered.

What's in This Book

The book is organised into the following sections:

- Section 1 covers the basics of trading.
- Section 2 defines various patterns and my observations about these patterns on Nifty.
- Section 3 lists specific formulas that can be used for money and risk management.
- Section 4 is perhaps the most important section in the book. It discusses a bunch of my favourite Nifty trading patterns, and will offer you guidance on how these patterns worked in the past.

By the time you reach the end of Section 4, and if I have done my job well, you should already have a strong sense of where your trading style will lead you over the next few years.

Acknowledgements

Many thanks to my significant other Yamini and the apple of my eye Tejas for making me smile everyday.

Thanks to my father Lakshmi Reddy who put me on to mathematics during my childhood.

I'm fortunate to have very understanding in-laws, Malathi and Vasu Reddy. They kindly babysat Tejas countless times otherwise the book would never have been completed.

My brother, Mouli, for all the encouragement and support he has given me in writing this book.

I also feel a debt of gratitude to so many professionals. I am thankful for their marvellous work in offering education for traders — you are an asset to the world of trading. It would be foolish and amiss of me not to mention that parts of this book are heavily influenced by market wizards and self-less teachers, such as Toby Crabel, Larry Williams and Andrew Goodwin.

I want to thank my colleagues at the hedge fund firm where I worked; they have greatly contributed to my knowledge of the world of short term trading. The fund closed back in 2005, once the fund manager, Владислав*, became a centi-millionaire in GBP terms and decided to quit the financial world to pursue philanthropic interests.

I have benefited from many helpful suggestions and comments from Deepak Longani, Kapil Tandon, Mukesh Rijhwani, N. Sreenivasa Rao, Raghavan Natarajan, Sam Costanzo, Sapna Reddy, Srilekha Reddy, Srinath Srinidhi and Suparna Rijhwani.

* That is Vladislav in English.

My special thanks to Vision Books. I particularly want to thank Kapil Malhotra, its Publisher, and the Editor of this book, as well as the rest of its staff. Kapil's reading and comments on the material and his eye for detail go well beyond my abilities, and his efforts are truly appreciated. I couldn't have chosen a better publisher.

Thanks to Vidur Chhabra of HatchDesign for the cover.

Finally, special thanks to all the traders in India and all over the globe; you are the source of inspiration for me to write this book. **This is a book for traders and by a day trader.**

A Word of Caution

This book relies on sources and information reasonably believed to be accurate, but the author doesn't guarantee accuracy or completeness.

Past results are not necessarily indicative of future performance. It should not be assumed that the pattern studies presented in this book will always be profitable, or that they will not result in significant losses. Often there are sharp differences between historical and hypothetical performance and the actual results subsequently achieved by a trading strategy. By the way, trading is risky. You and only you are 101% solely responsible for your trading decisions. The author cannot take any responsibility for your trading successes or setbacks.

Introduction

"If past history was all there was to the game,
the richest people would be librarians"
— Warren Buffett

When attempting to solve a problem, the most difficult task is to know where to start. In this specific case, the problem is how to find a persuasive answer to the above quote, a quote from none other than the "Oracle of Omaha", as the world's most successful investor is often called. You can well imagine how hard it was for me to find an answer, knowing very well that both my trading style and the musings in this book are about trading based on price patterns derived from past history.

I became a technical trader and I wanted to use price charts alone to determine my buy and sell signals. I realised this technical approach to analysing the markets could level the playing field between "professional insiders" in the markets and individual traders like me. I recognised this when I realised that I was not smart enough to gather all the news and assess its impact correctly in order to arrive at the market's behaviour. The obvious problem is that it is difficult to determine whether a news item is bad or good for the market, or, even worse, it could simply be rumour as well. And it is even more difficult to interpret how the thousands and thousand of investors and traders might interpret the same news. It is important to remember that it's not necessarily the news itself that is important; how the market reacts to the news is more important than the news. Therefore, instead of going through lots of news sources I started looking at price charts of the markets to understand how other market participants were interpreting the latest news and information.

It is interesting to see when a market makes an unexpected large move for no obvious reason, only to be confirmed by some news release at later time. Jesse Livermore,* a famous speculator, once wrote:

> Remember there is always a reason for a stock acting that way it does. But also remember the chances are you will not become acquainted with the reason until some time in the future, when it is too late to act on it profitably.

Confused, right? Markets discount all the fundamental news there is and also how market participants interpret it.

The fundamental news involves corporate earnings, profits, book value, and price per share earnings, and so on. The technical approach analyses past market movements and projects future actions.

"Price leads to fundamentals"

The above statement will probably surprise, or even upset, many investors. But it has been observed time and again that markets seem to top just when the fundamental news is the most bullish — and bottom out when the news reports are the most bearish. The price, thus, discounts the fundamental news in advance. Successful traders are already looking into the future, while novice traders are still trying to trade off past news. I'm not saying that fundamentals do not influence market prices but prices usually anticipate and adjust to changes in fundamentals well before these become common news. As the legendary Jesse Livermore wrote in his book *How to Trade in Stocks*:

> All through time, people have basically acted and reacted the same way in the market as a result of: greed, fear, ignorance, and hope. That is why the numerical formations and patterns recur on a constant basis.

---

* Jesse Lauriston Livermore (26 July 1877 - 28 November 1940), also known as the Boy Plunger, was an early 20th century stock trader. He was famed for making and losing several multi-million dollar fortunes and short selling during the stock market crashes in 1907 and 1929.

As a result of two human emotions that are as old as humanity, greed and fear, traders have a tendency to over-react to market behaviour. When things are going well, traders succumb to greed and over-buy in an effort to maximize profits. When the market is not going their way, fear kicks in, followed by a flurry of selling. These two opposing emotions have been around since the market began and will always continue to be a key factor in the movement of prices.

Many people reject the notion that market activity is repeatable or ordered because they believe that the previous price patterns occurred randomly, or without precedent. They believe that the ongoing trading conditions are unique and very unlike anything that happened in the past to make any type of valid comparison. Occasionally I read or hear people say "Markets have changed since the technology revolution", or something along those lines; in effect that "this time it's different".

The truth is that markets have always behaved in the same manner because human behaviour is the same. Humans acted the same way during my great grandfather's time and will act in the same manner during my great grandchild's time. Everything moves in cycles; so long as human nature doesn't change, history will continue to repeat itself. As W. D. Gann perceptively said, "The future is nothing but a repetition of the past".

Now let me conclude this chapter by presenting another famous saying, which many readers may have come across already:

> "We simply attempt to be fearful when others are greedy and to be greedy only when others are fearful". — **Warren Buffett**

Yes! It is from the same Warren Buffet. Although his investment methods are different, the premise of his approach, too, would appear to be the same. He believes that the natural cycles of greed and fear repeat throughout the market's history. Thus, the market's past history is there for him to learn from. In the real world, events won't repeat in exactly the way they unfolded in the past. Instead, history is more likely to play out again either in a kind of delayed reaction fashion or in a knee-jerk fashion:

> "I believe the future is only the past again, entered through another gate." — **Sir Arthur Wing Pinero, 1893**

Here, I must tell the reader that just because I'm using quotes by famous traders doesn't I mean I like their methods; neither do I necessarily disagree with them. I believe that having an idol when it comes to trading is a little dangerous to one's own trading as one's idol will be nowhere near when you are truly in need of help.

For example, consider the truth about Jesse Livermore, yes the same Jesse Livermore whom many traders idolize. The life of Jesse Livermore can be divided into three parts:

- The first part comprised the bucket-shop era from 1890-1910, when Livermore was able to make easy money by taking advantage of the bid-ask spread on inactive stocks with leverage of 100-to-1.
- The second part spanned his days as a trader on the New York Stock Exchange from 1910-1920, when he went bust over and over again despite his abilities and insights because he used too much leverage.
- Finally came his career as a stock manipulator (a criminal act in present times) in the 1920s, where the fees he charged were 25% of the market value of the manipulated stock.

After losing his fortune or going bust at least six times, Livermore committed suicide in 1940 at the age of 63 at the Sherry Netherland Hotel in Manhattan, New York.

Nevertheless, the book by Jesse Livermore and the references to Jesse Livermore in many a trading book will live on forever.

Section - 1

Trading Basics

Chapter-1

Day Trading

Chapter-2

Nifty Futures

Chapter-3

Chart Types

Chapter-4

Entries and Exits

Chapter-5

Market Structure

Chapter-6

Price Patterns

Chapter 1

Day Trading

No one knows for certain how many people in India are into day trading. But the numbers are unquestionably way up from ten years ago, thanks to the rapid penetration of online trading which has made buying and selling of stocks, etc. easy, convenient and economical.

So, any guesses on how many people are into day trading in India? Your guess is as good as mine but if I were to make a guestimate*, and were to additionally take into account those who trade online at home or between meetings at the office, and so on, one might well come up with a staggering number running into several millions. And, actually, that's no surprise: Technology, one would say, has made it all possible, and the lure of the periodic bull markets has made it irresistible.

What is Day Trading?

Day trading is all about trying to make money buying and selling stocks, etc. during the course of a day, taking advantage of their daily price movements. Day traders end the day flat, with no open positions left after the market closes.

What draws people to day trading? Here are some reasons that I can think of.

---

* Guestimate = Guess + Estimate.

Zero Overnight Risk

To avoid the risk of price gaps, namely any differences between the previous day's close and the subsequent day's open prices, day traders close all their positions at the end of a trading day. Because of this, they are not worried about the next day's opening price. In other words, they sleep easy.

Lower Trading Commissions

The commission structure in day trading is very low compared to trades taken on a delivery basis.

Increased Leverage

Day traders can avail of as much as four times their equity as intraday buying power. Used wisely, this margin can potentially increase their profits quite substantially. But leveragè, or margin, is a double edged sword; increased leverage makes day trading very risky, especially if one scores poorly on the three key attributes of discipline, risk management and money management.

Profit in Either Market Direction

Day traders often take recourse to short selling to take advantage of declining stock prices. The ability to profit even when markets fall during the trading day can obviously be extremely useful, particularly during bear market conditions.

Why Day Trade?

The most apparent answer to this basic question is quite simple: To make money.

The Profit Potential

This is, by far, the most obvious reason. In Nifty futures, the quintessential day trader's arena in India, market swings of over 100 points during a trading day are relatively common. A 100-point swing, it should be noted, translates to ₹ 5,000 per one Nifty futures contract, if caught in the right direction. That's certainly a large enough sum, if you consider that the investment required to buy or sell one Nifty contract at 5,000 Nifty levels is less than ₹ 50,000.

But the motivation to day trade is often not that simple; beyond profitability there might exist other reasons as well:.

The Challenge

Yet another reason is the very challenge of the game. Many day traders derive considerable personal satisfaction from a venture that not only offers the potential of making good money but tests one's mind and intellect, i.e. something which is challenging in itself.

Fame

The lure of fame cannot be ignored. An outstandingly successful trader has a more than reasonable chance of being in the limelight: he / she might gain recognition as an authority on the subject, choose to write books, become a widely-read columnist or be called upon by television channels to serve as a trading expert. So, it's not only about making money.

Dopamine Release

Many neurologists and psychiatrists, while explaining the workings of the human brain, talk about "a reward system" in the brain which releases dopamine when we do something pleasurable, challenging or exciting. Such acts where dopamine gets elevated include gambling, video gaming, having sex, watching pornography*, alcohol consumption, amongst others. I wouldn't hesitate to include day trading in this category!

Why Day Traders Lose Money

There's a popular belief that 80% to 90% of day traders lose money. That may perhaps be true. But many lose big because they lack the required discipline; the discipline needed to exit immediately when the price begins to move against them.

This book does not seek to elaborate on the psychological aspects of trading. Nor does it attempt to be a treatise on the kind of discipline required to make a successful day trader — and how to go about acquiring it. Still, it bears emphasis that a successful trader is one who not only has the "staying power" but is also endowed with a sense of calm and balance; not to act like a chicken with its head cut off, when the going gets tough — which is bound to happen again and again and happen at unpredictable times. Day trading has its rewards, no doubt, but the rewards come with risks attached. In order to keep the risks of day trading in check, keep the following guidelines in mind:

- **Abandon the adrenaline rush, forget the excitement.** Profit depends upon detached and disciplined execution.
- **Learn the numbers.** The nature of price movement must get inbuilt deeply enough in you to allow spontaneous decision-making during the trading day.
- **Cross-verify.** Objective measurements must filter unconscious bias.

In Section 3 of this book you will find additional discipline requirements based on mathematical formulas.

---

* I was initially very reluctant to use this word in this book, but Reserve Bank of India (RBI) governor D. Subbarao emboldened me, by his statement defining financial stability: "Financial stability is like pornography. You can't define it but when you see it, you know it."

Chapter 2

Nifty Futures

A futures contract is a standardized contract to buy or sell a particular commodity or financial instrument at a certain date in the future at a market determined price (the futures price). Futures contracts are traded on a futures exchange. The future date is called the delivery date or final settlement date. The official price of the futures contract at the end of a day's trading session on the exchange is called the settlement price for that business day.

A futures contract gives the holder the obligation to make, or take, delivery under the terms of the contract. Both parties — namely, the buyer and the seller of a futures contract — must fulfil the contract on the settlement date. The seller delivers the underlying asset to the buyer or, if it is a cash-settled futures contract, cash is transferred from the futures trader who sustained a loss to the one who made a profit. To exit the commitment prior to the settlement date, the holder of a futures position has to offset his / her position by either selling a long position or buying back (covering) a short position, effectively closing out the futures position and its contractual obligations.

Origins of Futures

The origins of futures contract can be traced to ancient Greece. Aristotle tells the story of Thales, a poor philosopher from Miletus who developed a "financial device, which involves a principle of universal application." Thales used his skill in forecasting and predicted that the olive harvest would be exceptionally good the next autumn. Confident in his prediction, he made agreements with local olive-press owners to deposit money with them for the guaranteed exclusive use of their olive presses when the harvest was ready. Thales could successfully negotiate low prices because no one knew whether the forthcoming harvest would be plentiful or poor and because the olive-press owners were willing to hedge against the possibility of a poor yield. At harvest time, when many presses were wanted all at once and of a sudden, he let them out at any rate he pleased, and made a large amount of money.

The first futures exchange market was the Dōjima Rice Exchange, which came up in Japan in the 1730s to meet the needs of the Samurai who, being paid in rice and after a series of bad harvests, needed a stable conversion to coin.

What is Margin?

To minimize credit risk to the exchange, traders must post a margin or a performance bond, typically 5%-20% of the contract's value.

To minimize counterparty risk to traders, trades executed on regulated futures exchanges are guaranteed by a clearing house. Effectively, the clearing house becomes the buyer to each seller, and the seller to each buyer so that in the event of a counterparty default, the clearer assumes the risk of loss. This enables traders to transact without performing due diligence on their counterparty.

Who Trades Futures?

Futures traders are traditionally placed in one of two groups:

- Hedgers, who have an interest in the underlying asset (which could include an intangible such as an index or interest rate) and are seeking to hedge out, namely insure against the risk of price changes; and
- Speculators, or traders, who seek to make a profit by predicting market moves and opening a derivative (finance) contract related to the asset "on paper", while they have no practical use or intent to actually take or make delivery of the underlying asset. In other words, the trader is seeking exposure to the asset in a long futures contract, or the opposite effect *via* a short futures contract.

Basics of Nifty Futures

In India, the National Stock Exchange (NSE) commenced trading in index futures on 12 June 2000. The index futures contracts are based on the popular market benchmark S&P CNX NIFTY index (National Index for Trading in Equity, or National Fifty). NSE defines the characteristics of the futures contract, such as the underlying index, market lot, and the maturity date of the contract. The futures contracts are available for trading from introduction to their expiry date.

The Nifty

S&P CNX* Nifty is a well-diversified 50-stock index accounting for 23 sectors of the Indian economy. It is used for a variety of purposes, such as benchmarking fund portfolios, index-based derivatives and index funds. S&P CNX Nifty is owned and managed by India Index Services and Products Ltd. (IISL), a joint venture between NSE and CRISIL. IISL is India's first specialised company focussed upon the index as a core product. IISL have a consulting and licensing agreement with Standard & Poor's (S&P), the world leaders in index services.

Security Descriptor of Nifty Futures

The security descriptor for the S&P CNX Nifty futures contracts is as follows:

- **Market Type:** N; Instrument type: FUTIDX; Underlying: NIFTY; Expiry date: Date of contract expiry.
- **Trading Cycle:** Currently, S&P CNX Nifty futures contracts have a maximum of 3-month trading cycle — the near-month (one), the next month (two), and the far-month (three). A new contract is introduced on the trading day following the expiry of the near-month contract. The new contract is introduced for 3-month duration. This way, at any point in time there are three contracts available for trading in the market, i.e.

* CNX stands for the Credit Rating Information Services of India Limited (CRISIL) and the National Stock Exchange of India (NSE).

one near-month, one mid-month and one of far-month duration, respectively.

- **Expiry Day:** S&P CNX Nifty futures contracts currently expire on the last Thursday of the expiry month. If the last Thursday is a trading holiday, the contracts expire on the previous trading day.
- **Contract Size:** Currently, the permitted lot size of S&P CNX Nifty futures contracts is 50, and for S&P CNX Mini Nifty futures contracts it is 20, and multiples thereof.
- **Price Bands:** There are no daily minimum or maximum price ranges applicable for S&P CNX Nifty futures contracts. However, in order to prevent erroneous order entry by trading members, currently operating ranges are kept at +10 % or, — 10 %. In respect of orders which have come under price freeze, members would be required to confirm to the exchange that there is no inadvertent error in the order entry and that the order is genuine. On receiving confirmation, the exchange may approve such an order.

Why Trade Nifty Futures?

By trading Nifty futures you can trade the "entire stock market" instead of individual securities. Index futures are highly liquid, are characterized by large intraday price swings and are easy to trade, both on the short side and the long side. The advice of many trading legends is to trade in liquid markets. Liquidity is like oxygen for traders; without it they are dead.

There is another reason for choosing Nifty futures. At the time of writing this book, Nifty futures ranked 7th among the top traded equity derivatives contracts worldwide (Table 2.1), based on rankings for 2008 by the Futures Industry Association (FIA).

All the studies and patterns presented in this book are based on Nifty futures. After reading this book, you may therefore wonder whether the patterns mentioned in this book also work on stocks and other commodities. The answer is, yes, they do. Since I only trade Nifty futures, the book mentions only these for all the patterns discussed. However, this in no way means that these patterns can be used only for trading Nifty futures.

Table 2.1

Top Traded Equity Futures in the World

Rank	*Contract*	*Jan-Jun 2008*	*Jan-Jun 2007*	*% Change*
1.	Kospi 200 Index Options, KRX	1,136,565,743	1,409,753,531	-19.38%
2.	E-mini S&P 500 Index Futures, CME	276,146,082	168,099,079	64.28%
3.	DJ Euro Stoxx 50 Index Futures, Eurex	194,904,054	149,795,207	30.11%
4.	DJ Euro Stoxx 50 Index Options, Eurex	180,666,460	117,930,165	53.20%
5.	SPDR S&P 500 ETF Options*	130,646,163	46,099,020	183,40%
6.	Powershares QQQ ETF Options*	108,675,023	72,705,317	49,47%
7.	S&P CNX Nifty Index Futures, NSE	87,072,050	60,111,533	44.85%
8.	iShares Russell 2000 ETF Options*	79,036,452	62,686,779	26.08%
9.	S&P 500 Index Options, CBOE	78,353,503	74,417,476	5.29%
10.	Financial Select Sector SPDR ETF Options*	56,602,328	7,285,360	676.93%
11.	E-mini Nasdaq 100 Futures, CME	53,295,145	42,977,486	24.01%
12.	Dax Index Options, Eurex	50,298,610	45,338,306	10.94%
13.	Talex Index Options, Taifex	46,833,114	45,523,800	2.88%
14.	TA-25 Index Options, TASE (Israel)	42,887,206	44,436,752	-3.49%
15.	Nikkei 225 Mini Futures, OSE	41,314,078	17,657,667	133.97%
16.	RTS Index Futures, FORTS (Russia)	40,893,224	7,379,193	454.17%
17.	S&P CNX Nifty Index Options, NSE India	36,975,918	23,579,538	56.81%
18.	E-mini Russell 2000 Futures, CME	33,574,781	26,361,538	27.36%
19.	Kospi 200 Index Futures, KRX	24,546,049	22,500,937	9.09%
20.	CAC 40 Futures, Litte	23,968,740	21,229,464	12.90%

** Traded on multiple US options exchanges*

Chapter 3

Chart Types

Price charts are a fundamental aspect of technical analysis. A chart pattern is a distinct formation on a stock's price chart that creates a trading signal, or a sign of future price movements. These patterns are used to identify current trends and trend reversals, and to trigger buy and sell signals. The underlying idea is that certain patterns are seen many times and that these patterns signal a certain high probability move in a stock. Depending on the information they seek and their individual skills, investors and traders use four main types of charts: the line chart, the bar chart, the candlestick chart and point and figure chart. Following is a brief discussion on each type of chart.

Line Chart

A line chart (Figure 3.1) is the simplest type of chart. The single line represents the stock's closing price on each day. Dates are displayed along the bottom of the chart and prices are displayed on the side(s). If you are confused, let's look at the pictorial presentation of a line chart. I am a big believer of the old saying, "A picture is worth a thousand words". I will, therefore, try to use charts wherever possible to illustrate what I'm saying.

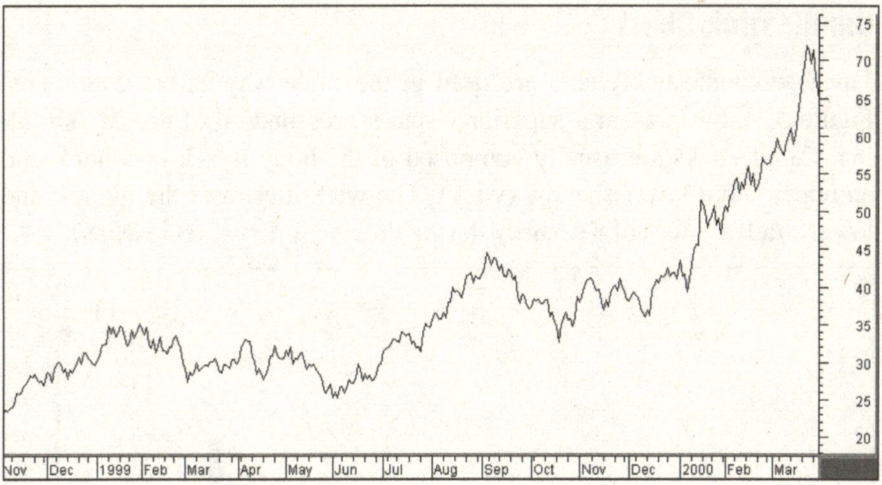

Figure 3.1: **A line chart**

Bar Chart

A bar chart displays a security's open, high, low, and closing prices. Bar charts are highly popular among technical analysts.

As illustrated in Figure 3.1 of a bar chart, the top of each vertical bar represents the highest price that the stock traded during the period, and the bottom of the bar represents the lowest price that it traded. A closing "tick" is displayed on the right side of the bar to designate the last price at which the security was traded. The opening price is represented by a tick on the left side of the bar.

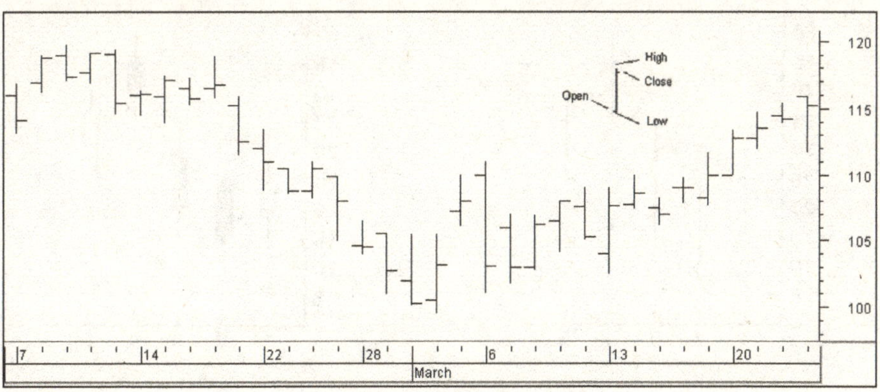

Figure 3.2: **A bar chart**

Candlestick Chart

Japanese candlestick charts are used in the same way as bar charts (*see* Figure 3.3), but present a superior visual representation of the day's trading. Candlesticks are usually composed of the body (black or white), and an upper and a lower shadow (wick). The wick illustrates the highest and lowest traded prices of a security during the time interval represented.

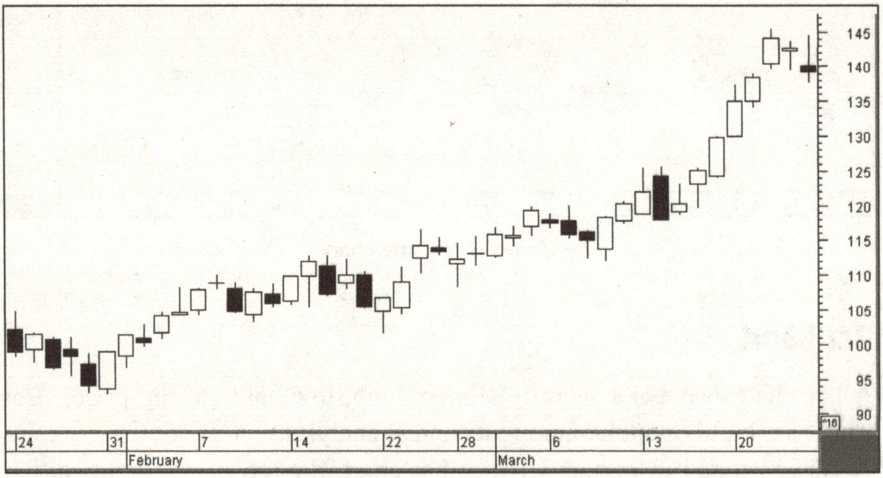

Figure 3.3: **Candlestick chart**

Elements of bar charts and candlesticks compare a bar chart and a candlestick chart based on the same open, high, low, and close data (Figure 3.4).

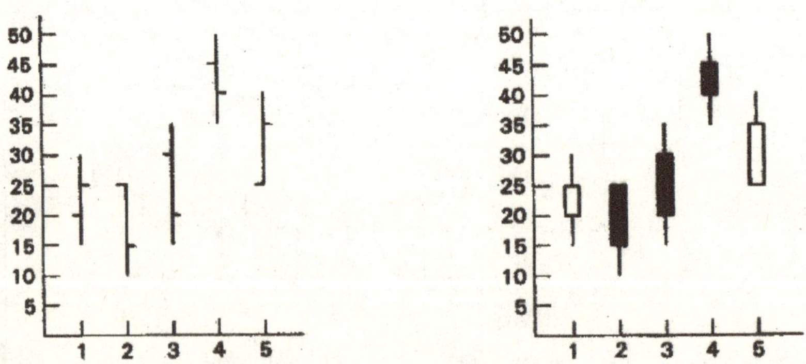

Figure 3.4: **Elements of bar charts and candlesticks**

The relationship between the open-price level and the close-price level forms the body colour of the candlestick chart. If the close is below the opening, the body is black. If the close is above the opening, the body is white. The price moves above or below the candlestick body is called the "shadow." Depending on how large the distance is between high and low of a price bar to the body of the candlestick, the shadows can be long or short (Figure 3.5).

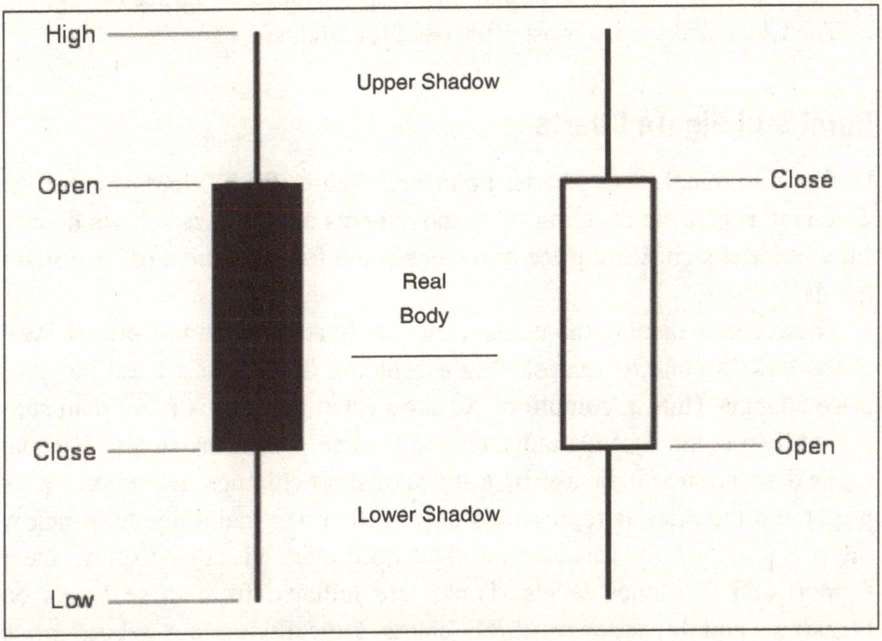

Figure 3.5: **Elements of candlesticks**

A Bit More on Price Fields

- **Open:** This is the price of the first trade for the period, e.g. the first trade of the day in a daily chart. When analysing daily data, the Open is especially important as it is the consensus price after all interested parties have "slept on it".
- **High:** This is the highest price that the security traded at during the period. It is the point at which there were more sellers than there were buyers. While there are always sellers willing to sell at higher prices,

but the High represents the highest price buyers were willing to pay during the period.

- **Low:** This is the lowest price that the security traded at during the period. It is the point at which there were more buyers than there were sellers. While there are always buyers willing to buy at lower prices, but the Low represents the lowest price sellers were willing to accept during the trading period.
- **Close:** This is the last price that the security traded at during the period. The Close is the price most often used for analysis.

Point and Figure Charts

Unlike traditional price charts, point and figure (P&F) charts ignore the time factor, concentrating on price movements alone. These charts help to filter out less-significant price movements and focus on the most important trends.

These charts display the underlying supply and demand of prices. P&F charts have Xs and 0s representing ascent and descent of a fixed box size price change. Thus, a column of Xs shows that demand is more than supply while a column of Os indicates the reverse. When the supply is equal to the demand, it is indicated by a series of short columns. Each box size is preset and the price is represented only if the price trades above or below the previous box by that amount. The P&F chart visually displays clear support and resistance levels. Trades are initiated from these levels on breakouts and breakdowns. P&F charts typically do not record price moves in a congestion range, hence choppy trading can be avoided. Box sizes can be a function of price range, average true range, or a fixed size based on the closing prices.

P&F charts are ideal for observing market activity, and as such are very helpful in identifying support / resistance lines, and chart patterns. There are several chart patterns that regularly appear in P&F charts. These include Double Tops and Bottoms, Bullish and Bearish Signal Formations, Bullish and Bearish Symmetrical Triangles, Triple Tops and Bottoms.

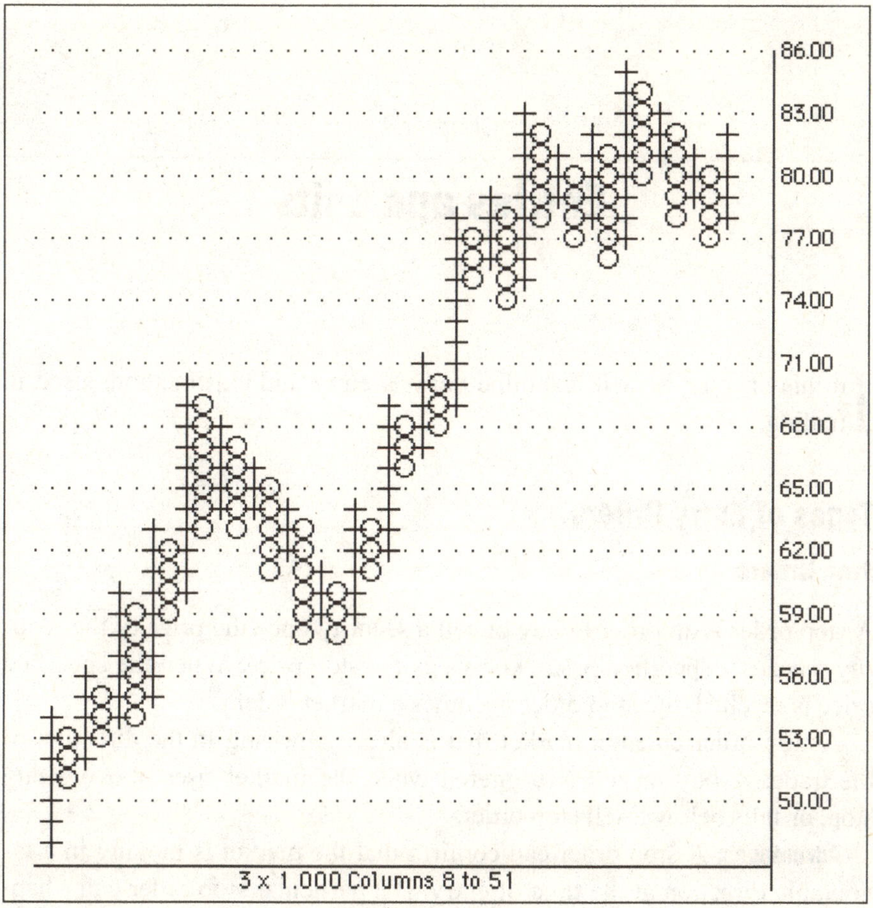

Figure 3.6: **P&F chart**

As would be evident from Figure 3.6, this type of chart is used to filter out non-significant price movements, and it enables the trader to easily determine critical support and resistance levels.

Chapter 4

Entries and Exits

In this chapter we will examine various entry and exit methods used in trading.

Types of Entry Orders

Stop Orders

A stop order is an order to buy or sell a security once the price of the security reaches a specified price, known as the stop price. When the specified price is reached, the stop order becomes a market order.

A stop order enters a market that is already moving in the direction of the trade. A buy or sell is triggered when the market rises above a buy stop, or falls below a sell stop order.

Advantages: A stop order can confirm that the market is moving in a favourable direction at the time of entry. If a particular stop order entry happens to be a good one, momentum will cause the trade to quickly become profitable.

Shock Circumstance: A highly unpleasant situation can arise when the entry order gets filled past the stop and the market then begins to reverse! Because an order is entered on a stop, market entry occurs at a poor price.

Consider another case wherein prices begin to move rapidly in favour of a trade. Buying or selling into such movement is like jumping on to a fast-moving train and is likely to result in large amounts of slippage; the faster the move, the greater the slippage. Slippage is the difference between the price at which the stop is set and the price at which the order is actually filled. Slippage is plainly undesirable as it eats into the profit generated by a trade.

Limit Orders

A limit order is an order to buy or to sell at a specified, or better, price.

For a buy limit order to be filled, the market must move below the limit price; for a sell order, the market must move above the limit price.

Advantages: The advantage of a limit order is that there is no slippage, and entry takes place at a favourable — and known — price.

Shock Circumstance: Consider this; the market never trades below X+1 points and moves in the desired direction considerably, whereas your limit order to buy is at X points.

Market Orders

A market order is a simple order to buy or sell at the current market price.

Advantages: Once placed, a market order is the fastest to get executed. Another advantage is guaranteed execution; after a market order has been placed, entry into the trade will definitely take place.

Shock Circumstance: The problem with the market order is that of possible slippage. However, in contrast to a stop order, slippage can go either way — sometimes in the trade's favour, sometimes against it, depending on the market movement.

Selecting Suitable Entry Orders

Determining which kind of order to use for an entry would depend on the nature of the model that generates the entry signals, and the market logic that underpins it:

- A limit order can be used to enter at or near the retracement level and when you are expecting the market to bounce from that retracement level.
- If you require some kind of confirmation before entering the market, a stop order might be a good choice.
- A market order is suitable when the timing provided by the system is critical.

Two types of orders — entry at open or at close, and entry on stop — appear throughout the study of various patterns in this book.

Strategies Used in Exit

Money Management Exit

A money management exit is usually implemented using a stop order. Such a stop closes out at a specified price below (if long), or above (if short) the price at which the trade was entered.

Trailing Exits

Typically, a trailing exit is implemented with a so-called trailing stop. The purpose behind this type of exit is to lock in some of the profits from a trade. As the market moves further in favour of the trade, the trailing stop can be moved up if you are going long — or down, if in a short position — which is why it is called a trailing stop.

The following example is based on the assumption that a trade has been entered as a long position. If a ₹ 1,000 money management stop has been put in place and the market moves more than ₹ 1,000 against the trade, the position is closed with a ₹ 1,000 loss. However, if the market moves ₹ 1,000 in the trade's favour, it might be wiser to move the original money management stop closer to the market's current price, perhaps to ₹ 500 below the current market price. Now, if the market reverses and the stop gets hit, the trade will be closed out with a profit of ₹ 500.

Profit Target Exits

A profit-target exit is generally implemented with a limit order placed to exit the position when the market has moved by a specified amount in favour of the trade. For example, if a profit target of ₹ 1,000 is set on a long trade on the Nifty, a sell-at-limit order has been placed.

Time-Based Exits

Time-based exits involve getting out of the market on a market order after having held the trade for a fixed period of time, usually at the time of the market close the same day, or on next day's open, or after two days at the market close, etc.

Selecting a Suitable Exit Strategy

A good exit strategy is more critical and difficult to achieve than a good entry. If one opportunity to enter is missed, another will always come along. Once a trade is entered, however, failing to exit at an appropriate moment can prove costly, even leading to that dreaded margin call from your broker!

There are a number of issues to be taken into consideration when attempting to exit the market. Some orders, such as stops, may result in premature exit; other orders, such as limits, may simply not be filled at all. There are also trade-offs to consider; e.g. tight stops might keep losses small. A 2-point stop loss on Nifty, it needs to be pointed out, gets filled almost 95% of the time. But at the same time it could kill potentially winning trades and increase the number of losses.

Only one type of exit strategy, exit at close, appears throughout the study of various patterns featured in this book.

It might shock you to know that many professional traders almost never use stop orders to exit losing positions. Contrary to the advice found in most trading manuals, the dozen or so large fund traders whom I have spoken with do not use intraday protective stops. This is because such stops tend to get triggered at the extreme price levels of the day thereby resulting in giving up positions at the very worst possible moments. Professional traders hang on to their trades until time runs out on their trades.

You might want to know what kind of stop loss they use. The answer is that they set mental stops. Mental stops are simply price levels you set in your mind that, once met, prompt you to exit the trade. This is the method used by most professional traders who monitor their positions closely throughout the day and don't want to reveal to the market where their entry and exit points are. It is somewhat akin to rummy or poker players not wanting to show their hand to other players. Think of such market traders as your opponents in a card game.

Later in the book I will present a strategy to protect you from ending up with a zero balance account if you intend not to use intraday protective stops.

Chapter 5

Market Structure

"The game of speculation is the most uniformly fascinating game in the world. But it is not a game for the stupid, the mentally lazy, the person of inferior emotional balance, or the get-rich-quick adventurer. They will die poor."

— Jesse Livermore

Investors keen to outperform the market — that is, investors looking for returns higher than the market average — take to active trading, employing various methods and strategies.

Active trading, including day trading, is better understood by distinguishing it from buy-and-hold investing. In buy-and-hold investing, investors disregard day-to-day market fluctuations essentially for two reasons: one, they believe that effects of short-term movements are really minor and, two, because they believe that short-term movements are almost impossible to predict with any degree of precision.

Active traders, on the other hand, are a different breed. Active traders are driven by the urge to look for profit potential in the market's temporary trends, which means trying to sense a trend as it begins, and to predict the direction in which it would head in the near future.

However, a larger number of trades does not necessarily translate into greater profits. Outperforming the market, which is what active trading is all about, is not to be mistaken for doing many trades; rather, the focus is on maximizing opportunities by employing a conscious strategy.

"Speculation, in its truest sense, calls for anticipation."

— **Richard D. Wyckoff***

Technical Indicators

Technical indicators are the squiggly lines often found above, below and on top of the price information on a technical chart. Indicators that use the same scale as prices are typically plotted on top of the price bars and are therefore referred to as "overlays".

A technical indicator is a series of data points that are derived by applying a formula to the price data of a security. Price data includes any combination of the open, high, low or close price over a period of time. Some indicators use only the closing prices, while others also incorporate volume and open interest into their formulas. The price data is entered into the formula and a data point is produced.

For example, the average of three closing prices is one data point [5,200 + 5,300 + 5,400) / 3 = 5,300]. However, one data point does not offer much information and does not make an indicator. A series of data points over a period of time is required to create valid reference points to enable analysis. By creating a time series of data points, a comparison can be made between the present and past levels. For analysis purposes, technical indicators are usually shown in a graphical form above or below a security's price chart. Once shown in graphical form, an indicator can then be compared with the corresponding price chart of the security. Sometimes indicators are plotted overlaid on the price plot for a more direct comparison.

* Richard Demille Wyckoff (2 November 1873 — 19 March 1934) was a stock market authority, founder and one-time editor of the *Magazine of Wall Street* which he founded in 1907, and editor of *Stock Market Technique*. Wyckoff implemented his methods in the financial markets, and grew his account such that he eventually owned nine-and-a-half acres and a mansion next door to the General Motors' chief's, Alfred Sloan Estate, in Great Neck, New York (Hamptons).

What Does a Technical Indicator Offer?

A technical indicator offers a different perspective from which to analyse the price action. Some, such as moving averages, are derived from simple formulas and the mechanics are relatively easy to understand. Others, such as stochastics, have complex formulas and require more study to fully understand

My Take on Technical Indicators

Technical indicators prove disappointing. Over the years I have tried many different indicators and each one, in turn, has proved more disappointing than the other. Perhaps for those who trade much longer time frames — weeks, months or years — some of the indictors may help, but for short-term traders there is not much help from most of these technical indicators. And virtually all indictors are correct after the day is over. For example, simple systems such as moving average cross-over will be correct *post-facto* but simply do not have the ability to do the business before hand.

Taylor Trading

Another method, the Taylor Trading Technique — so called after its creator George Douglas Taylor — is essentially a short-term method for trading daily price movements that relies entirely on odds and percentages. Taylor's book, *The Taylor Trading Technique*, published way back in 1950, is considered a classic and a reference manual for swing trading. The 3-day method, also called "The Book Method", elaborated upon in this book explains in greater detail how the markets move with a natural rhythm that is made up of a buy day, a sell day, and a sell short day.

The book may appear confusing at times, but for me the book offers a very organized method for determining whether the short-term trend is up or down. Tests of previous highs and lows, as well as systematic counting form the basis for determining whether to buy, sell, or sell short.

Elliott Waves

In the 1930s, Ralph Nelson Elliott, an accountant, developed a concept now well-known as the Elliot Wave Theory (EWT). It attempts to forecast trends in the financial markets and other collective activities. Outlining his theory in 1939, Elliott wrote that stock prices move in cycles based upon the Fibonacci numbers, namely 1, 2, 3, 5, 8, 13, 21, 34, 59, 93 . . . each successive number in the sequence being the sum of the two previous ones. The market rises in five distinct waves and declines in three distinct waves. Elliott also believed that these patterns exist at many levels and that any given wave or cycle is part of a larger one and also contains within it smaller waves and cycles. The Wave Principle holds that collective investor psychology swings from optimism to pessimism — and back again to pessimism. What these swings create are patterns — patterns evident, for instance, in the price movements of a market at every degree of trend.

The cult of Elliott Wave Theory (EWT) intimidates even the most experienced of traders. But simple elements of this arcane practice add great insight to pattern cycle analysis. Strong trends routinely print orderly action-reaction waves. Each wave has its own "signature", which often reflects the psychology of the moment. Understanding how and why the waves develop is the key to applying the Wave Principle.

Wave impulses correspond with the crowd's emotional participation. A surging first wave represents the fresh enthusiasm of an initial breakout. The new crowd then hesitates and prices drop into a counter-trend second wave. This coils the action for the rising greed of the runaway third wave. Then after another pullback slowly awakens fear and the manic crowd exhausts itself in a final fifth wave blowoff.

The Wave Principle provides a probability framework as to when to enter a particular market and when to get out, whether for a profit or a loss. But the principle is not without critics, however. Many technical analysts question its value, calling it too vague since it cannot consistently identify when a wave begins or ends.

Gann Angles

Reference should also be made to W. D. Gann, a financial trader and prolific writer on trading, who developed the technical analysis tool known as

Gann Angles. Gann's forecasting methods are based on a combination of geometry, astrology and ancient mathematics. In his book, *The Basis of My Forecasting Method* (published in 1935), Gann describes the use of angles in the stock market.

Each geometrical angle divides time and price into proportionate parts. The most important angle, the 1x1, or the 45° angle, represents — according to Gann — one unit of price for one unit of time. Other important angles are the 2x1 (moving up two points per day), the 3x1, the 4x1, the 8x1, and the 16x1. When the angles are drawn in a group, they are often called a Gann fan. Angles may either be drawn ascending from price bottoms, as just described, or descending from price tops.

In an interview published way back in 1909, when Gann was relatively unknown, he was quoted as saying:

> From my extensive investigations, studies and applied tests, I find that not only do the various stocks vibrate, but that the driving forces controlling the stocks are also in a state of vibration. These vibratory forces can only be known by the movements they generate on the stocks and their values in the market. Since all great swings or movements of the market are cyclic, they act in accordance with periodic law.

However, the value and relevance of Gann Angles continue to be debated. While Gann has his fans, he has more than his share of critics as well. There is controversy as to whether Gann was completely transparent with his methods or chose to reveal them only partially.

My Take on Gann

With so many angles, many time scales and dubious rules it should be quite easy to find many examples that come "close" to turning points in the markets. In fact, it is probably quite difficult to find many failures. This is especially true if one is allowed to define "close" as whatever one needs to make the current data fit.

Surprisingly, it is notable though that there are no well-known fund managers that I've met who claim to have applied Gann's lessons and become successful. The Gann "industry" seems to be a bunch of seminar peddlers claiming that they can teach novices how to trade successfully.

The usual bait is making extraordinary claims for which there is no evidence, and then comes an offer for a course, followed by an advanced course, followed by an even more advanced course, and so on and so forth.

In his book, *Trading for a Living*, Alexander Elder had this to say about Gann:

> Various opportunists sell 'Gann courses' and 'Gann software'. They claim that Gann was one of the best traders who ever lived, that he left a $50 million estate, and so on. I interviewed W. D. Gann's son, an analyst for a Boston bank. He told me that his famous father could not support his family by trading but earned his living by writing and selling instructional courses. When W. D. Gann died in the 1950s, his estate, including his house, was valued at slightly over $100,000. The 'legend' of W. D. Gann, the giant of trading, is perpetuated by those who sell courses and other paraphernalia to gullible customers.

How Can We Effectively Trade the Market's Next Move?

In case you wonder why I've discussed so many patterns in Section 2 of this book, the reason is to be able to arrive at a few short-term trading strategies for daily price movements — strategies that rely entirely on odds and percentages — and to capture the market rhythms of large ranges, both on the long and short sides.

In short, the art of speculation is about figuring out the most probable direction the future will take. The future is seldom predictable to a precise degree but we can make investment predictions that have higher odds. The way to make money in trading is to be able to anticipate the market direction by using some trading techniques, enter the trade, and use appropriate exit strategies either with profit, or with a loss.

Chapter 6

Price Patterns

"Are price moves random? Is there any basis for trends? What makes prices move? The 'aha!' process lies at the heart of price change. For instance, consider the series: OTTFFSSE. What is the next letter? This puzzle creates tension. Until you see the first letters of the ordinal numbers, one, two. 'Aha!' you say. A lot happens during an 'aha'. The puzzle dies and the tension dissipates. A societal 'aha!' drives price. Read the newspapers and the news magazines during a major move. At first, no one gets why the move is happening. There's a lot of confusion. Part of the move is way up, some people get it. At the end, everybody gets it. The tension is resolved and the move ends."

— Ed Seykota* in *Technical Analysis Magazine*

Technical analysis, by its very nature, deals not in certainties but in probabilities. The key to success in trading lies in focusing — more often than not — on what has already happened in the market. Too often investors buy and sell a stock not knowing whether it is in an uptrend or in a downtrend, near a top or near a bottom, or at a resistance or support level. That is where price patterns come in handy. Knowing what to look for as prices change helps the investor make better informed buy and sell decisions.

The four basic price patterns are: rising prices (upside), declining prices (downside), sideways prices, and repeating cycles of rising and falling prices.

---

* Edward Arthur Seykota (born 7 August 1946) is a commodities trader. In 1970 he pioneered systems trading by using early punch card computers to test his ideas on trading the markets.

Contrary to popular belief, you do not need to know what the price will be in the future to make money. Your goal should rather be to improve the odds of making profitable trades. The use of technical analysis will give you an edge; an edge that you would not have gained without technical analysis, even if your analysis is as simple as determining the long-, intermediate- and short-term trends of the security you are trading.

Short-term Price Patterns

A short-term price pattern is an analysis of recent price action in terms of:

1. Previous closes;
2. Previous opens;
3. Range size; and
4. Moves off the open.

Price patterns attempt to quantify market action so as to test for a significant directional movement. Price patterns allow us to take large amounts of information about the market and condense it into workable units. Market action can thus be tested. The tendencies found within the testing period can then be used as a partial basis for taking real action in the market.

I hasten to clarify that the phrase price patterns used throughout this book is not to be confused with chart patterns, such as head and shoulders, double bottoms, double tops, etc. used in technical analysis.

Many people reject the notion that market activity is repeatable or ordered, because they feel that patterns occur purely randomly. They believe that present trading conditions are much too unlike anything that happened in the past to make any type of valid comparison. The market has no memory and every situation is unique. There is a fallacy in this way of thinking. Every day and every market situation is indeed unique, but there are common patterns which may be generalised, just as every person is unique, but generalities exist for all humans. Everyone may not have the same likes and dislikes, but everyone has likes and dislikes.

Price patterns evolve through the engine of greed and fear. The crowd's emotions act in a predictable manner and are captured as chart patterns. This herd behaviour translates into directional movement that, in turn, translates into common, repeated and predictable elements.

Price patterns provide a complete, powerful method to locate opportunity regardless of market conditions. Since markets cannot move upward to infinity, nor downward below zero, well-marked patterns evolve within each time frame. An intelligent trader needs to recognize the various separate stages of the market's evolution, learn the well-marked pattern cycle, and develop and discover the hidden language of price patterns.

There is no pattern, relationship, or indicator that will always turn out right. The best we can do is to aim at a high degree of accuracy as a limit. All patterns will have their losing episodes. When these come about, the disciplined trader will take his or her loss in stride and exit the trade. There is, to my mind, no other way to trade if you want to be successful over the long term.

And always remember Murphy's Law: "Anything that can go wrong will go wrong".

Why No Volume?

Throughout this book I've not included volume in my pattern analysis as volume details are not available for the early 2000s specific to Nifty futures. The test data I have selected, therefore, doesn't have the full volume data. But that is not the sole reason. Here is my opinion on volume.

Volume breathes differently than does price. Volume as a tool works well on daily charts but consistently damages intraday signals. It offers both early warnings and dead ends, often at the same time. Volume reflects crowd psychology that often makes little sense in the short term but turns highly predictable at key intersections of trend and time. A successful trader needs to have an intelligent interpretation of the herd mentality that drives price change, develop an understanding of volume's impact on the chart, learn when to use it and how to ignore it when required.

Opportunity arises from recognition of key volume events and a correct interpretation of the crowd behaviour. You need to invoke both left- and right-brain functions to measure the complex struggle between greed and fear. But keep in mind that profits depend on price change alone. The price itself offers the best indicator for price changes throughout the pattern cycles. As price rises, it predicts that further gains will follow. As it falls, odds increase that it will fall even further.

Section - 2

Price Patterns on Nifty

Chapter-7

Moves from Open and Close

Chapter-8

Multiple Day Action from Open and Close

Chapter-9

Day of the Week

Chapter-10

New High and New Low

Chapter-11

Gaps and Laps

Chapter-12

Range Expansion and Contraction

Chapter-13

NR4, NR7 & WS4, WS7 Days

Chapter-14

Opening Range Breakout

Chapter-15

Inside Day

Chapter-16

Doji

Chapter-17

Pivot Points

Chapter-18

Tri- and Penta-Section

Chapter-19

Hook Days

Chapter 7

Moves from Open and Close

Data Sample

Throughout this book, the data chosen for testing the short-term patterns is S&P Nifty 50 Index data for the period 3 January 2000 to 30 June 2009. The sample includes many major market surges to the upside, including the biggest increase that the Nifty has ever seen, whether in terms of points or percentage, that occurred on 18 May 2009. Likewise, it includes a couple of major price shocks to the downside; on 14 May 2004 — in the wake of the uncertainty over the UPA government formation — and another one on 23 October 2008 when all the global markets tanked over the sub-prime mortgage crisis that triggered a global recession and the collapse of Lehman Brothers.

The sample data also includes many historic global and national events, such as the New York terrorist attacks on 11 September 2001, and several heinous terrorist attacks that occurred on Indian soil. In terms of economic events, the sample data covers a bubble burst, which was followed by the early 2000 technology and dot-com boom, the unprecedented GDP growth levels witnessed in India's economy the likes of which were never seen before, and the global recession that followed in 2008, which Warren Buffett called the Pearl Harbour of the American financial system. We all know that when NASDAQ and DJIA sneeze, the Nifty catches a cold. The sample data period had its share of scams, too, as for instance the infamous Ketan Parekh episode and the later Satyam scandal.

The point is, I firmly believe that this sample data is an accurate — and comprehensive — representation, what with many so many Black Swan events* included in the market movements. Therefore the sample data is a reasonably true mirror of both the past and what the future may witness.

"Er, have you counted and tested that?" — **Victor Niederhoffer**

When someone suggests a trading idea, always ask the above question. I owe an appreciation and indebtedness for this theme, i.e. to count and test to Victor Niederhoffer. The whole idea of this book is to test and count every market hypothesis as I'm a firm believer that every trading idea must be quantified and tested for its veracity. Victor's blog www.dailyspeculations.com — oops, I am revealing a very important resource of mine; anyway, try and make it a habit to read it once a day — and books have added greatly to market literature. Victor is the most profound generator of trading ideas of our time — his blog is a must read. The key idea is that, as a trader you should think about markets in the manner of a scientist. You make observations, you formulate theories about what is happening in markets, you express those theories as hypotheses, and then you test those hypotheses with specific trades that you place.

I hold Victor in higher regard than even Владислав for his ability to generate numerous trading ideas at the blink of the eye. I consider him an amazing modern day polymath and, mind you, there haven't been many of these in the 20th century, where one could achieve greatness in at most two fields. Victor has attained extraordinary distinction in many separate areas:

- **Athlete:** He was the US National intercollegiate squash champion. He won the US Nationals five times, a record exceeded only by Stanley Pearson. He also won three national doubles titles. In 1975, he defeated one of the greatest players in the history of the game, Sharif Khan, in the finals of the North American Open. It was the only time that Khan failed to win the title in the 13-year period between 1969 and 1981.
- **Academician:** It requires educational endurance to earn a PhD. Victor earned a PhD in statistics at the University of Chicago, and published a

* Black Swans" — undirected and unpredicted as popularised by Nassim Nicholas Taleb in his book, *The Black SwanTheory*. "Black Swan" events are considered extreme outliers. He gives the rise of the Internet, the personal computer, World War I, and the 11 September 2001 attacks as examples of Black Swan events.

few dozen groundbreaking scientific papers in respected journals. His work disproving the random walk theory on financial markets is still cited, decades later.

- **Trader:** In the context of this book, this point should have been first in the list but I am proceeding in chronological order. He once used to trade for the legendary sultan of speculation, the man who broke the Bank of England and made a billion USD and some change with a single trade, the palindrome, George Soros. Using various trading systems Niederhoffer made many millions of dollars for himself and his clients. In 1996 he was ranked the best-performing hedge fund manager for all time periods. After a debacle in 1997, he went on to achieve one of the greatest comebacks ever. Niederhoffer is proudest of having had a benevolent influence on people who came in contact with him. At least a dozen of his employees who he started out with or taught became billionaires or multi-cent millionaires, including Monroe Trout, Stu Rose, Toby Crabel, John Hummer and Victor Niederhoffer, all of whom became famous as traders or in the M&A business.
- **Author:** His first book, *The Education of a Speculator*, hit the *New York Times* business bestseller list. His second book, *Practical Speculation*, further established his reputation as an illuminator of statistical and scientific thinking towards financial markets.

Open-to-Close Observations

Traders need to use percentages to describe their results. The use of percentages is a simple way of accurately comparing different results. The absolute gain or loss in terms of points is not as important as the percentage gain or loss. Consider this: if you make a gain of 50 points when the Nifty is trading around 2,500, it translates into a 2% gain, whereas the same 50-point gain when Nifty is trading at 5,000 levels translates into a gain of only 1%. If you think in terms of percentage gains or losses, you can correctly compare the results of one trade with that of another. Accordingly, throughout this book I would consider the moves on percentage basis rather than in absolute points.

Let's start with a simple study to find out to what extent the Nifty's close moved from the open in a trading day. The findings have been organized in Table 7.1.

The condition observed can be found in the left column of the table and the number of occurrences of a particular condition features in the middle of the table. The column at right provides the number of occurrences in percentage terms.

Table 7.1
Open to Close in a Single Day

Condition	*# Occurrences*	*% Occurrences*
Close above the Open	1,272	53.6%
Close above the Open +1%	575	24.2%
Close above the Open +2%	213	9.0%
Close above the Open +3%	81	3.4%
Close above the Open +4%	39	1.6%
Close below the Open	1,095	46.2%
Close below the Open -1 %	517	21.8%
Close below the Open -2%	229	9.7%
Close below the Open -3%	109	4.6%
Close below the Open -4%	50	2.1%
Close equal to Open	4	0.2%

From Table 7.1, it can be seen that the market (Nifty) moved either 4% up or 4% down during a single day only on 3.7% of the occasions.

Let us now extend the above study to find out the differences between Nifty's closing levels on two successive days (Table 7.2).

Table 7.2
Close to Close on Successive Days

Today's close versus Yesterday's close	*Occurrences*	*% Occurrences*
Positive	1,297	54.7%
More than 1%	581	24.5%
More than 2%	221	9.3%
More than 3%	84	3.5%
More than 4%	38	1.6%

(Contd . . .)

Table 7.2 (contd.)

Close to Close on Successive Days

Today's close versus Yesterday's close	*Occurrences*	*% Occurrences*
Negative	1,071	45.2%
Less than 1%	510	21.5%
Less than 2%	227	9.6%
Less than 3%	110	4.6%
Less than 4%	51	2.2%
Equal	3	0.1%

From Table 7.2, it can be seen that the market moved either 4% up or 4% down on two successive days only on 3.8% of the occasions.

What both the open-close (Table 7.1) and the close-close (Table 7.2) moves suggest to us is that **on more than 96% of the occasions the Nifty moved less than 4% either way, be it up or down.**

In the next study, I present my findings on where the Nifty closed when the market moved above or below the open by a certain percentage.

The findings are presented in Table 7.3 and Table 7.4; the former bearing on market rallies and the latter on the declines.

Each of the two tables has eight columns. The first column shows where the market's intraday high. For example, the row "Open +4%" means that the market traded at an intraday high of open +4% levels. The next column features the number of occurrences of the condition mentioned in the first column. The next six columns indicate where the market closed for that trading day.

Table 7.3

Closes from Open When the Market Rallied

Nifty Intraday High		*Nifty Closed At*					
	Occurrences	*Open +*	*Open +1%*	*Open +2%*	*Open +3%*	*Open -*	*Open -1%*
Open	2,230	1,272	575	213	81	954	406
Open +1%	1,066	887	575	213	81	179	85
Open +2%	366	339	306	213	81	27	17
Open +3%	150	138	126	116	81	12	7
Open +4%	64	61	57	56	52	3	1

Let's consider an example from Table 7.3. In the row "Open +3%", the occurrences column says 150, and the "Open +" column says 138. This means that there were 138 closes above the open out of the 150 occurrences when Nifty made an intraday high above Open +3%. In the same row, the column "Open -" mentions 12, which means there were 12 occurrences when the Nifty closed below the open despite making an intraday high above Open +3%.

From Table 7.3 it can be observed that when the market traded above 4% from the open during a day, i.e. when Nifty made an intraday high of more than 4% above the day's open, it invariably closed above that day's open. A possible application of this data for an intraday trade could be that it makes sense to sit on all the open long positions once the market moves above 4% from the open as the chances of it closing below its open is only 3 out of 64, i.e. less than 5%.

The reason why I have not included (in some tables) Nifty's actions where the open and close were the same is because I would be presenting in detail a price pattern* around such occurrences in Chapter 16.

Table 7.4 summarises the corresponding position when the market declined:

Table 7.4

Closes from Open When the Market Declined

Nifty Intraday High	*Nifty Closed At*							
	Occurrences	*Open+*	*Open +1%*	*Open -*	*Open -1%*	*Open -2%*	*Open -3%*	*Open -4%*
Open -	2,067	968	367	1095	517	229	109	50
Open -1%	932	148	57	784	517	229	109	50
Open -2%	132	42	20	371	335	229	109	50
Open -3%	213	19	7	194	184	164	109	50
Open -4%	112	5	1	107	104	95	84	50

* That's the Doji for the curious minds.

Table 7.4 reveals an interesting fact: when the market traded 4% below from its open during market declines, it has a tendency to bounce back. This happened on 62 occasions out of a total of 112, including 5 positive closes, i.e., close above the open.

This book seeks to explore and present precisely such high-probability tradable opportunities on Nifty. A tradable opportunity, in simple terms, is one having higher odds of winning, enhanced with probability, statistics, common sense, and crowd psychology. I do, however, want to caution you that just because a pattern seems profitable with a nice average profit per trade, you cannot start using that pattern based on historical statistics alone. But more on that later in Chapter 23.

Chapter 8

Multiple Day Action from Open and Close

The objective of this chapter is to observe whether there exists any tradable bias from open-to-close or close-to-close *vis-a-vis* the previous day's closing prices. If so, such a bias could offer possible profitable trading patterns. In this study, I have tested all possible 2-, 3-, 4- and 5-day close-to-close, and open-to-close patterns on Nifty.

How to Read the Tables

The tables presented in this chapter contain the following columns:

- **Pattern:** In the first column, U symbolizes an up closing while D represents a down closing. **Throughout this chapter down closings include even those closings where the difference between successive closes was zero.** I have used two decimal point precision, since Nifty is calculated up to two decimal points, to determine if the difference between two closes was, indeed, zero.

  The notation used to represent multiple days is as follows:

- For a close-to-close pattern, the letter on the far right represents the current (latest) day's direction of the close and the preceding letters indicate the direction of the closes of the previous days, in chronological order.
- When presenting open-to-close patterns, the letter on the far right side represents the current (latest) day's direction of the open as compared to the previous day's close.

- Similar to the zero close consideration, I have considered an open as a down opening when the latest day's open is the same as the previous day's close.

Now a few examples to help clarify the close-to-close patterns:

- **DDUUD:** The latest day (today) was a down close, yesterday was an up close, the day before yesterday was an up close, 3 day ago was a down close, 4 days ago was also a down close.
- **UDDDU:** The latest day (today) was an up close, yesterday was a down close, the day before yesterday (i.e., 2 days ago) was a down close, 3 days earlier was a down close, 4 days ago was an up close.
- **DDDUU:** The latest day (today) was an up close, yesterday was also an up close, the day before yesterday (i.e., 2 days earlier) was a down close, 3 days ago was a down close, and 4 days ago was also a down close.
- **UUDDD:** The latest day (today) was a down close, yesterday was a down close, the day before yesterday (i.e., 2 days earlier) was a down close, 3 days ago was an up close, and 4 days ago was also an up close.

Now a few examples to explain the notation in the case of open-to-close patterns:

- **DDUUD:** Today was a down open, yesterday was an up close, the day before yesterday was an up close, 3 days ago was a down close, 4 days ago was also a down close.
- **UDDDU:** Today was an up open, yesterday was a down close, the day before yesterday was a down close, two days before yesterday (i.e., 3 days earlier) was a down close, while 4 days ago was an up close.
- **DDDUU:** Today was an up open, yesterday was an up close, the day before yesterday (i.e., 2 days earlier) was a down close, 3 days ago was a down close, and 4 days ago was a down close.
- **UUDDD:** Today was a down open, yesterday was a down close, the day before yesterday (i.e., 2 days ago) was a down close, 3 days ago was an up close, and 4 days ago was also an up close.

Please note that throughout this book I have used the same notation, with the right most alphabet representing the current (latest) day.

- **Action:** This column will have either of the two entries, i.e., "long" or "short". If it is "long", it means going long would have been profitable; conversely, if it is "short", going short would have been profitable.
- **# Winning trades:** Total number of trades that were profitable.
- **# Losing trades:** Total number of trades that were unprofitable.
- **Avg Profit:** Average amount of profit for the profitable trades.
- **Avg Loss:** Average amount of loss for the losing trades.
- **Win / Loss Ratio:** The average profit of all winning trades divided by the average loss of all losing trades. Please note that it is not the number of winning trades divided by the number of losing trades.
- **Gross Profit:** Total profit achieved by following the profitable action. The reason why I'm calling it gross profit is simple; I'm not including slippage and brokerage charges.
- **Profit per Trade:** Total profit divided by the total number trades, i.e. sum of the winning and losing trades.

Readers must also note that we tested thousands of price patterns. In this and the following chapters, we are presenting only such patterns which showed promise of profitable trading based on how they performed during our nine-and-a-half year test period of the Nifty.

Close-to-Close Patterns

Table 8.1 features close-to-close study for 2-, 3- and 4-day Nifty patterns. The entry for the trade is assumed at the latest day's close, and exit at the next day's close.

Please note that throughout Section 2:,

- **"Gross Profit" and the "Profit per Trade" are calculated under the assumption of trading one unit of Nifty Cash Index.**
- **The results reported are based on a test of Nifty price data from 3 January 2000 to 30 June 2009.**

Table 8.1

2-, 3- and 4-day Close-to-Close Patterns

Pattern	*Action*	*Winning Trades*	*Losing Trades*	*Avg Profit*	*Avg Loss*	*W / L Ratio*	*Gross Profit*	*Profit per Trade*
DD	Short	262	260	1.6	-1.5	1.08	33	0.1
DU	Long	329	213	1.3	-1.2	1.04	158	0.3
UD	Short	261	283	1.4	-1.1	1.30	61	0.1
UU	Long	410	332	1.0	-1.1	0.97	67	0.1
DDD	Long	133	128	1.7	-1.6	1.08	24	0.1
DDU	Long	149	110	1.4	-1.4	1.01	58	0.2
DUD	Short	116	97	1.5	-1.2	1.26	58	0.3
DUU	Long	186	143	1.0	-1.3	0.80	7	0.0
UDD	Short	134	127	1.7	-1.3	1.27	56	0.2
UDU	Long	180	102	1.1	-1.0	1.11	100	0.4
UUD	Short	145	186	1.4	-1.1	1.30	3	0.0
UUU	Long	223	187	1.0	-0.9	1.17	63	0.2
DDDD	Long	68	60	1.7	-1.7	1.01	15	0.1
DDDU	Long	74	59	1.4	-1.6	0.86	7	0.1
DDUD	Short	60	51	1.7	-1.4	1.20	29	0.3
DDUU	Short	67	82	1.8	-1.2	1.53	24	0.2
DUDD	Short	66	50	1.4	-1.5	0.93	17	0.1
DUDU	Long	53	44	1.5	-1.2	1.26	27	0.3
DUUD	Short	67	77	1.6	-1.1	1.47	23	0.2
DUUU	Long	100	87	1.1	-0.9	1.11	23	0.1
UDDD	Long	65	68	1.6	-1.4	1.14	9	0.1
UDDU	Long	75	51	1.5	-1.2	1.25	51	0.4
UDUD	Short	56	46	1.3	-1.0	1.36	29	0.3
UDUU	Long	104	76	0.9	-0.9	1.06	31	0.2
UUDD	Short	68	77	1.9	-1.2	1.62	39	0.3
UUDU	Long	127	58	1.0	-0.9	1.08	73	0.4
UUUD	Long	109	78	1.1	-1.2	0.87	20	0.1
UUUU	Long	123	100	1.0	-0.8	1.23	40	0.2

Table 8.2 features the study of 5-day close-to-close patterns.

Table 8.2
5-day Close-to-Close Patterns

Pattern	*Action*	*Winning Trades*	*Losing Trades*	*Avg Profit*	*Avg Loss*	*W/L Ratio*	*Gross Profit*	*Profit per Trade*
DDDDD	Long	34	26	1.9	-1.9	0.98	14	0.2
DDDDU	Long	39	29	1.5	-1.4	1.08	19	0.3
DDDUD	Short	32	27	1.5	-1.3	1.15	13	0.2
DDDUU	Short	34	40	2.2	-1.4	1.54	17	0.2
DDUDD	Short	32	28	1.4	-1.5	0.94	3	0.0
DDUDU	Long	29	22	1.5	-1.2	1.25	17	0.3
DDUUD	Short	32	37	2.2	-1.0	2.16	33	0.5
DDUUU	Long	47	35	1.2	-0.8	1.42	27	0.3
DUDDD	Long	34	31	1.5	-1.2	1.23	13	0.2
DUDDU	Long	28	21	1.9	-1.3	1.48	27	0.5
DUDUD	Short	21	23	1.3	-1.0	1.31	5	0.1
DUDUU	Long	32	21	1.1	-0.8	1.29	17	0.3
DUUDD	Short	37	30	2.1	-1.3	1.68	41	0.6
DUUDU	Long	51	26	1.0	-0.7	1.36	31	0.4
DUUUD	Long	56	31	1.2	-1.5	0.83	23	0.3
DUUUU	Long	54	46	1.1	-0.7	1.58	26	0.3
UDDDD	Short	34	34	1.5	-1.5	0.99	1	0.0
UDDDU	Short	30	35	1.8	-1.2	1.49	12	0.2
UDDUD	Short	28	24	1.8	-1.5	1.25	16	0.3
UDDUU	Short	33	42	1.4	-0.9	1.48	6	0.1
UDUDD	Short	34	22	1.4	-1.5	0.92	14	0.3
UDUDU	Long	24	22	1.5	-1.2	1.27	10	0.2
UDUUD	Long	40	35	1.1	-1.0	1.12	10	0.1
UDUUU	Short	52	53	1.0	-0.9	1.10	4	0.0
UUDDD	Short	37	31	1.6	-1.8	0.91	5	0.1
UUDDU	Long	47	30	1.2	-1.1	1.10	24	0.3
UUDUD	Short	35	23	1.3	-0.9	1.41	24	0.4
UUDUU	Long	72	55	0.9	-0.9	0.97	13	0.1
UUUDD	Long	47	31	1.1	-1.6	0.68	2	0.0
UUUDU	Long	76	32	1.0	-1.1	0.93	43	0.4
UUUUD	Short	47	53	1.1	-0.9	1.20	3	0.0
UUUUU	Long	69	54	0.9	-0.9	1.01	13	0.1

Open-to-Close Patterns

The next two tables, namely Table 8.3 and Table 8.4, present the results of my study of open-to-close Nifty patterns. The entry is assumed at the open on the day following the pattern listed in the first column of the table and exit at the end of that same day's close. Thus, for example, the first pattern listed in Table 8.3 in the column captioned "Pattern" is "DD" and the action listed in the column captioned "Action" is "Short". This means that the action tested was to go short after ascertaining that today's open is down and if the previous day's close was also down, as indicated by DD.

Table 8.3

2-, 3- and 4-Day Open-to-Close Patterns

Pattern	*Action*	*Winning Trades*	*Losing Trades*	*Avg Profit*	*Avg Loss*	*W / L Ratio*	*Gross Profit*	*Profit per Trade*
DD	Short	244	184	1.8	-1.3	1.41	200	0.5
DU	Long	318	257	1.4	-1.3	1.07	107	0.2
UD	Short	201	209	1.3	-1.1	1.16	27	0.1
UU	Long	464	333	1.2	-1.0	1.13	195	0.2
DDD	Short	118	93	2.0	-1.5	1.34	95	0.4
DDU	Long	141	131	1.6	-1.3	1.23	56	0.2
DUD	Long	97	83	1.2	-1.3	0.91	8	0.0
DUU	Long	202	127	1.3	-1.2	1.15	122	0.4
UDD	Short	126	90	1.6	-1.0	1.53	107	0.5
UDU	Long	177	126	1.2	-1.2	0.94	51	0.2
UUD	Long	202	127	1.3	-1.2	1.15	122	0.4
UUU	Long	260	205	1.0	-0.9	1.08	70	0.2
DDDD	Short	57	56	1.9	-1.6	1.20	20	0.2
DDDU	Long	68	66	1.9	-1.3	1.48	43	0.3
DDUD	Short	45	42	1.4	-1.2	1.14	11	0.1
DDUU	Long	95	64	1.6	-1.4	1.11	59	0.4
DUDD	Short	60	32	1.8	-1.0	1.83	77	0.8
DUDU	Long	59	57	1.3	-1.2	1.11	10	0.1
DUUD	Long	95	64	1.6	-1.4	1.11	59	0.4
DUUU	Long	118	86	1.0	-1.1	0.89	21	0.1
UDDD	Short	61	37	2.0	-1.3	1.57	75	0.8

(Contd . . .)

Table 8.3 (contd.)
2-, 3- and 4-Day Open-to-Close Patterns

Pattern	*Action*	*Winning Trades*	*Losing Trades*	*Avg Profit*	*Avg Loss*	*W / L Ratio*	*Gross Profit*	*Profit per Trade*
UDDU	Long	73	65	1.4	-1.4	1.02	13	0.1
UDUD	Long	55	38	1.2	-1.3	0.96	19	0.2
UDUU	Long	107	63	1.1	-0.9	1.24	63	0.4
UUDD	Short	66	58	1.4	-1.1	1.31	30	0.2
UUDU	Long	118	69	1.1	-1.3	0.86	41	0.2
UUUD	Long	107	63	1.1	-0.9	1.24	63	0.4
UUUU	Long	142	119	1.0	-0.8	1.26	49	0.2

Table 8.4
5-day Open-to-Close Patterns

Pattern	*Action*	*Winning Trades*	*Losing Trades*	*Avg Profit*	*Avg Loss*	*W / L Ratio*	*Gross Profit*	*Profit per Trade*
DDDDD	Short	25	26	2.1	-1.5	1.36	12	0.2
DDDDU	Long	38	32	2.0	-1.4	1.42	30	0.4
DDDUD	Short	26	21	1.6	-1.2	1.29	15	0.3
DDDUU	Long	49	31	1.5	-1.8	0.83	17	0.2
DDUDD	Short	33	20	2.2	-1.0	2.25	52	1.0
DDUDU	Long	29	26	1.7	-1.1	1.57	21	0.4
DDUUD	Long	49	31	1.5	-1.8	0.83	17	0.2
DDUUU	Long	57	37	1.0	-1.3	0.74	7	0.1
DUDDD	Short	25	11	1.4	-1.7	0.81	16	0.4
DUDDU	Short	33	32	1.5	-1.5	0.97	0	0.0
DUDUD	Long	19	16	1.7	-1.3	1.34	12	0.4
DUDUU	Long	30	26	1.4	-1.2	1.16	10	0.2
DUUDD	Short	33	23	1.6	-1.1	1.55	30	0.5
DUUDU	Long	49	29	1.1	-1.5	0.70	8	0.1
DUUUD	Long	30	26	1.4	-1.2	1.16	10	0.2
DUUUU	Long	63	54	1.1	-0.9	1.20	19	0.2
UDDDD	Short	32	30	1.7	-1.6	1.08	8	0.1
UDDDU	Long	30	34	1.7	-1.1	1.52	13	0.2
UDDUD	Long	21	19	1.2	-1.2	1.07	4	0.1
UDDUU	Long	46	33	1.7	-1.1	1.59	42	0.5

(Contd . . .)

Table 8.4 (contd.)

5-day Open-to-Close Patterns

Pattern	*Action*	*Winning Trades*	*Losing Trades*	*Avg Profit*	*Avg Loss*	*W / L Ratio*	*Gross Profit*	*Profit per Trade*
UDUDD	Short	27	12	1.4	-1.0	1.32	24	0.6
UDUDU	Short	31	30	1.3	-0.9	1.37	12	0.2
UDUUD	Long	46	33	1.7	-1.1	1.59	42	0.5
UDUUU	Long	61	49	1.0	-0.9	1.05	14	0.1
UUDDD	Short	36	26	2.4	-1.1	2.25	59	0.9
UUDDU	Long	41	32	1.3	-1.2	1.04	13	0.2
UUDUD	Long	36	22	0.9	-1.2	0.76	7	0.1
UUDUU	Long	77	37	1.0	-0.7	1.45	52	0.5
UUUDD	Short	33	35	1.2	-1.1	1.07	1	0.0
UUUDU	Long	69	40	1.1	-1.1	1.01	33	0.3
UUUUD	Long	77	37	1.0	-0.7	1.45	52	0.5
UUUUU	Long	79	65	1.0	-0.8	1.32	30	0.2

Application

From these studies one can conclude that a tradable bias does exist for Nifty's multiple day close-to-close and open-to-close action. This is established by the fact that quite a few patterns produced high enough gross profits. You can use some of the patterns — as for example, UUDU (Long), UDDU (Long), and DUUDD (Short) from among the close-to-close patterns, and DUU (Long), DUDD (Short), DDUDD (Short), UUDDD (Short) from among the open-to-close patterns — as a starting point in your trading. However, when clubbed with other patterns that I will be presenting in the subsequent chapters of this section, these will provide you with some very reliable trading entries.

Chapter 9

Day of the Week

The daily life of a typical Indian is governed by several dos and don'ts for each day of the week. Some believe that Monday is not an auspicious day for shaving, while some others hold Tuesday inauspicious for washing one's hair, and for others still, buying cooking oil on a Saturday is a no-no, and so on. Most of these beliefs are linked to the movement of planets presiding over each day, or so believe the believers.

Could financial markets, too, be similarly influenced by planets? Do planetary positions have a bearing on how each trading day fares? Let me hasten to add that I'm not attempting to establish a direct association between planetary positions or movements and their impact, or otherwise, on trading days in a given week. But my study does show that certain days of the week are indeed "special" for trading Nifty.

Let's take a look. Table 9.1 shows the closes above the open for different days of the week. One of the reasons to consider point-based moves here rather than percentage moves as in the rest of the book is to determine when the largest point-based declines or rallies tend to occur. A 200-point move (however small or big in relative percentages) will definitely make a headline in most financial newspapers.

Table 9.1

Open-to-Close Relationship for Rallies by Weekday

Day of the Week	*Above*	*Above +50*	*Above +100*	*Above +200*
Monday	253	43	16	4
Tuesday	245	37	13	3
Wednesday	257	47	16	3
Thursday	254	39	9	1
Friday	255	47	21	2

Similarly, Table 9.2 presents occurrences of Nifty's closes below the open for each day of the week.

Table 9.2

Open-to-Close Relationship for Declines by Weekday

Day of the Week	*Below*	*Below -50 Points*	*Below -100 Points*	*Below -200 Points*
Monday	223	48	27	7
Tuesday	227	39	15	2
Wednesday	218	38	15	1
Thursday	217	43	17	3
Friday	208	46	17	3

Table 9.3 summarises closes above the open for each day of the week in terms of percentage moves instead of in points.

Table 9.3

Open- to-Close Relationship for Rallies by Weekday (in Percentage)

Day of the Week	*Open +1%*	*Open +2%*	*Open +3%*
Monday	116	52	14
Tuesday	97	36	14
Wednesday	117	43	25
Thursday	119	34	10
Friday	124	48	18

Table 9.4 summarises closes below the open for each day of the week in terms of percentage moves.

Table 9.4

Open-to-Close Relationship for Declines by Weekday (in Percentage)

Day of the Week	*Open -1%*	*Open -2%*	*Open -3%*
Monday	108	58	34
Tuesday	100	39	17
Wednesday	98	42	16
Thursday	103	39	23
Friday	108	51	19

At first glance it may appear that there isn't anything significant in Table 9.1, 9.2, 9.3 and 9.4, but a closer look would reveal some truly explosive moves, i.e. moves of more than 100 points in either direction, and these seem to occur mostly on either Mondays or Fridays.

Then, too, a closer look at the percentage-based moves would reveal an anomaly; the 3% down moves tend to occur most often on Mondays, whereas the 3% up moves tend to occur most frequently on Wednesdays.

Extending the same study to close-to-close action, Table 9.5 summarises the results.

Table 9.5

Close-to-Close Relationship for Rallies by Weekday

Day of the Week	*Above*	*Above +50*	*Above +100*	*Above +200*
Monday	257	44	17	6
Tuesday	253	38	14	3
Wednesday	266	46	16	3
Thursday	256	40	9	1
Friday	257	47	21	2

Table 9.6 summarises the close to close moves for each day of the week in terms of percentage gains during rallies and Table 9.7 summaries the close to close moves in percentage terms for each day of the week during declines.

Table 9.6

Close-to-Close Relationship for Rallies by Weekday (in Percentage)

Day of the Week	*1% gains*	*2% gains*	*3% gains*
Monday	101	39	14
Tuesday	110	40	24
Wednesday	122	37	13
Thursday	135	55	20
Friday	110	50	12

Table 9.7

Close-to-Close relationship for Declines by Weekday

Day of the Week	*Below*	*Below -50*	*Below -100*	*Below -200*
Monday	218	48	25	7
Tuesday	220	39	14	2
Wednesday	208	37	16	1
Thursday	216	44	17	3
Friday	207	44	17	3

Table 9.8 summarises the close to close moves for each day of the week in terms of percentage declines during declines.

Table 9.8
Close-to-Close Relationship for Declines by Weekday (in Percentage)

Day of the Week	*1% decline*	*2% decline*	*3% decline*
Monday	98	38	15
Tuesday	96	38	17
Wednesday	106	44	26
Thursday	104	46	17
Friday	106	59	35

The close-to-close studies, summarised from Table 9.5 to Table 9.8 reveal that most of the 3% down moves are clustered on Fridays

The data presented so far still does not reveal anything significant to establish a definite tradable relationship between any particular day of the week and the market. So, we will go a little further and examine how matters play out if we enter Nifty every day on open and exit on close.

Before you take a look at the tables that follow, here is a quick explanation on what each column in the tables means:

- **Day of the Week:** Weekday
- **Action:** This column indicates "long" or "short", as the case may be. If it's long, it means going long was profitable; conversely, if it's short, going short was profitable.
- **# Winning Trades:** Total number of trades that were profitable.
- **# Losing Trades:** Total number of trades that were not profitable.
- **Avg Profit:** Average amount of profit for the profitable trades.
- **Avg Loss:** Average amount of loss for the losing trades.
- **Win / Loss Ratio:** Average profit of all winning trades divided by average loss of all losing trades.
- **Total Profit:** Total profit achieved by following the profitable action.

Table 9.9 examines a strategy when trades are taken at the open of the day and we exit the same day at close for each day of the week.

Table 9.9

Open-to-Close for Each Day of the Week

Day of the Week	*Action*	*Winning Trades*	*Losing Trades*	*Avg Profit*	*Avg Loss*	*W/L Ratio*	*Gross Profit*	*Profit per Trade*
MON	Short	223	253	1.5	-1.3	1.17	10	0.0
TUE	Long	245	227	1.1	-1.2	0.94	3	0.0
WED	Long	257	218	1.2	-1.2	1.07	66	0.1
THU	Long	254	217	1.1	-1.3	0.90	14	0.0
FRI	Long	255	208	1.3	-1.4	0.88	24	0.1

Table 9.10 examines a strategy when trades are taken at the close of a day and exited the next day at close.

Table 9.10

Close-to-Close for Each Day of the Week

Day of the Week	*Action*	*Winning Trades*	*Losing Trades*	*Avg Profit*	*Avg Loss*	*W/L Ratio*	*Gross Profit*	*Profit per Trade*
MON	Long	261	215	1.1	-1.2	0.94	35	0.1
TUE	Long	261	210	1.2	-1.2	0.99	59	0.1
WED	Long	256	219	1.2	-1.3	0.90	17	0.0
THU	Long	262	209	1.3	-1.4	0.95	54	0.1
FRI	Short	216	248	1.5	-1.2	1.26	28	0.1

Let's extend the above two strategies a little further. For the open-to-close trades, we will add another condition, namely we trade only after the open direction is known, i.e. once we know whether the open is up or down (Tables 9.11 and 9.12).

Table 9.11

Open-to-Close for Each Weekday if Open is Up

Day of the Week	*Action*	*Winning Trades*	*Losing Trades*	*Avg Profit*	*Avg Loss*	*W/L Ratio*	*Gross Profit*	*Profit per Trade*
MON	Long	155	120	1.4	-1.3	1.10	64	0.2
TUE	Long	142	127	1.2	-1.0	1.12	33	0.1
WED	Long	157	117	1.2	-1.0	1.28	82	0.3
THU	Long	169	120	1.2	-1.1	1.02	60	0.2
FRI	Long	161	107	1.2	-1.2	1.02	70	0.3

Table 9.12

Open-to-Close for Each Weekday if Open is Down

Day of the Week	*Action*	*Winning Trades*	*Losing Trades*	*Avg Profit*	*Avg Loss*	*W/L Ratio*	*Gross Profit*	*Profit per Trade*
MON	Short	139	139	1.5	-1.2	1.31	50	0.2
TUE	Short	129	140	1.4	-1.0	1.33	32	0.1
WED	Long	148	137	1.3	-1.3	0.96	6	0.0
THU	Short	130	136	1.3	-1.0	1.25	27	0.1
FRI	Short	134	143	1.6	-1.2	1.30	38	0.1

Let's similarly extend the above strategy for close-to-close basis. Thus, the trade is entered at the close of a trading day, once we know whether the close is down or up, and we exit the next day at the close (*see* Table 9.13 and 9.14).

Table 9.13

Close-to-Close for Each Weekday if the Close is Down

Day of the Week	*Action*	*Winning Trades*	*Losing Trades*	*Avg Profit*	*Avg Loss*	*W/L Ratio*	*Gross Profit*	*Profit per trade*
MON	Long	261	210	1.1	-1.3	0.89	29	0.1
TUE	Long	269	213	1.2	-1.2	1.07	86	0.2
WED	Short	230	247	1.3	-1.2	1.14	17	0.0
THU	Short	231	244	1.5	-1.3	1.10	14	0.0
FRI	Short	238	213	1.5	-1.1	1.37	125	0.3

Table 9.14

Close-to-Close for Each Weekday if Close is Up

Day of the Week	*Action*	*Winning Trades*	*Losing Trades*	*Avg Profit*	*Avg Loss*	*W/L Ratio*	*Gross Profit*	*Profit per Trade*
MON	Long	254	218	1.0	-1.0	0.92	16	0.0
TUE	Long	264	202	1.1	-1.1	1.06	81	0.2
WED	Long	266	215	1.1	-1.2	0.92	36	0.1
THU	Long	270	203	1.2	-1.2	0.97	74	0.2
FRI	Long	259	206	1.2	-1.3	0.94	49	0.1

Application

The six tables, from Table 9-9 to Table 9-14, reveal some interesting facts, which also perhaps explain how labels such as Black Monday and Black Thursday came into being. Black Monday refers to Monday, 19 October 1987. It was on this day that the Dow Jones Industrial Average lost over 500 points, or a staggering 22% of its value!

Black Thursday, the first of the many "black days" known, occurred during the era of the Great Depression. The Dow had climbed from 100 in 1926 to 381 points on 3 September 1929. On 24 October 1929, which subsequently came to be called Black Thursday, the market experienced its first major decline which continued through Tuesday, during this 5-day period the Dow shed 62 percent of its value.

Coming back to the tables presented above, a closer look reveals that the "best days to buy" were Mondays, Wednesdays and Fridays, whereas the best "sell days" were Mondays and Thursdays.

Monday and Friday tend to share similar characteristics in trading patterns. That is, if Friday closes negative, Monday also tends to close down. Conversely, if Friday closes up, Monday too tends to close up.

Counter-trends, that is, reversal from the general trend of the recent market moves, often occur on a Tuesday for a reversal from downtrend to an uptrend, or Wednesday for a reversal from an uptrend to downtrend.

Larry Williams in his book *Long Term Secrets to Short Term Trading* exploits these day-of-the-week patterns to build some tradable strategies. This idea of exploiting the day-of–the-week is the inspiration behind some of the patterns presented in the subsequent sections of this book.

Now that I've mentioned Larry Williams, let me introduce him to you, in case you haven't fully heard his story. In 1987, Williams won the World Cup Championship of Futures Trading, sponsored by Robbins Trading Company, trading $10,000 in real money up to $1,147,000 in 12 months — a feat no one else has since come even close to matching. Williams ran his winnings to more than $2,000,000 by the end of September, dropped down to $750,000 after the October 1987 crash, and traded back to the $1,147,000 mark by the end of the year.

As a trader, if you haven't still got goose bumps whether in admiration or wonder, read on.

He has a daughter named Michelle Ingrid Williams (born 9 September 1980), an American actress, and who received an Academy Award nomination for Best Actress in 2010 for the movie *Blue Valentine*. Now, listen to this. In 1997, at the age 16, Michelle Williams won the same Robbins competition with exactly 1,000 percent returns on her US$10,000 investment, a true inheritor of her father's trading genes.

[In case you wish to repeat the weekday exercise or any other observations presented in this book, by downloading data from www.nseindia.com website, please do note that the Indian market sometimes traded on Saturdays for some trial runs, or if Diwali happened to fall on either a Saturday or a Sunday. I have removed the trading data for such Saturdays and Sundays. — Author]

Chapter 10

New High and New Low

20-Day High: This is the highest price at which the security traded during the 20-day period. It represents the point where there were more sellers than buyers for the security. While there are always sellers willing to sell at higher prices, the High represents the highest price buyers were willing to pay.

20-Day Low: This is the lowest price at which the security traded during the 20-day period. It represents the point where there were more buyers than sellers. While there are always buyers willing to buy at lower prices, the Low represents the lowest price sellers were willing to accept.

There are well-known trading systems developed around the 20-day High / Low prices. Among them is the Turtle Trading System, popularised by Richard Donchian*, an American commodities and futures trader. The famous Turtle Trading System is not at all complicated; in fact, some people consider it be childishly simple. One of the basic guidelines it advocates is that if prices make a new 20-day high, buy; if prices make a new 20-day low, sell.

Whenever the Nifty trades at a 20-day high or low, the news is significant enough to make it to the headlines of financial dailies. With so many trend-following, breakout players in the investment arena, the action around 20-day high / low increases dramatically. Due to the liveliness of the market action around these 20-day high and low points, you would do

---

* Richard Davoud Donchian (b. September 1905, Hartford, Connecticut — d. 1993) developed a rule based trading approach which became known as trend following. It is based on the assumption that commodity prices moved in long, sustained moves. He became known as the father of trend following.

well to monitor such developments carefully so that you are well equipped to take advantage of any subsequent trading opportunity.

20-Day High / Low Patterns

Let's examine the trading action around 20-day high and low points on Nifty. I'm observing the 20-day high or 20-day low on close values and not on the intraday high or intraday low values as most of the fund managers and institutional investors I have talked to do the same.

Pattern 1

We enter the trade when the price hits either a 20-day high or a 20-day low at the close, and exit at the next day's close. The way I mark a 20-day high is to take all the closing prices from the previous 19 trading days, plus the current day's trading price, and if today's close is the highest in those 20 days, then I mark it as a 20-day high — and *vice-versa* for the 20-day-low.

Table 10.1 presents the results.

Table 10.1
20-Day High and Low on Nifty

Condition	*Action*	*Winning Trades*	*Losing Trades*	*Avg Profit*	*Avg Loss*	*W / L Ratio*	*Gross Profit*	*Profit per Trade*
20-day Low	Short	110	118	2.2	-1.8	1.21	28	0.1
20-day High	Long	282	205	0.9	-0.8	1.10	82	0.2

Pattern 2

Even Richard Donchian used to delay entering the trade by a day if the 20-day high or low signal occurred on certain specific weekdays. In this pattern study we will break the action around Nifty's 20-day highs / lows into specific weekdays.

Table 10.2 presents the study around 20-day low broken against specific weekdays.

Table 10.2

20-Day Low Action on Nifty on Specific Weekdays

Day of Week	*Action*	*Winning Trades*	*Losing Trades*	*Avg Profit*	*Avg Loss*	*W/L Ratio*	*Gross Profit*	*Profit per Trade*
MON	Long	32	24	1.7	-1.8	0.93	11	0.2
TUE	Long	29	18	2.0	-1.9	1.07	24	0.5
WED	Short	18	15	1.8	-2.0	0.91	3	0.1
THU	Short	22	23	2.4	-2.0	1.20	7	0.2
FRI	Short	28	21	2.8	-1.3	2.06	49	1.0

Table 10.3 presents the results of the same study around Nifty's 20-day highs against specific weekdays.

Table 10.3

20-day High Action on Nifty on Specific Weekdays

Weekday	*Action*	*Winning Trades*	*Losing Trades*	*Avg Profit*	*Avg Loss*	*W/L Ratio*	*Gross Profit*	*Profit per Trade*
MON	Long	54	59	0.8	-0.7	1.15	2	0.0
TUE	Long	49	39	0.8	-0.8	1.04	10	0.1
WED	Long	50	41	0.9	-0.7	1.23	14	0.2
THU	Long	61	32	0.9	-0.8	1.10	28	0.3
FRI	Long	69	35	1.0	-1.1	0.90	29	0.3

Application

What if you were long whenever the market closed at a 20-day high on Thursdays and Fridays and were short on Fridays and long on Tuesdays whenever the market closed at 20-day lows on these days? That would have meant a gain of around 3,400 points, i.e. more than the absolute gains achieved by employing the buy-and-hold strategy from January 2000 till June 2009, where the gains were 2,699 points. And, remember, you were in the market for only 292 days, as against 2,362 days with the buy-and-hold strategy. Even in percentage terms, the above 292 days of trading would have yielded roughly about 130% of gross returns, or about close to 0.5% of average gains on each trading day. One can conclude from the above patterns that profitable trading strategies can be developed by incorporating the 20-day high and low points coupled with the day of the week.

Chapter 11

Gaps and Laps

Definitions

Gap trading is a disciplined approach to buying and shorting stocks. That leads us to the question: What is a gap? A gap is a change in price levels between the close and open of two consecutive days.

- A "Full Gap Up" or simply "Gap Up" is defined as one when the opening price of a day is higher than the previous day's high price.
- A "Partial Gap Up" is one when a day's opening price is higher than the previous day's close, but not higher than the previous day's high.

To make it even simpler, I've have borrowed the term "Lap" from the book *Dave Landry on Swing Trading*. The precise terminologies I have taken from this book are Lap Up and Lap Down. So, our definitions now are:

- **Gap Up:** Open is above yesterday's high (Figure 11.1).
- **Lap Up:** Open above yesterday's close but below yesterday's high (Figure 11.2).
- **Gap Down:** Open below yesterday's low (Figure 11.3).
- **Lap Down:** Open below yesterday's close but above yesterday's low (Figure 11.4).

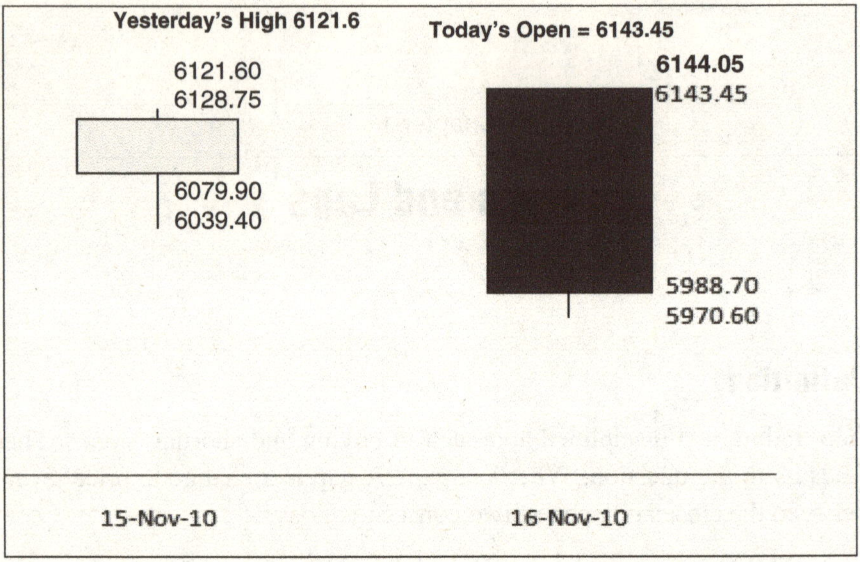

Figure 11.1: **Gap up**

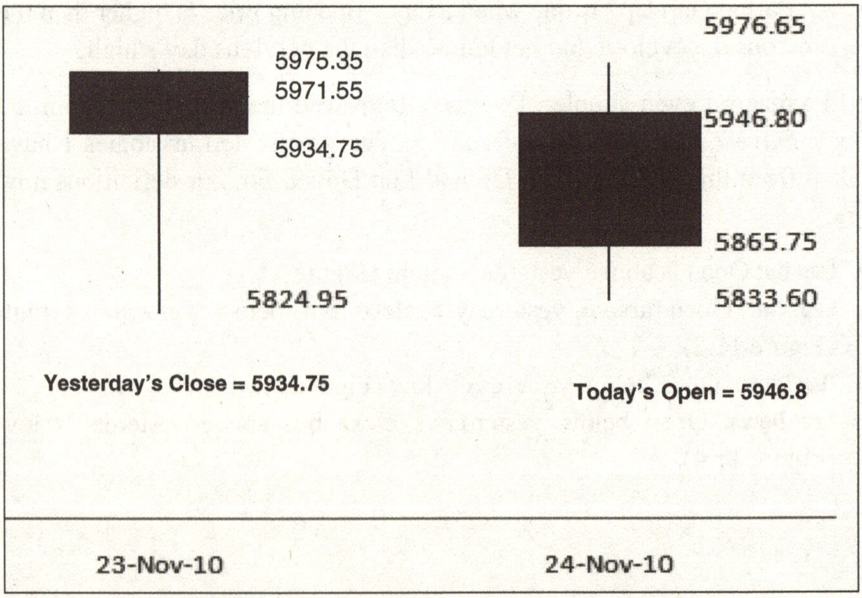

Figure 11.2: **Lap up**

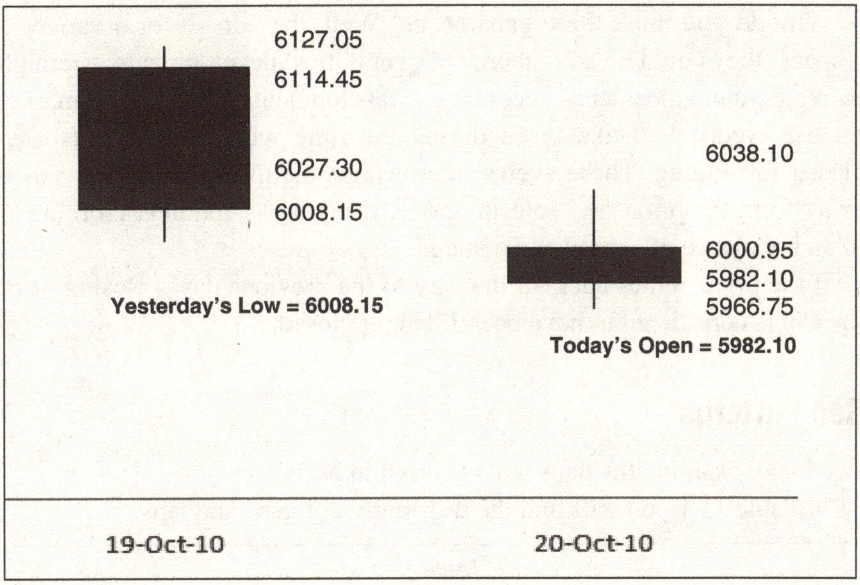

Figure 11.3: **Gap down**

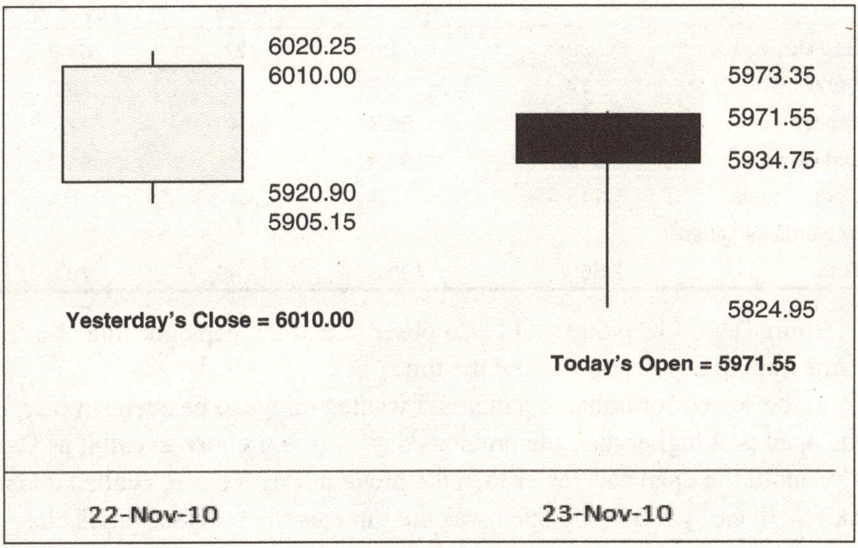

Figure 11.4: **Lap down**

Why do you think these gaps occur? Well, they do so for a variety of reasons; they could be an outcome of geopolitical developments, overnight earnings announcements, economic developments and other market-related events that take place during the time when the markets were closed for trading. These events often trigger significant price movement away from the prior day's closing price, resulting — the next morning — in an imbalance of supply and demand.

If the price comes back all the way to the previous day's closing price, the gap is considered to have been filled, or closed.

Gap Patterns

Let's now examine the gaps that occurred in Nifty.

In Table 11.1 you will find the distribution of gaps and laps:

Table 11.1
Distribution of Gaps and Laps in Nifty

Condition	*Occurrences*	*Occurrences (%)*	*Occurrences Filled*	*Occurrences Filled (%)*
Gap Up	39	1.6	27	69.2
Gap Down	17	0.7	13	76.5
Lap Up	1,338	56.7	1,040	77.7
Lap Down	823	34.9	669	81.3
Open Equals Yesterday's Close	143	6.1	NA	NA
Total	2,360	100.0	1,749	78.9

From Table 11.1 you would also observe that the gaps got filled on the same trading day nearly 80% of the time.

In the search for tradable patterns, I wanted things to be even simpler: if the open was higher than the previous day's close, I chose to call it as Gap Up, and if the open was lower than the previous day's close, I called it Gap Down. In cases where the open was the same as the previous day's close I ignored them for the moment and left them as they were.

Let's now reconstruct Table 11.1 as Table 11.2 using the above definitions:

Table 11.2
Distribution of Nifty Gaps

Condition	*Occurrences*	*Occurrences (%)*	*Occurrences Filled*	*Occurrences Filled (%)*
Gap Up	1,377	62.1	1,067	77.5
Gap Down	840	37.9	682	81.5
Total	2,217	100.0	1,749	78.9

Now, let's test the following trading patterns for high probability and reliable entries.

Gap Pattern 1

We enter the trade at a predefined level above or below the open on a Gap Up day, and exit at the close of the same day.

Table 11.3 shows the results. Beware of one of the mistakes people often make — as I did, too, for quite some time. For longs, for example, one unthinkingly assumes that a price tick is indeed traded by looking only at the intraday high. That may not be so. You must also look at the intraday low since that has to be lower than your entry point. Let us take the current day's hypothetical OHLC values as 5,230, 5,250, 5,225, 5,240. Now suppose yesterday high was at 5,210, and as per our pattern study we want to go short at yesterday's high level, i.e. is 5,210. Do you think it is possible? No!, Any entry value of above 5,225 is possible on that day, but not an entry value below 5,225. So to arrive at practicable intraday trading results for any entry point, the entry point should be tested to confirm whether it is indeed in between the intraday high and intraday low.

Table 11.3
Gap Up on Nifty

Trade Entry	*Action*	*Winning Trades*	*Losing Trades*	*Avg Profit*	*Avg Loss*	*W/L Ratio*	*Gross Profit*	*Profit per Trade*
OPN +1/2%	Long	555	523	1.1	-1.0	1.12	101	0.1
OPN +1%	Long	357	333	1.2	-1.1	1.04	41	0.1
OPN +2%	Long	140	109	1.3	-1.3	1.00	40	0.2
OPN -1/2 %	Short	389	340	1.1	-0.8	1.30	140	0.2
OPN -1%	Short	244	216	1.1	-0.9	1.25	79	0.2
OPN -2%	Short	104	76	1.1	-1.0	1.08	36	0.2

The corresponding results for Gap Down on Nifty are summarised in Table 11.4.

Table 11.4
Gap Down on Nifty

Pattern	*Action*	*Winning Trades*	*Losing Trades*	*Avg Profit*	*Avg Loss*	*W/L Ratio*	*Gross Profit*	*Profit per Trade*
OPN +1/2 %	Long	613	567	1.1	-1.0	1.09	104	0.1
OPN +1%	Long	393	354	1.1	-1.1	0.99	40	0.1
OPN +2%	Long	145	118	1.3	-1.3	0.99	33	0.1
OPN -1/2%	Short	426	379	1.1	-0.8	1.31	148	0.2
OPN -1%	Short	267	237	1.1	-0.9	1.27	90	0.2
OPN -2%	Short	112	84	1.1	-1.0	1.10	39	0.2

In both Table 11.3 and Table 11.4 you can observe the profit potential is skewed towards the short entries, taken at the same distance from the open for the long entries (for example, Open +1% and/or Open -1%). What can we conclude from this? Simply, that markets fall faster than they go up. And why do you think they do so?

Compare the two emotions and put yourself in that situation and decide:

- **Greed:** "Honey, you shouldn't have spent that fifty thousand on buying jewellery, instead we should have bought more stocks. We could then have been worth ₹ 5 lakh."
- **Fear:** "Oh God, if the market goes down any more, I will lose everything I have."

You see, once the market starts going down you start praying to God. Fear is a stronger emotion than greed and that is why markets fall faster than they go up.

Gap Pattern 1A

This is a variation of Pattern 1. In this case we enter the trade at a pre-defined level — in terms of points instead of percentages — above or below the open on a Gap Up day, and exit at the day's close. The point moves I chose for this study are 50, 100, and 200 above or below the open.

The first column has the trade entry point. If it says Open +50, it means the trade is entered once the Nifty starts trading 50 points above the open, and so on. This study is meant to see the how Nifty moves after large point-based moves.

The results are given in Table 11.5.

Table 11.5
Gap Up on Nifty

Pattern	*Action*	*Winning Trades*	*Losing Trades*	*Avg Profit*	*Avg Loss*	*W/L Ratio*	*Gross Profit*	*Profit per Trade*
OPN +50	Long	133	106	1.5	-1.5	1.04	47	0.2
OPN +100	Long	51	30	1.6	-1.6	1.01	34	0.4
OPN +200	Long	11	1	2.1	-0.1	20.64	23	1.9
OPN -50	Short	97	86	1.3	-1.1	1.19	32	0.2
OPN -100	Short	33	22	1.2	-0.8	1.50	23	0.4
OPN -200	Long	7	3	0.9	-1.0	0.95	4	0.4

The corresponding results for Gap Down are given in Table 11.6.

Table 11.6
Gap Down on Nifty

Pattern	*Action*	*Winning Trades*	*Losing Trades*	*Avg Profit*	*Avg Loss*	*W/L Ratio*	*Gross Profit*	*Profit per Trade*
OPN +50	Long	70	49	1.1	-1.0	1.13	30	0.3
OPN +100	Long	21	13	1.1	-1.0	1.11	11	0.3
OPN +200	Short	3	2	0.5	-0.9	0.52	0	0.1
OPN -50	Short	110	104	1.8	-1.5	1.21	43	0.2
OPN -100	Short	52	39	1.7	-1.5	1.11	28	0.3
OPN -200	Long	15	13	2.2	-1.5	1.53	15	0.5

It is a little difficult to conclude anything from the above study apart from a small noticeable anomaly; namely, that if the Nifty moves by 200 points after a positive open, it pays to stick to one's long entries and exit at the close rather than booking profits intraday at a point of Open +200.

Gap Pattern 2

This is an extension of Pattern 1A. This pattern additionally considers the position of the Open compared to the previous day's range. Thus, if the

Open is above the mid-point of the previous day's price range, I have marked it "Top Range Open"; otherwise, as "Bottom Range Open".

Figure 11.5 simplifies things.

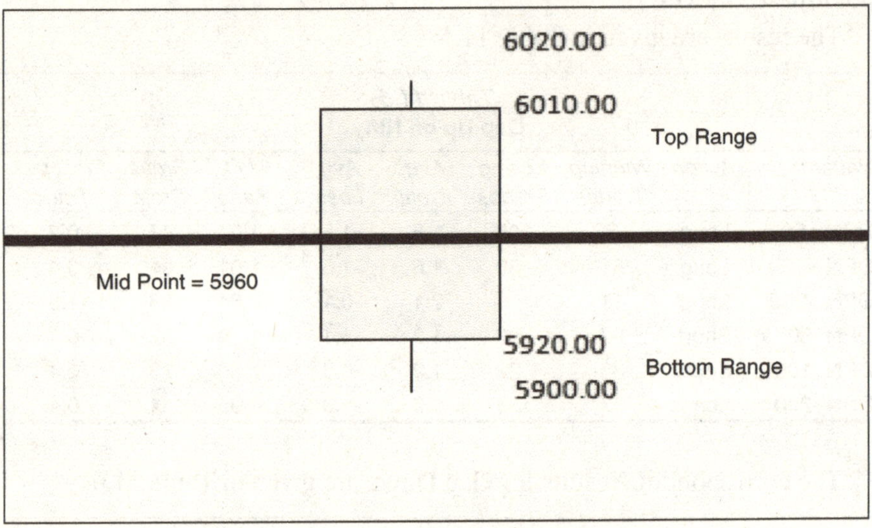

Figure 11.5: **Top Range and Bottom Range**

Table 11.7 summarises the results for the four various possible combinations, i.e. top range open and bottom range open for each, gap up openings and gap down openings.

Table 11.7

Gap Up and a Top Range Open

Pattern	*Action*	*Winning Trades*	*Losing Trades*	*Avg Profit*	*Avg Loss*	*W/L Ratio*	*Gross Profit*	*Profit per Trade*
OPN +1/2	Long	330	334	1.1	-1.0	1.18	54	0.1
OPN +1	Long	209	217	1.2	-1.1	1.11	16	0
OPN +2	Long	81	69	1.4	-1.4	0.96	13	0.1
OPN -1/2	Short	221	190	1.1	-0.7	1.55	105	0.3
OPN -1	Short	137	110	1.1	-0.8	1.42	66	0.3
OPN -2	Short	62	35	1.0	-1.0	1.02	27	0.3

Table 11.8 summarises the results for the bottom range and gap up occurrences on Nifty.

Table 11.8
Gap Up and a Bottom Range Open

Pattern	*Action*	*Winning Trades*	*Losing Trades*	*Avg Profit*	*Avg Loss*	*W/L Ratio*	*Gross Profit*	*Profit per Trade*
OPN +1/2	Long	225	189	1.2	-1.1	1.03	47	0.1
OPN +1	Long	148	116	1.1	-1.2	0.93	26	0.1
OPN +2	Long	59	40	1.2	-1.0	1.12	27	0.3
OPN -1/2	Short	168	150	1.1	-1.0	1.09	34	0.1
OPN -1	Short	107	106	1.1	-1.0	1.11	13	0.1
OPN -2	Short	42	41	1.2	-1.0	1.18	9	0.1

Table 11.9 and Table 11.10 summarise the corresponding gap-down occurrences on Nifty.

Table 11.9
Gap Down and a Top Range Open

Pattern	*Action*	*Winning Trades*	*Losing Trades*	*Avg Profit*	*Avg Loss*	*W/L Ratio*	*Gross Profit*	*Profit per Trade*
OPN +1/2	Long	127	115	1	-1.0	1.06	19	0.1
OPN +1	Long	82	69	1.0	-1.1	0.86	2	0.0
OPN +2	Long	30	15	0.9	-1.5	0.60	4	0.1
OPN -1/2	Short	116	96	1.3	-1.0	1.35	60	0.3
OPN -1	Short	84	57	1.2	-0.9	1.35	52	0.4
OPN -2	Short	28	33	1.9	-1.3	1.52	12	0.2

Table 11.10
Gap Down and a Bottom Range Open

Pattern	*Action*	*Winning Trades*	*Losing Trades*	*Avg Profit*	*Avg Loss*	*W / L Ratio*	*Gross Profit*	*Profit per Trade*
OPN +1/2	Long	156	114	1.1	-1.1	0.98	44	0.2
OPN +1	Long	97	66	1.1	-0.9	1.33	54	0.3
OPN +2	Long	37	20	1.2	-1.0	1.29	27	0.5
OPN -1/2	Short	216	160	1.6	-1.1	1.50	174	0.5
OPN -1	Short	166	121	1.5	-1.2	1.24	103	0.4
OPN -2	Short	89	67	1.4	-1.4	0.99	30	0.2

Application

From the above analyses we can conclude that Nifty generally displayed continuation in the direction of a gap down. A selection of tradable gap patterns, together with some other patterns presented in other chapters of this book, are featured in Section 4.

Chapter 12

Range Expansion and Contraction

Contraction / Expansion

Range contraction / expansion is the market phenomenon of change from a period of rest to a period of movement, and back to a period of rest. Many traders assume that range expansion and range contraction have an impact on price action on the day or days following range expansion or contraction.

- A range contraction, or a narrow range (NR) day, can be defined as the day whose daily range (the difference between the day's high and low) is less than the previous day's range.
- Conversely, a range expansion day, or a wide spread (WS) day, can be defined as one when the daily range is more than the previous day's range.

If yesterday's range was 100 points, and the market's range today is less than 100 points, then it is an NR (narrow range) day while if the range today is more than 100 points then it is a WS (widespread) day.

What if today's range is exactly the same as yesterday's? Such a day is called as "control" and occurred only twice in the Nifty during the period of this study. Let us now study the price movements after the NR and WS days.

NR / WS Patterns

Let's now examine the NR / WS that occurred on Nifty on close-to-close basis.

NR Close-to-Close Pattern

The pre-condition for entering a trade is that the day of entry should be an NR day. Entry is set at the NR day's close and exit is assumed at the next day's close. Table 12.1 show the results for this pattern.

Table 12.1

NR Close-to-Close Observations on Nifty

Pattern	*Action*	*Winning Trades*	*Losing Trades*	*Avg Profit*	*Avg Loss*	*W/L Ratio*	*Gross Profit*	*Profit per Trade*
DD	Short	110	124	1.6	-1.4	1.19	9	0.0
DU	Long	191	136	1.3	-1.3	1.03	79	0.2
UD	Short	123	118	1.3	-1.1	1.25	38	0.2
UU	Short	195	218	1.1	-1.0	1.16	8	0.0
DDD	Long	66	56	1.5	-1.4	1.07	21	0.2
DDU	Long	84	74	1.6	-1.4	1.11	27	0.2
DUD	Short	60	41	1.6	-1.2	1.33	46	0.5
DUU	Short	86	96	1.4	-1.1	1.38	24	0.1
UDD	Short	54	58	1.8	-1.2	1.54	30	0.3
UDU	Long	107	62	1.1	-1.1	1.00	52	0.3
UUD	Long	77	63	1.0	-1.1	0.92	8	0.1
UUU	Long	121	108	0.9	-0.8	1.06	18	0.1
DDDD	Long	34	26	1.7	-1.5	1.17	20	0.3
DDDU	Short	42	36	1.6	-1.5	1.10	15	0.2
DDUD	Short	34	20	1.6	-1.6	0.99	23	0.4
DDUU	Short	39	45	2.0	-1.3	1.54	20	0.2
DUDD	Long	22	17	1.3	-1.5	0.85	3	0.1
DUDU	Long	35	25	1.3	-1.2	1.02	13	0.2
DUUD	Long	38	24	1.1	-1.0	1.06	16	0.3
DUUU	Short	57	58	1.0	-0.8	1.19	8	0.1
UDDD	Short	30	32	1.3	-1.3	1.04	1	0.0
UDDU	Long	48	32	1.6	-1.1	1.44	42	0.5
UDUD	Short	26	21	1.5	-0.8	2.00	24	0.5
UDUU	Short	47	51	1.0	-0.8	1.18	3	0.0
UUDD	Short	37	36	2.0	-1.2	1.74	33	0.4
UUDU	Long	72	37	1.1	-1.1	1.01	38	0.4
UUUD	Short	39	39	1.2	-0.9	1.22	8	0.1
UUUU	Long	63	51	1.0	-0.7	1.40	26	0.2

WS Close-to-Close Pattern

The pre-condition for entering a trade is that the day of entry should be a WS day. Exit is assumed at the next day's close. Table 12.2 contains the results for this pattern.

Table 12.2

WS Close-to-Close Observations on Nifty

Pattern	*Action*	*Winning Trades*	*Losing Trades*	*Avg Profit*	*Avg Loss*	*W/L Ratio*	*Gross Profit*	*Profit per Trade*
DD	Short	160	147	1.6	-1.6	1.02	25	0.1
DU	Long	147	92	1.2	-1.2	1.06	74	0.3
UD	Short	148	172	1.6	-1.2	1.40	40	0.1
UU	Long	205	143	1.1	-1.0	1.09	81	0.2
DDD	Long	67	72	1.9	-1.7	1.10	3	0.0
DDU	Long	65	36	1.3	-1.4	0.88	31	0.3
DUD	Short	56	56	1.4	-1.2	1.18	12	0.1
DUU	Long	90	57	1.0	-1.1	0.94	30	0.2
UDD	Short	80	69	1.5	-1.4	1.10	26	0.2
UDU	Long	73	40	1.1	-0.9	1.31	49	0.4
UUD	Short	82	109	1.6	-1.1	1.45	11	0.1
UUU	Long	102	79	1.1	-0.9	1.28	45	0.3
DDDD	Short	34	34	1.9	-1.7	1.08	5	0.1
DDDU	Long	38	17	1.3	-1.6	0.81	22	0.4
DDUD	Short	26	31	1.8	-1.3	1.39	7	0.1
DDUU	Short	28	37	1.4	-1.0	1.45	4	0.1
DUDD	Short	49	28	1.4	-1.7	0.81	20	0.3
DUDU	Long	18	19	1.9	-1.1	1.74	14	0.4
DUUD	Short	43	39	1.9	-1.1	1.75	40	0.5
DUUU	Long	42	30	1.4	-0.9	1.54	31	0.4
UDDD	Long	33	38	2.0	-1.5	1.31	8	0.1
UDDU	Long	27	19	1.2	-1.3	0.95	8	0.2
UDUD	Short	30	25	1.2	-1.2	1.00	6	0.1
UDUU	Long	53	29	1.1	-0.8	1.38	34	0.4
UUDD	Short	31	41	1.8	-1.2	1.50	7	0.1
UUDU	Long	55	21	0.9	-0.7	1.33	35	0.5
UUUD	Long	70	39	1.1	-1.3	0.86	28	0.3
UUUU	Long	60	49	0.9	-0.9	1.09	14	0.1

We shall now extend the above patterns to the open-to-close situation.

NR Open-to-Close Pattern

Now, we will consider narrow range days on an open to close basis.

The pre-condition for entering a trade is that the previous day should have been an NR day. Entry is assumed at the following (current) day's open and exit is assumed at the day's close. Table 12.3 shows the results for this pattern.

Table 12.3

NR Open-to-Close Observations on Nifty

Pattern	*Action*	*Winning Trades*	*Losing Trades*	*Avg Profit*	*Avg Loss*	*W/L Ratio*	*Gross Profit*	*Profit per Trade*
DD	Short	92	82	1.8	-1.0	1.79	83	0.5
DU	Long	145	132	1.4	-1.2	1.09	32	0.1
UD	Short	130	120	1.3	-1.2	1.06	21	0.1
UU	Long	250	198	1.1	-1.1	0.99	58	0.1
DDD	Short	37	46	2.1	-1.2	1.85	26	0.3
DDU	Long	69	70	1.5	-1.4	1.14	12	0.1
DUD	Long	58	54	1.4	-1.3	1.04	8	0.1
DUU	Long	114	85	1.4	-1.3	1.09	50	0.3
UDD	Short	55	36	1.6	-0.8	1.94	58	0.6
UDU	Long	76	62	1.2	-1.1	1.05	20	0.1
UUD	Short	76	62	1.2	-1.1	1.18	29	0.2
UUU	Long	136	113	0.9	-1.1	0.88	7	0.0
DDDD	Long	26	16	1.2	-1.7	0.71	4	0.1
DDDU	Long	37	42	1.8	-1.3	1.39	12	0.2
DDUD	Short	31	26	1.2	-1.4	0.86	1	0.0
DDUU	Long	48	47	1.8	-1.5	1.19	16	0.2
DUDD	Short	32	16	1.8	-0.9	2.15	45	0.9
DUDU	Short	27	24	1.3	-1.3	0.99	4	0.1
DUUD	Short	37	29	1.7	-1.3	1.26	24	0.4
DUUU	Short	46	60	1.3	-0.9	1.45	6	0.1
UDDD	Short	21	20	2.5	-1.1	2.20	30	0.7
UDDU	Short	28	32	1.5	-1.3	1.15	0	0.0
UDUD	Long	32	24	1.3	-1.4	0.96	9	0.2
UDUU	Long	66	38	1.1	-1.0	1.12	35	0.3
UUDD	Short	23	20	1.2	-0.8	1.56	12	0.3
UUDU	Long	52	35	1.1	-1.0	1.15	24	0.3
UUUD	Short	40	33	0.9	-0.8	1.07	8	0.1
UUUU	Long	76	67	1.0	-0.9	1.09	14	0.1

WS Open-to-Close Pattern

Now let us review the open-to-close patterns for WS days.

The precondition for entering a trade is that the previous day should have been a WS day. Entry is assumed at the following (current) day's open and exit is assumed at the day's close. Table 12.4 shows the results for this pattern.

Table 12.4
WS Open-to-Close Observation on Nifty

Pattern	*Action*	*Winning Trades*	*Losing Trades*	*Avg Profit*	*Avg Loss*	*W/L Ratio*	*Gross Profit*	*Profit per Trade*
DD	Short	160	105	1.8	-1.5	1.22	132	0.5
DU	Long	187	134	1.4	-1.4	1.00	71	0.2
UD	Short	78	95	1.4	-1.1	1.29	6	0.0
UU	Long	228	150	1.2	-0.9	1.30	134	0.4
DDD	Short	81	47	1.9	-1.8	1.07	69	0.5
DDU	Long	72	61	1.7	-1.3	1.34	44	0.3
DUD	Short	29	39	1.4	-1.0	1.37	1	0.0
DUU	Long	88	42	1.3	-1.0	1.33	72	0.6
UDD	Short	71	54	1.6	-1.2	1.34	49	0.4
UDU	Long	101	64	1.2	-1.4	0.86	31	0.2
UUD	Short	42	50	1.4	-1.1	1.32	6	0.1
UUU	Long	124	92	1.1	-0.8	1.38	62	0.3
DDDD	Short	41	30	2.0	-1.9	1.03	24	0.3
DDDU	Long	31	24	1.9	-1.2	1.60	31	0.6
DDUD	Short	15	16	1.7	-0.9	1.80	10	0.3
DDUU	Long	47	17	1.4	-1.2	1.13	44	0.7
DUDD	Short	28	16	1.8	-1.1	1.57	31	0.7
DUDU	Long	35	30	1.3	-1.1	1.22	14	0.2
DUUD	Short	16	24	1.8	-1.0	1.82	5	0.1
DUUU	Long	58	40	1.0	-0.8	1.25	27	0.3
UDDD	Short	40	17	1.7	-1.4	1.22	45	0.8
UDDU	Long	41	37	1.5	-1.3	1.16	13	0.2
UDUD	Long	23	14	1.1	-1.1	1.00	10	0.3
UDUU	Long	41	25	1.2	-0.8	1.47	28	0.4
UUDD	Short	43	38	1.5	-1.2	1.23	18	0.2
UUDU	Long	66	34	1.1	-1.6	0.68	17	0.2
UUUD	Short	26	26	1.2	-1.2	1.02	1	0.0
UUUU	Long	66	52	1.1	-0.8	1.50	36	0.3

Application

Noted stocks and commodities trader Larry Williams believes there is a "clear-cut, precise cadence" to range activity. As he puts it in his book, *Long-term Secrets to Short-term Trading*, "At all times, in all markets, ranges fluctuate — and this is critical — from a series of small ranges to a cluster of large ranges."

What's more, the cycle repeats itself year on year, with smaller ranges following large ones, and larger ranges following small ones. In other words, large ranges give way to small ranges, and small ranges to large ranges. This cycle is both continuous and powerful because of the simple reason that traders bank on price change to make money, and greater the price change, the greater the potential to make profit. Conversely, if there is nil or negligible price change, speculators find themselves just twiddling their thumbs as price fails to trend.

Often, narrow range periods (i.e., periods of range contraction) presage range expansion. You can think of the market movement being akin to a spring — it needs to coil itself up tightly (contract) in order to build up enough potential energy for its next expansion.

An expansion-contraction strategy tracks the old wisdom that advises us to "enter in mild times but exit in wild times."

Now, what if we were to consider the range against several earlier trading days instead of the previous day alone? This sets the context for Chapter 13.

Chapter 13

NR4, NR7 & WS4, WS7 Days

In his book, *Day Trading with Short Term Price Patterns and Opening Range Breakout*, Toby Crabel defines the price patterns NR4, NR7, WS4, and WS7. I borrowed — and despite several reminders never returned, in short stole — this book from Влади* back in 1999, and was filled with an amazing "a-ha" feeling after reading it. Let me describe that feeling.

Have you heard of or seen Wordlock? Here is a picture.

When I saw the Wordlock** for the first time, I had the same amazing "a-ha" feeling. Why? How many times you have seen a great idea and

* That's Vladi, short name for Владислав.

** The Wordlock won the Staples invention quest in 2005 and the US patent and trademark office included Wordlock among the Top 100 New Inventions, a distinction it won at the Invent Now America competition.

been amazed at its simplicity. When I saw the Wordlock for the first time, I was similarly amazed. Here is why.

The number-based combination lock that we use has been in existence for more than one hundred and fifty years. It has two serious problems that I can think of. Firstly, we ourselves often forget the number combination that we put for the lock, particularly if we are not using it frequently. In order to overcome this, we might decide to put an easy-to-remember number. For instance, the "Bond, James Bond" in me tells me to use 007 for my number lock. But this leads to the second problem; easy-to-remember numbers are easier for other people to crack with some luck or practice. So the very purpose of using number locks, namely securing your valuables, is lost. Imagine your luggage in the hands of a thief capable of breaking a number lock in less than five seconds.

Enter Wordlock. The person behind creating and patenting wordlock is Todd Basche who has twenty years of experience in the software industry. His last job before he started a company to manufacture Wordlock was at Apple, where he was responsible for creating iTunes. The fact that such a simple invention had not been thought of by any of the world's existing lock manufactures for over 150 years gives rise to that amazing "a-ha" feeling.

Definitions

- **NR4:** If a price bar's range is less than those of the previous 3 bars (measured independently), it is said to have the narrowest range in 4 days and such a day is called an NR4 day, or simply NR4.
- **NR7:** If a price bar's range is less than those of the previous 6 bars (measured independently), it is said to have the narrowest range in 7 days. This is an NR7 day, or simply NR7.
- **WS4:** If a price bar's range is wider than those of the previous 3 bars (measured independently), it is said to have the widest range in 4 days, or WS4, or simply WS4.
- **WS7:** If a price bar's range is wider than those of the previous 6 bars (measured independently), it is said to have the widest range in 7 days, or WS7, or simply WS7.

Figure 13.1 depicting NR7 will also be able to help you visualize NR4, WS4 and WS7.

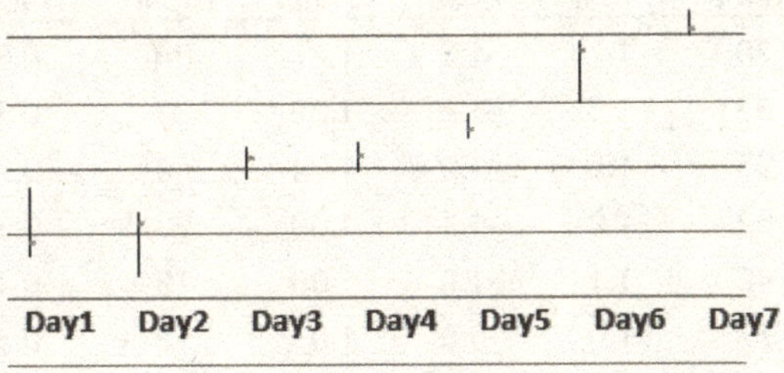

Range - Day1	35.4
Range - Day2	90.8
Range - Day3	35.7
Range - Day4	43.7
Range - Day5	47.65
Range - Day6	95.55
Range - Day7	103

Day7	05-Nov-10
Day6	04-Nov-10
Day5	03-Nov-10
Day4	02-Nov-10
Day3	01-Nov-10
Day2	29-Oct-10
Day1	28-Oct-10

Figure 13.1: **NR7**

Close-to-Close Observations

NR4 Close-to-Close Pattern

The pre-condition for entering such a trade is that the day of entry should be an NR4 day. Entry is assumed at the day's close and exit at the following day's close. Table 13.1 shows the results for this pattern.

Table 13.1

NR4 Close-to-Close Study on Nifty

Pattern	*Action*	*Winning Trades*	*Losing Trades*	*Avg Profit*	*Avg Loss*	*W/L Ratio*	*Gross Profit*	*Profit per Trade*
DD	Short	47	44	1.4	-1.4	0.98	3	0.0
DU	Long	87	59	1.4	-1.2	1.12	48	0.3
UD	Short	72	62	1.4	-1.2	1.15	25	0.2
UU	Short	131	122	1.2	-1.0	1.17	32	0.1
DDD	Long	19	21	1.7	-1.3	1.33	5	0.1
DDU	Long	34	27	1.7	-1.4	1.21	20	0.3

(Contd . . .)

Table 13.1 (contd.)
NR4 Close-to-Close Study on Nifty

Pattern	*Action*	*Winning Trades*	*Losing Trades*	*Avg Profit*	*Avg Loss*	*W/L Ratio*	*Gross Profit*	*Profit per Trade*
DUD	Short	36	20	1.7	-1.3	1.27	34	0.6
DUU	Short	61	53	1.5	-1.2	1.32	32	0.3
UDD	Short	26	25	1.5	-1.2	1.24	9	0.2
UDU	Long	53	32	1.2	-1.1	1.08	28	0.3
UUD	Long	50	42	1.1	-1.0	1.09	13	0.1
UUU	Long	84	77	1.0	-0.9	1.07	12	0.1
DDDD	Long	12	11	2.0	-1.3	1.57	10	0.4
DDDU	Short	16	15	1.6	-1.3	1.25	6	0.2
DDUD	Short	23	9	1.8	-2.0	0.89	23	0.7
DDUU	Short	31	27	2.0	-1.4	1.49	26	0.5
DUDD	Short	10	13	1.5	-1.1	1.34	0	0.0
DUDU	Long	19	13	1.4	-1.2	1.14	10	0.3
DUUD	Long	25	17	1.2	-1.2	1.06	11	0.3
DUUU	Short	39	41	1.1	-0.8	1.29	8	0.1
UDDD	Short	10	7	1.3	-1.2	1.08	4	0.3
UDDU	Long	19	11	2.0	-1.1	1.79	26	0.9
UDUD	Short	13	11	1.5	-0.8	1.95	11	0.5
UDUU	Short	30	26	1.0	-1.0	1.07	6	0.1
UUDD	Short	16	12	1.4	-1.2	1.17	8	0.3
UUDU	Long	34	19	1.1	-1.1	1.05	18	0.3
UUUD	Short	19	17	0.9	-0.9	0.97	1	0.0
UUUU	Long	27	30	1.0	-0.6	1.70	10	0.2

WS4 Close-to-Close Pattern

The pre-condition for entering a trade, at the day's close, is that the day of entry should be a WS4 day. Exit is assumed at next day's close. Table 13.2 shows the results for this pattern.

Table 13.2
WS4 Close-to-Close Study on Nifty

Pattern	*Action*	*Winning Trades*	*Losing Trades*	*Avg Profit*	*Avg Loss*	*W/L Ratio*	*Gross Profit*	*Profit per Trade*
DD	Short	96	86	1.6	-1.7	0.95	9	0.1
DU	Long	68	39	1.0	1.0	0.94	26	0.2
UD	Short	81	79	1.7	-1.1	1.47	46	0.3
UU	Long	76	57	1.0	-0.9	1.06	21	0.2
DDD	Long	43	46	1.9	-1.7	1.13	5	0.1
DDU	Long	31	22	1.1	-1.3	0.86	6	0.1
DUD	Short	31	26	1.6	-1.3	1.23	16	0.3
DUU	Long	36	25	0.9	-1.2	0.77	3	0.1
UDD	Short	50	43	1.5	-1.5	1.05	14	0.2
UDU	Long	37	16	0.9	-0.8	1.17	20	0.4
UUD	Short	50	53	1.7	-1.1	1.62	30	0.3
UUU	Long	40	32	1.0	-0.7	1.44	18	0.3
DDDD	Short	20	20	1.9	-1.6	1.18	6	0.1
DDDU	Long	20	10	1.2	-1.6	0.72	7	0.2
DDUD	Short	10	13	2.6	-1.4	1.82	7	0.3
DDUU	Short	14	18	1.6	-0.8	1.98	8	0.2
DUDD	Short	28	18	1.5	-1.6	0.94	13	0.3
DUDU	Long	6	6	1.3	-1.1	1.21	1	0.1
DUUD	Short	27	22	1.9	-1.0	2.05	32	0.6
DUUU	Long	19	6	1.1	-1.0	1.17	16	0.6
UDDD	Long	23	26	2.2	-1.5	1.44	11	0.2
UDDU	Short	12	11	1.0	-1.0	1.03	1	0.1
UDUD	Short	21	13	1.2	-1.3	0.95	9	0.3
UDUU	Long	18	11	1.0	-0.7	1.53	11	0.4
UUDD	Short	22	25	1.6	-1.4	1.17	1	0.0
UUDU	Long	31	10	0.8	-0.5	1.46	19	0.5
UUUD	Long	31	23	1.1	-1.4	0.78	2	0.0
UUUU	Long	21	26	0.9	-0.6	1.41	2	0.0

NR7 Close-to-Close Pattern

The pre-condition for entering a trade, at the day's close, is that the day of entry should be an NR7 day. Exit is assumed at the following day's close.

An obvious point to be noted is that an NR7 is also an NR4 (similarly a WS7 is WS4 as well). Table 13.3 shows the results for this pattern.

Table 13.3

NR7 Close-to-Close Study on Nifty

Pattern	*Action*	*Winning Trades*	*Losing Trades*	*Avg Profit*	*Avg Loss*	*W/L Ratio*	*Gross Profit*	*Profit per Trade*
DD	Short	27	20	1.7	-1.5	1.13	15	0.3
DU	Long	44	36	1.3	-1.0	1.20	18	0.2
UD	Short	39	37	1.5	-1.1	1.38	19	0.2
UU	Short	95	69	1.2	-1.1	1.11	39	0.2
DDD	Short	11	6	1.6	-2.2	0.75	5	0.3
DDU	Short	15	12	1.1	-0.8	1.36	7	0.3
DUD	Short	16	13	2.1	-1.0	2.01	20	0.7
DUU	Short	42	32	1.6	-1.0	1.55	34	0.5
UDD	Short	16	14	1.7	-1.2	1.43	11	0.4
UDU	Long	32	21	1.4	-1.0	1.44	25	0.5
UUD	Long	24	23	1.1	-1.2	1.00	1	0.0
UUU	Short	52	36	0.9	-1.2	0.74	3	0.0
DDDD	Short	6	1	1.5	-5.5	0.27	3	0.5
DDDU	Short	6	4	1.2	-0.9	1.41	4	0.4
DDUD	Short	11	4	2.0	-1.4	1.41	16	1.1
DDUU	Short	19	13	2.2	-1.1	2.07	28	0.9
DUDD	Short	6	4	1.7	-1.1	1.55	6	0.6
DUDU	Long	9	6	1.8	-1.3	1.38	8	0.6
DUUD	Long	12	9	1.6	-1.3	1.22	7	0.3
DUUU	Short	30	18	1.0	-1.3	0.82	8	0.2
UDDD	Short	5	5	1.8	-1.5	1.19	1	0.1
UDDU	Short	9	8	1.1	-0.8	1.32	3	0.2
UDUD	Short	5	9	2.3	-0.9	2.66	4	0.3
UDUU	Short	23	19	1.1	-1.0	1.08	6	0.1
UUDD	Short	10	10	1.7	-1.2	1.40	5	0.2
UUDU	Long	23	15	1.3	-0.8	1.49	16	0.4
UUUD	Short	14	12	1.1	-0.7	1.46	6	0.2
UUUU	Long	18	22	1.0	-0.6	1.69	5	0.1

WS7 Close-to-Close Pattern

The pre-condition for entering a trade, at close, is that the day of entry should be a WS7 day. Exit is assumed at the following day's close. Table 13.4 shows the results for this pattern.

Table 13.4

WS7 Close-to-Close Study on Nifty

Pattern	*Action*	*Winning Trades*	*Losing Trades*	*Avg Profit*	*Avg Loss*	*W/L Ratio*	*Gross Profit*	*Profit per Trade*
DD	Short	66	49	1.6	-1.9	0.88	17	0.1
DU	Long	41	20	1.0	-1.2	0.87	19	0.3
UD	Short	34	42	2.0	-1.0	1.94	25	0.3
UU	Long	42	26	0.9	-1.0	0.92	12	0.2
DDD	Short	34	25	1.7	-2.0	0.84	7	0.1
DDU	Long	19	14	1.0	-1.1	0.93	4	0.1
DUD	Short	11	13	2.0	-1.0	1.95	9	0.4
DUU	Short	14	22	1.2	-0.8	1.58	0	0.0
UDD	Short	32	24	1.6	-1.7	0.93	10	0.2
UDU	Long	22	6	1.0	-1.3	0.77	14	0.5
UUD	Short	23	29	2.0	-1.0	1.93	16	0.3
UUU	Long	20	12	1.0	-0.7	1.53	12	0.4
DDDD	Short	16	11	1.9	-1.7	1.10	12	0.4
DDDU	Long	15	7	1.1	-1.5	0.76	6	0.3
DDUD	Short	4	6	3.5	-0.8	4.57	9	0.9
DDUU	Short	10	12	1.4	-0.6	2.32	7	0.3
DUDD	Short	18	13	1.7	-1.6	1.03	9	0.3
DUDU	Long	3	4	1.9	-1.0	1.84	2	0.2
DUUD	Short	12	9	2.5	-0.9	2.92	22	1.1
DUUU	Long	11	2	1.2	-1.0	1.11	11	0.8
UDDD	Long	14	18	2.3	-1.5	1.49	4	0.1
UDDU	Short	7	4	0.8	-0.8	1.00	2	0.2
UDUD	Short	7	7	1.2	-1.3	0.95	0	0.0
UDUU	Long	10	4	1.0	-0.8	1.27	7	0.5
UUDD	Short	14	11	1.4	-1.8	0.81	1	0.0
UUDU	Long	19	2	0.9	-1.9	0.46	13	0.6
UUUD	Long	20	11	1.1	-1.5	0.76	6	0.2
UUUU	Long	9	10	0.8	-0.6	1.42	2	0.1

Open-to-Close Observations

The next four studies are based on open-to-close patterns.

NR4 Open-to-Close Pattern

The pre-condition for entering a trade is that the previous day should have been an NR4 day. Entry is assumed at the day's open, and exit at the day's close. Table 13.5 shows the results for this pattern.

Table 13.5
NR4 Open-to-Close Study on Nifty

Pattern	*Action*	*Winning Trades*	*Losing Trades*	*Avg Profit*	*Avg Loss*	*W/L Ratio*	*Gross Profit*	*Profit per Trade*
DD	Short	52	31	1.6	-0.9	1.74	55	0.7
DU	Long	67	62	1.4	-1.1	1.28	27	0.2
UD	Short	82	60	1.4	-1.4	1.04	34	0.2
UU	Long	127	108	1.2	-1.1	1.12	36	0.2
DDD	Short	17	11	1.6	-1.1	1.40	14	0.5
DDU	Long	28	28	1.6	-1.2	1.26	9	0.2
DUD	Long	24	26	1.6	-1.3	1.21	4	0.1
DUU	Long	53	34	1.4	-1.1	1.24	36	0.4
UDD	Short	35	20	1.6	-0.8	1.98	41	0.7
UDU	Long	39	34	1.3	-1.0	1.32	18	0.2
UUD	Short	56	36	1.4	-1.2	1.22	38	0.4
UUU	Short	74	73	1.0	-1.0	1.03	3	0.0
DDDD	Short	7	4	1.8	-1.0	1.84	9	0.8
DDDU	Long	15	14	1.8	-1.1	1.64	12	0.4
DDUD	Short	14	9	1.3	-1.8	0.72	2	0.1
DDUU	Long	21	15	1.8	-1.4	1.27	17	0.5
DUDD	Short	20	7	2.0	-1.1	1.79	32	1.2
DUDU	Short	16	12	1.3	-1.5	0.89	3	0.1
DUUD	Short	30	16	1.9	-1.6	1.22	32	0.7
DUUU	Short	31	33	1.2	-1.0	1.26	6	0.1
UDDD	Short	10	7	1.4	-1.2	1.19	6	0.3
UDDU	Short	14	13	1.4	-1.3	1.06	2	0.1
UDUD	Long	15	13	1.5	-1.3	1.15	6	0.2

(Contd . . .)

Table 13.5 (contd.)

NR4 Open-to-Close Study on Nifty

Pattern	*Action*	*Winning Trades*	*Losing Trades*	*Avg Profit*	*Avg Loss*	*W/L Ratio*	*Gross Profit*	*Profit per Trade*
UDUU	Long	32	19	1.1	-0.9	1.27	19	0.4
UUDD	Short	15	13	1.2	-0.7	1.73	9	0.3
UUDU	Long	27	18	1.3	-0.8	1.70	21	0.5
UUUD	Short	27	20	0.9	-0.9	1.09	8	0.2
UUUU	Long	40	43	1.0	-0.9	1.15	3	0.0

WS4 Open-to-Close Pattern

The pre-condition for entering a trade is that the previous day should have been a WS4 day. Entry is assumed at the day's open, and exit at the day's close. Table 13.6 shows the results for this pattern.

Table 13.6

WS4 Open-to-Close Study on Nifty

Pattern	*Action*	*Winning Trades*	*Losing Trades*	*Avg Profit*	*Avg Loss*	*W/L Ratio*	*Gross Profit*	*Profit per Trade*
DD	Short	91	57	1.8	-1.5	1.22	79	0.5
DU	Long	94	77	1.5	-1.4	1.03	28	0.2
UD	Short	31	44	1.5	-0.9	1.62	6	0.1
UU	Long	89	60	1.0	-0.8	1.28	42	0.3
DDD	Short	50	32	1.9	-1.8	1.06	37	0.5
DDU	Long	43	39	1.8	-1.3	1.40	27	0.3
DUD	Short	12	19	1.7	-0.8	2.07	5	0.2
DUU	Long	45	23	1.0	-0.9	1.14	25	0.4
UDD	Short	41	24	1.7	-1.0	1.59	43	0.7
UDU	Short	38	51	1.6	-1.2	1.32	1	0.0
UUD	Short	19	25	1.4	-1.0	1.36	1	0.0
UUU	Long	43	36	0.9	-0.7	1.29	14	0.2
DDDD	Short	24	20	2.1	-1.9	1.14	14	0.3
DDDU	Long	18	17	2.2	-1.2	1.90	20	0.6
DDUD	Short	8	8	1.7	-1.1	1.54	5	0.3
DDUU	Long	23	12	1.1	-1.2	0.91	11	0.3

(Contd . . .)

Table 13.6 (contd.)
WS4 Open-to-Close Study on Nifty

Pattern	Action	Winning Trades	Losing Trades	Avg Profit	Avg Loss	W/L Ratio	Gross Profit	Profit per Trade
DUDD	Short	16	6	2.0	-1.1	1.85	25	1.1
DUDU	Long	17	16	1.4	-1.3	1.15	4	0.1
DUUD	Short	8	9	2.0	-1.2	1.74	6	0.3
DUUU	Long	21	17	0.8	-0.8	1.00	3	0.1
UDDD	Short	26	12	1.6	-1.6	1.02	23	0.6
UDDU	Long	25	22	1.5	-1.4	1.08	7	0.1
UDUD	Short	4	11	1.7	-0.6	2.72	0	0.0
UDUU	Long	22	11	1.0	-0.6	1.62	15	0.4
UUDD	Short	25	18	1.5	-1.0	1.41	18	0.4
UUDU	Short	22	34	1.8	-1.1	1.70	4	0.1
UUUD	Long	16	11	0.9	-0.9	1.03	5	0.2
UUUU	Long	22	19	1.1	-0.7	1.60	11	0.3

NR7 Open-to-Close Pattern

The pre-condition for entering a trade is that the previous day should have been an NR7 day. Entry is assumed at the current day's open, and exit at the day's close. Table 13.7 shows the results for this pattern.

Table 13.7
NR7 Open-to-Close Study on Nifty

Pattern	Action	Winning Trades	Losing Trades	Avg Profit	Avg Loss	W/L Ratio	Gross Profit	Profit per Trade
DD	Short	31	20	1.8	-0.9	2.12	39	0.8
DU	Long	33	33	1.5	-1.4	1.10	5	0.1
UD	Short	57	29	1.4	-1.2	1.16	44	0.5
UU	Long	74	74	1.2	-1.0	1.25	18	0.1
DDD	Short	10	8	1.8	-1.0	1.78	10	0.5
DDU	Short	15	10	1.6	-2.1	0.76	3	0.1

(Contd . . .)

Table 13.7 (contd.)
NR7 Open-to-Close Study on Nifty

Pattern	Action	Winning Trades	Losing Trades	Avg Profit	Avg Loss	W/L Ratio	Gross Profit	Profit per Trade
DUD	Short	15	9	1.0	-1.7	0.59	0	0.0
DUU	Long	31	20	1.1	-1.0	1.08	14	0.3
UDD	Short	21	12	1.8	-0.8	2.41	29	0.9
UDU	Long	23	18	1.2	-1.2	1.07	8	0.2
UUD	Short	42	20	1.5	-0.9	1.60	45	0.7
UUU	Long	42	54	1.2	-0.9	1.32	1	0.0
DDDD	Short	4	2	2.1	-0.6	3.34	7	1.2
DDDU	Long	4	7	2.9	-1.4	2.12	2	0.2
DDUD	Short	7	1	0.8	-1.1	0.70	4	0.5
DDUU	Short	8	10	1.5	-0.7	2.01	4	0.2
DUDD	Short	9	5	2.5	-0.9	2.62	18	1.3
DUDU	Short	7	7	1.5	-1.1	1.33	3	0.2
DUUD	Short	22	8	2.1	-1.1	1.92	37	1.2
DUUU	Short	21	21	1.1	-1.1	1.03	1	0.0
UDDD	Short	6	6	1.6	-1.1	1.40	3	0.2
UDDU	Short	8	6	1.8	-1.6	1.16	5	0.4
UDUD	Long	8	9	1.8	-1.1	1.60	4	0.3
UDUU	Long	21	12	1.3	-0.8	1.74	19	0.6
UUDD	Short	12	7	1.3	-0.6	2.15	12	0.6
UUDU	Long	16	11	1.3	-1.0	1.36	10	0.4
UUUD	Short	21	12	1.0	-0.9	1.13	10	0.3
UUUU	Long	21	33	1.4	-0.8	1.69	2	0.0

WS7 Open-to-Close Pattern

The pre-condition for entering a trade is that the previous day should have been a WS7 day. Entry is assumed at the current day's open, and exit at the day's close. Table 13.8 below shows the results for this pattern.

Table 13.8
WS7 Open-to-Close Study on Nifty

Pattern	Action	Winning Trades	Losing Trades	Avg Profit	Avg Loss	W/L Ratio	Gross Profit	Profit per Trade
DD	Short	55	31	1.9	-1.6	1.17	53	0.6
DU	Long	51	39	1.5	-1.7	0.86	8	0.1
UD	Short	13	24	1.9	-1.0	1.89	1	0.0
UU	Long	52	30	1.0	-0.8	1.25	27	0.3
DDD	Short	34	18	2.0	-2.0	1.03	34	0.6
DDU	Long	24	27	2.0	-1.2	1.65	15	0.3
DUD	Long	11	4	0.8	-2.0	0.41	1	0.1
DUU	Long	28	13	1.1	-1.2	0.89	14	0.3
UDD	Short	26	14	1.9	-1.1	1.81	35	0.9
UDU	Short	15	29	2.4	-0.9	2.53	8	0.2
UUD	Short	14	14	1.8	-1.1	1.58	9	0.3
UUU	Long	31	22	0.9	-0.7	1.16	10	0.2
DDDD	Short	18	11	2.2	-1.8	1.23	20	0.7
DDDU	Long	11	12	2.5	-1.1	2.29	15	0.6
DDUD	Short	2	4	1.5	-1.0	1.58	1	0.1
DDUU	Long	15	10	1.0	-1.3	0.82	3	0.1
DUDD	Short	8	3	1.8	-0.7	2.55	13	1.1
DUDU	Short	3	8	2.6	-1.1	2.42	1	0.1
DUUD	Short	5	5	2.3	-1.2	1.93	5	0.5
DUUU	Long	13	9	0.6	-0.5	1.09	3	0.1
UDDD	Short	16	7	1.8	-2.2	0.81	13	0.6
UDDU	Short	15	13	1.3	-1.6	0.83	1	0.0
UDUD	Short	2	7	2.6	-0.8	3.30	0	0.0
UDUU	Long	13	3	1.1	-1.0	1.12	11	0.7
UUDD	Short	13	10	1.5	-1.2	1.22	7	0.3
UUDU	Short	9	19	2.9	-0.9	3.10	8	0.3
UUUD	Long	8	4	1.2	-1.4	0.82	4	0.3
UUUU	Long	10	8	1.0	-0.4	2.77	7	0.4

Application

The thinking behind the NR4 / NR7 patterns is that price behaviour is similar to a spring being wound, and the range is the spring. The smaller the range, the tighter the spring. The direction of the coming release cannot be accurately predicted at the time of NR4 / NR7 observation, but the coming move is sometimes a violent one. By seeing the direction of the open the next day, one could anticipate the coming move. You can also observe from Table 13.7 ("NR7 Open-to-Close Study on Nifty") a concentration of high win / loss trades with the average profit per trade being more than 0.5 % for quite a few entries.

Chapter 14

Opening Range Breakout

Entering the trade at the market open can be quite tough and, because the market moves very briskly at the open, you never know at what price your order might get filled if it is placed immediately after the open. Traders, therefore, often use a stop order to enter the market after the open.

Here are some of reference points that you can employ before entering the trade:

- Previous day's high or low;
- Pivot points; pivot points are discussed in detail in Chapter 17;
- Open plus or minus stretch;
- Open plus or minus a percentage of the previous day's range.

Some Concepts

In this context, the following concepts have been conceived by Tony Crabel:

- **Stretch:** The stretch is calculated by taking the SMA (simple moving average) of the absolute difference between the open and either the high or low, whichever is smaller, for the previous 10 trading days.

  For example, if for a particular day the open is 4,200, the high is 4,250, and the low is 4,170, then we would take the value of 30 for that day because 4,200-4,170 is 30, which is smaller than 4,250-4,200 which is 50. We then add up all such values for the previous 10 trading days and divide it by 10 to get the 10-day simple moving average (SMA). The value thus obtained is called the stretch.
- **ORB:** ORB is an abbreviation for opening range breakout. Using this strategy, the trader places a buy stop just above the open price plus the

stretch, and a sell stop just below the open price minus the stretch. The first stop triggered enters the trader into the trade and the other stop becomes the protective stop.

- **ORBP:** ORBP is the abbreviation for opening range breakout preference. An ORBP trade is a one-sided ORB trade. If other technical indicators show a strong trend in one direction, then the trader will exercise a "preference" for the direction in which to trade the ORB trade. A stop to open a position would be placed only on the side of the trend — and, if filled, a protective stop would then be placed. The calculation of where to place the "stop to open" would be the same as that for the ORB trade: namely, for longs, the open price plus the stretch, and for shorts, the open price minus the stretch. The ORBP trade is a specialized form of the ORB trade.

High / Low ORB

Entries with Previous Day's High / Low as Reference

We will now study the above entry techniques on Nifty.

Here are the results for the 2-, 3- and 4-day pattern trades, with the Nifty's previous day's high or low used as reference. Entry takes place if Nifty trades above yesterday's high during the day, and exit is at the close on the same day. Table 14.1 summarises the results.

Table 14.1

Open-to-Close Patterns — Entry if Nifty Trades Above the Previous Day's High

Pattern	*Action*	*Winning Trades*	*Losing Trades*	*Avg Profit*	*Avg Loss*	*W/L Ratio*	*Gross Profit*	*Profit per Trade*
DD	Short	27	48	1.1	-0.5	1.98	3	0.0
DU	Long	126	94	0.8	-0.9	0.95	23	0.1
UD	Long	143	123	1.0	-0.9	1.19	40	0.2
UU	Long	351	312	1.0	-0.9	1.14	81	0.1
DDD	Short	12	28	1.4	-0.6	2.34	0	0.0
DDU	Long	57	43	1.0	-0.8	1.24	23	0.2

(Contd . . .)

Table 14.1 (contd.)

Open-to-Close Patterns — Entry if Nifty Trades Above the Previous Day's High

Pattern	*Action*	*Winning Trades*	*Losing Trades*	*Avg Profit*	*Avg Loss*	*W/L Ratio*	*Gross Profit*	*Profit per Trade*
DUD	Long	66	53	1.1	-0.8	1.32	29	0.2
DUU	Long	162	115	1.2	-1.1	1.09	67	0.2
UDD	Short	15	19	0.8	-0.5	1.67	3	0.1
UDU	Short	51	69	1.0	-0.7	1.35	0	0.0
UUD	Long	77	70	0.9	-0.9	1.08	11	0.1
UUU	Long	188	196	0.9	-0.8	1.13	14	0.0
DDDD	Long	15	3	0.7	-0.3	2.43	9	0.5
DDDU	Long	32	25	1.1	-0.9	1.24	13	0.2
DDUD	Long	29	27	1.1	-1.1	0.99	2	0.0
DDUU	Long	73	57	1.5	-1.3	1.13	34	0.3
DUDD	Short	5	4	0.7	-0.1	5.71	3	0.4
DUDU	Short	16	17	1.1	-0.8	1.35	4	0.1
DUUD	Long	40	27	0.9	-1.1	0.84	7	0.1
DUUU	Short	79	86	1.0	-0.9	1.13	3	0.0
UDDD	Short	9	13	1.8	-0.5	3.45	9	0.4
UDDU	Long	25	18	0.9	-0.7	1.25	10	0.2
UDUD	Long	37	26	1.2	-0.6	1.88	27	0.4
UDUU	Long	89	58	0.9	-0.9	1.10	34	0.2
UUDD	Short	10	15	0.8	-0.6	1.44	0	0.0
UUDU	Long	52	35	0.7	-0.9	0.76	4	0.0
UUUD	Long	37	43	0.9	-0.7	1.30	4	0.0
UUUU	Long	102	117	1.0	-0.7	1.38	16	0.1

Table 14.2 summarises the results when entry is made using the Nifty's previous day's low as reference. Entry will take place if Nifty trades below the previous day's low; exit is at the same day's close.

I'm not able to identify with conviction any trading biases in the case of trades taken at the previous day's high level as the average profit per trade in most trades is never above 0.5 %, but the trades taken at the previous day's low level do provide some edge in terms of going short during intraday.

Table 14.2

Open-to-Close Patterns — Entry with Reference to the Previous Day's Low

Pattern	*Action*	*Winning Trades*	*Losing Trades*	*Avg Profit*	*Avg Loss*	*W/L Ratio*	*Gross Profit*	*Profit per Trade*
DD	Short	205	141	1.5	-1.2	1.22	133	0.4
DU	Short	178	135	1.1	-1.0	1.11	59	0.2
UD	Short	95	57	1.0	-0.9	1.06	41	0.3
UU	Short	80	85	0.9	-0.7	1.33	14	0.1
DDD	Short	98	72	1.7	-1.3	1.26	68	0.4
DDU	Short	88	65	1.0	-1.0	1.02	25	0.2
DUD	Short	37	20	0.9	-1.0	0.90	13	0.2
DUU	Long	29	29	0.9	-0.9	1.05	1	0.0
UDD	Short	107	68	1.3	-1.1	1.20	67	0.4
UDU	Short	90	70	1.1	-0.9	1.20	34	0.2
UUD	Short	58	37	1.0	-0.9	1.16	27	0.3
UUU	Short	51	56	0.9	-0.6	1.65	16	0.1
DDDD	Short	50	42	1.5	-1.7	0.89	4	0.0
DDDU	Short	42	31	1.0	-1.1	0.93	9	0.1
DDUD	Short	19	11	0.8	-0.8	1.08	7	0.2
DDUU	Short	16	13	0.8	-0.8	0.99	2	0.1
DUDD	Short	52	25	1.4	-1.2	1.14	42	0.5
DUDU	Short	45	28	1.0	-1.0	0.98	16	0.2
DUUD	Short	30	12	1.2	-1.2	1.01	22	0.5
DUUU	Short	26	12	1.0	-0.5	1.90	19	0.5
UDDD	Short	48	30	1.8	-0.7	2.39	64	0.8
UDDU	Short	46	34	1.1	-1.0	1.11	16	0.2
UDUD	Short	18	9	1.0	-1.3	0.76	6	0.2
UDUU	Long	16	13	1.0	-1.0	1.04	4	0.1
UUDD	Short	55	43	1.3	-1.0	1.21	25	0.3
UUDU	Short	45	42	1.2	-0.8	1.41	18	0.2
UUUD	Short	28	24	0.9	-0.8	1.10	5	0.1
UUUU	Long	44	25	0.6	-0.9	0.66	3	0.0

Stretch ORB

Entries with Stretch as Reference

Entry will take place if Nifty trades above open plus stretch, and exit is at the same day's close. Table 14.3 summarises the results.

Table 14.3

2-, 3- and 4-day Nifty Open-to-Close Patterns — Entry with Open plus Stretch as Reference

Pattern	*Action*	*Winning Trades*	*Losing Trades*	*Avg Profit*	*Avg Loss*	*W/L Ratio*	*Gross Profit*	*Profit per Trade*
DD	Long	147	112	1.1	-1.1	0.96	32	0.1
DU	Long	250	223	1.2	-1.1	1.18	75	0.2
UD	Long	163	140	1.0	-1.0	1.04	28	0.1
UU	Long	373	316	1.0	-1.0	1.05	72	0.1
DDD	Long	79	50	1.2	-1.3	0.96	33	0.3
DDU	Long	111	106	1.5	-1.2	1.24	38	0.2
DUD	Long	78	54	1.0	-1.0	1.02	26	0.2
DUU	Long	166	121	1.2	-1.1	1.11	67	0.2
UDD	Short	62	67	1.0	-0.9	1.12	2	0.0
UDU	Long	139	117	1.0	-0.9	1.14	37	0.1
UUD	Long	85	86	1.0	-0.9	1.04	2	0.0
UUU	Long	206	194	0.9	-0.9	0.97	6	0.0
DDDD	Long	49	24	1.3	-1.2	1.11	36	0.5
DDDU	Long	55	54	1.7	-1.2	1.45	30	0.3
DDUD	Long	35	23	1.0	-1.2	0.80	6	0.1
DDUU	Long	75	57	1.5	-1.1	1.32	48	0.4
DUDD	Short	24	25	0.9	-0.7	1.20	3	0.1
DUDU	Long	44	48	1.2	-0.9	1.33	10	0.1
DUUD	Long	42	29	1.0	-1.1	0.93	11	0.2
DUUU	Short	77	94	1.0	-0.8	1.30	5	0.0
UDDD	Short	26	30	1.4	-1.1	1.26	3	0.1
UDDU	Long	56	52	1.3	-1.3	1.04	8	0.1
UDUD	Long	43	30	1.1	-0.8	1.24	20	0.3
UDUU	Long	91	64	0.9	-1.0	0.91	19	0.1
UUDD	Short	38	42	1.1	-1.0	1.09	1	0.0
UUDU	Long	95	69	0.9	-0.9	1.05	28	0.2
UUUD	Short	56	43	0.8	-0.9	0.90	7	0.1
UUUU	Long	112	117	0.9	-0.8	1.16	11	0.0

Table 14.4 summarises the results if entry is made once Nifty starts trading below open minus stretch; exit is at the same day's close.

Table 14.4

2-, 3- and 4-day Open-to-Close Patterns, Entry Reference as Open Minus Stretch

Pattern	*Action*	*Winning Trades*	*Losing Trades*	*Avg Profit*	*Avg Loss*	*W/L Ratio*	*Gross Profit*	*Profit per Trade*
DD	Short	198	148	1.7	-1.1	1.52	167	0.5
DU	Short	198	171	1.2	-1.0	1.17	61	0.2
UD	Short	158	120	1.2	-0.8	1.44	91	0.3
UU	Short	236	211	1.0	-0.7	1.45	88	0.2
DDD	Short	97	76	1.9	-1.3	1.43	82	0.5
DDU	Short	104	74	1.2	-1.0	1.12	44	0.2
DUD	Short	65	47	1.2	-0.9	1.39	38	0.3
DUU	Short	96	72	1.0	-0.8	1.33	44	0.3
UDD	Short	101	72	1.5	-0.9	1.67	86	0.5
UDU	Short	94	97	1.2	-1.0	1.21	17	0.1
UUD	Short	93	73	1.2	-0.8	1.48	53	0.3
UUU	Short	140	138	0.9	-0.6	1.52	45	0.2
DDDD	Short	47	49	1.8	-1.6	1.12	6	0.1
DDDU	Short	53	34	1.1	-1.2	0.94	19	0.2
DDUD	Short	37	18	1.2	-0.8	1.54	31	0.6
DDUU	Short	53	35	1.2	-0.9	1.31	32	0.4
DUDD	Short	49	31	1.7	-1.0	1.75	53	0.7
DUDU	Long	39	45	1.2	-1.0	1.19	1	0.0
DUUD	Short	46	32	1.5	-1.0	1.49	36	0.5
DUUU	Short	63	48	1.0	-0.7	1.49	31	0.3
UDDD	Short	50	27	2.0	-0.8	2.40	76	1.0
UDDU	Short	51	40	1.2	-0.9	1.33	25	0.3
UDUD	Short	27	29	1.3	-0.9	1.36	7	0.1
UDUU	Short	43	37	0.9	-0.7	1.29	12	0.2
UUDD	Short	52	41	1.3	-0.8	1.55	33	0.4
UUDU	Short	49	58	1.3	-0.8	1.64	18	0.2
UUUD	Short	46	41	0.9	-0.7	1.35	14	0.2
UUUU	Short	77	90	0.9	-0.6	1.50	15	0.1

Taking trades at the open +/- stretch gives us some breathing space rather than taking a trade immediately after the open.

Range ORB

Pattern: Entries with Yesterday's Range as Reference

Many trading books and experts advocate entries around open plus or minus the previous day's range, and there are a few related technical indicators, like average true range (ATR), etc. which are derived from the previous trading's days ranges), so I have applied the same concept to Nifty.

Entry takes place if Nifty trades above open plus yesterday's range and exit is at the same day's close. Table 14.5 summarises the results:

Table 14.5

Open-to-Close Patterns — Entry at Open plus Yesterday's Range

Pattern	Action	Winning Trades	Losing Trades	Avg Profit	Avg Loss	W/L Ratio	Gross Profit	Profit per Trade
DD	Long	22	18	0.4	-0.3	1.48	4	0.1
DU	Short	50	53	0.7	-0.6	1.17	3	0.0
UD	Long	41	24	0.5	-0.3	1.34	11	0.2
UU	Long	85	87	0.8	-0.7	1.18	9	0.1
DDD	Long	10	10	0.5	-0.2	2.61	3	0.2
DDU	Long	24	20	0.7	-0.4	1.72	8	0.2
DUD	Long	20	10	0.5	-0.4	1.40	7	0.2
DUU	Long	40	44	1.0	-0.8	1.30	6	0.1
UDD	Short	7	12	0.4	-0.3	1.34	1	0.0
UDU	Short	30	29	0.9	-0.6	1.66	11	0.2
UUD	Long	21	14	0.4	-0.3	1.26	4	0.1
UUU	Long	45	43	0.7	-0.7	1.07	3	0.0

Now let's consider the case when entry takes place if Nifty trades below open minus yesterday's range; exit is at the same day's close. Table 14.6 summarises the results:

Table 14.6
Open-to-Close Patterns — Entry at Open Minus Yesterday's Range

Pattern	*Action*	*Winning Trades*	*Losing Trades*	*Avg Profit*	*Avg Loss*	*W / L Ratio*	*Gross Profit*	*Profit per Trade*
DD	Long	59	54	1.2	-1.3	0.95	3	0.0
DU	Short	45	46	0.8	-0.7	1.16	4	0.0
UD	Short	43	49	1.0	-0.8	1.32	6	0.1
UU	Short	48	50	0.8	-0.5	1.80	16	0.2
DDD	Short	29	22	1.4	-1.6	0.89	6	0.1
DDU	Short	18	23	0.9	-0.7	1.35	1	0.0
DUD	Short	15	21	1.1	-0.7	1.64	3	0.1
DUU	Short	18	18	0.7	-0.5	1.48	4	0.1
UDD	Long	37	25	1.0	-1.2	0.87	8	0.1
UDU	Short	27	23	0.7	-0.7	1.03	3	0.1
UUD	Short	28	28	1.0	-0.8	1.15	3	0.1
UUU	Short	30	32	0.9	-0.4	2.02	12	0.2

As you can see from Tables 14.5 and 14.6, if we take the previous day's range of Nifty as our reference for entry, we are neither presented with many active trading opportunities nor trades where there is an edge of at least 0.5%. average profit per trade.

I have done another study by taking half of the previous day's range of Nifty but I am still not able to find any patterns which offer a significant trading edge. The study indicates that the range as a reference does not seem to provide any edge for short term Nifty trades.

Pivot Point Based ORB

Entries with Pivot Points as a Reference

As you may be aware, many brokerage houses in India provide the support and resistance levels for each trading day, which are nothing but pivot point levels.

Let us now consider pivot point levels for making trade entries.

Entry will take place if Nifty trades above resistance level 1 (R1) and we will exit at the same day's close. Table 14.7 summarises the results.

Table 14.7
Open-to-Close Patterns with a R1 Level as an Entry Point

Pattern	*Action*	*Winning Trades*	*Losing Trades*	*Avg Profit*	*Avg Loss*	*W/L Ratio*	*Gross Profit*	*Profit per Trade*
DD	Long	62	36	0.6	-0.7	0.93	15	0.2
DU	Long	151	121	0.9	-1.0	0.90	14	0.1
UD	Long	111	94	0.8	-0.8	1.09	20	0.1
UU	Short	270	285	1.0	-0.9	1.07	2	0.0
DDD	Long	35	17	0.7	-0.7	1.05	14	0.3
DDU	Long	67	64	1.0	-1.0	1.06	6	0.0
DUD	Long	53	40	0.9	-0.9	1.05	13	0.1
DUU	Long	129	106	1.1	-1.0	1.09	34	0.1
UDD	Short	19	26	0.7	-0.5	1.32	0	0.0
UDU	Long	84	57	0.8	-1.0	0.77	8	0.1
UUD	Long	58	54	0.8	-0.7	1.11	7	0.1
UUU	Short	163	154	1.0	-0.8	1.23	36	0.1

Now let us consider the case when entry takes place if Nifty trades below support level 1 (S1) and exit is at the same day's close. Table 14.8 summaries the results.

Table 14.8
Open-to-Close Patterns with a S1 Level as an Entry Point

Pattern	*Action*	*Winning Trades*	*Losing Trades*	*Avg Profit*	*Avg Loss*	*W/L Ratio*	*Gross Profit*	*Profit per Trade*
DD	Short	162	126	1.4	-1.2	1.12	67	0.2
DU	Short	136	104	1.0	-1.0	1.02	33	0.1
UD	Short	99	78	1.1	-0.8	1.34	44	0.2
UU	Short	106	93	0.8	-0.7	1.28	28	0.1
DDD	Short	75	63	1.6	-1.3	1.18	34	0.2
DDU	Short	67	57	0.9	-1.0	0.98	9	0.1
DUD	Short	37	33	1.1	-0.9	1.23	11	0.2
DUU	Short	42	26	0.8	-0.9	0.87	10	0.1
UDD	Short	87	63	1.2	-1.1	1.07	34	0.2
UDU	Short	69	47	1.0	-0.9	1.05	24	0.2
UUD	Short	62	45	1.1	-0.7	1.44	33	0.3
UUU	Short	64	67	0.9	-0.6	1.55	18	0.1

I'm not able to conclude any trading biases taken at the R1 level, but the trades taken at S1 level do tell us that it is not so wise to hold the longs during intraday as evident by the concentration of short bias in all rows in Table 14.8, and the winning trades out-numbering the losing trades in all the rows.

Conclusion

The open is a primary market action for the day and on certain days it acts as an ideal point of entry for a trade. On certain days it is ideal to place trade entries at either yesterday's low / high, or at pivot point levels, or open +/- stretch. The stretch concept is not so popular in India or in various charting packages.

A breakout can be defined as a situation when the price moves outside a defined support or resistance level with increased volume. A breakout trader enters a long position after the stock price breaks above a price level or enters a short position after the stock breaks below a price level. Once the stock trades beyond the price barrier, volatility tends to increase and the price usually trends in the breakout's direction. The reason breakouts are such an important trading strategy is because these set-ups are the starting point for future large price swings. In many circumstances, breakouts are the starting point for major price trends.

There is always an if, but or a however situation when dealing with the market because nothing works a hundred percent of the time. However, in case you miss the entry at the point of occurrence for any breakout trade, be it open or open+/- stretch, any retracement of up to half of the established range can be used as a secondary entry point. The disadvantage of waiting for the retracement is that when the market trend is extremely strong after the open, the market will usually not retrace even close to the 75 percent level, and not make even a small correction. Kindly note that the retracement levels need to be calculated on the range (high and low so far in the trading day) established in the first minute for the trading day.

In general, the earlier in the session the entry is taken, the better the chances for success. In fact, the ideal is an entry within the first 10 minutes of the session. In that case, an immediate continuation in the direction of the breakout is likely. When you get a large price movement in one direction within the first 15 minutes of the session (early entry), the protective stop can be moved to break-even very quickly and the trade is then free.

The more the time that passes between the open and trade entry, the lower the probability of success. Adjust the size of your position downward as the day goes on. The worst entry is just before the close when time is running out and it is difficult to realize a profit. The objective of these entry techniques is to establish a position for a two- to three-day run, but this is successful only if a substantial profit is realized by the end of the first session.

Chapter 15

Inside Day

Definitions

- **Inside Day (ID):** An inside day is defined as a trading day whose range lies completely within the previous day's range. More specifically, an inside day's high is lower than the previous day's high and its low is higher than the previous day's low.
- **Range:** Range is simply the difference between the high and the low of the day.

  Figure 15.1 demonstrates an inside day.

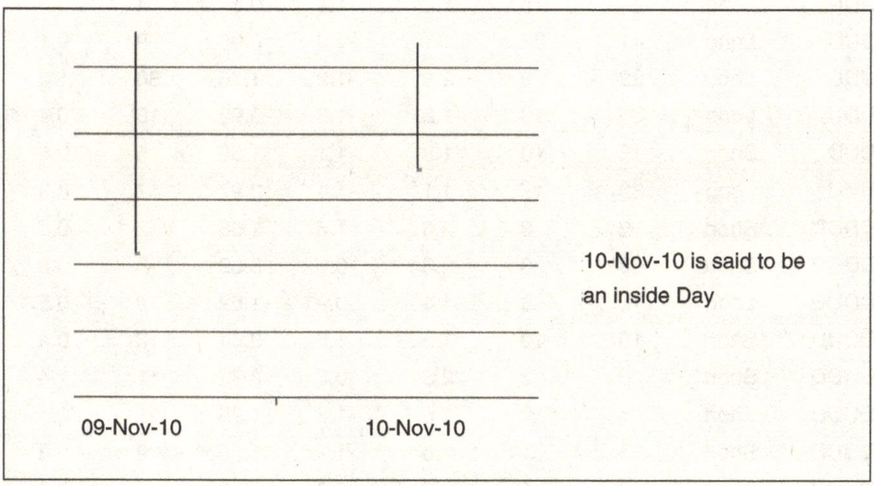

Figure 15.1: **Inside day**

ID Patterns

ID Open-to-Close Pattern

I have tested several patterns in order to find reliable entries. The precondition for entering the trade is that the previous day should have been an inside day. Entry is assumed at the open on the day following an inside day and exit at its close. Here are the studies of the price movements on Nifty after an ID occurs (Table 15.1).

Table 15.1
ID Open-to-Close Study

Pattern	*Action*	*Winning Trades*	*Losing Trades*	*Avg Profit*	*Avg Loss*	*W/L Ratio*	*Gross Profit*	*Profit per Trade*
DD	Short	13	10	2.1	-1.2	1.75	16	0.7
DU	Long	29	19	1.2	-1.6	0.75	4	0.1
UD	Short	24	29	1.6	-1.1	1.43	6	0.1
UU	Long	54	40	1.2	-1.2	1.05	19	0.2
DDD	Short	3	3	2.5	-1.2	2.11	4	0.7
DDU	Short	5	4	1.8	-0.8	2.31	6	0.7
DUD	Long	24	18	1.2	-1.4	0.87	4	0.1
DUU	Long	41	32	1.1	-1.2	0.96	9	0.1
UDD	Short	22	8	2.1	-1.2	1.76	36	1.2
UDU	Long	35	18	1.2	-1.3	0.93	19	0.4
UUD	Short	15	10	1.8	-1.1	1.59	15	0.6
UUU	Long	33	17	1.1	-1.1	0.97	17	0.3
DDDD	Short	2	2	2.6	-1.6	1.66	2	0.5
DDDU	Short	3	3	2.3	-0.6	3.62	5	0.8
DDUD	Long	12	8	1.4	-0.9	1.52	10	0.5
DDUU	Short	19	10	1.5	-1.6	0.94	13	0.4
DUDD	Short	6	2	2.2	-0.8	2.72	11	1.4
DUDU	Short	8	9	1.6	-1.3	1.25	1	0.1
DUUD	Short	4	1	2.6	-1.7	1.55	9	1.8
DUUU	Long	6	1	0.9	0.0	86.8	6	0.8
UDDD	Short	1	1	2.4	-0.5	4.94	2	1.0
UDDU	Short	2	1	1.1	-1.3	0.90	1	0.3
UDUD	Short	10	12	1.8	-1.1	1.71	5	0.2

(Contd . . .)

Table 15.1 (contd.)
ID Open-to-Close Study

Pattern	Action	Winning Trades	Losing Trades	Avg Profit	Avg Loss	W/L Ratio	Gross Profit	Profit per Trade
UDUU	Long	31	13	1.0	-0.7	1.36	21	0.5
UUDD	Short	4	5	1.8	-1.4	1.27	0	0.0
UUDU	Long	16	6	1.2	-1.3	0.93	11	0.5
UUUD	Short	2	4	1.4	-0.4	3.56	1	0.2
UUUU	Long	7	7	1.8	-1.1	1.58	5	0.3

ID Open-to-Close Pattern: Opening Range as Reference

In this case, I have considered the open against the previous day's range. I would consider the open as top range if the open is in the top half of the previous day's range, as explained in the Gaps and Laps chapter (Chapter 11). The pre-condition for entering the trade is that the previous day should have been an inside day. Entry is assumed at the day's open on the day following an inside day, which must be in the top range, and exit at the day's close (*see* Table 15.2).

Table 15.2
ID Open-to-Close Study, Open in the Top Range

Pattern	Action	Winning Trades	Losing Trades	Avg Profit	Avg Loss	W/L Ratio	Gross Profit	Profit per Trade
DD	Short	4	1	1.2	-0.7	1.65	4	0.8
DU	Long	12	4	1.3	-1.2	1.13	11	0.7
UD	Short	15	20	1.8	-1.1	1.54	4	0.1
UU	Long	49	35	1.2	-1.2	1.03	18	0.2
DDD	Short	1	0	1.8	NA	NA	2	1.8
DDU	Short	0	1	NA	-0.4	NA	0	0.4
DUD	Long	19	11	1.2	-1.7	0.71	4	0.1
DUU	Long	36	28	1.1	-1.2	0.94	7	0.1
UDD	Short	3	1	1.0	-0.7	1.40	2	0.6
UDU	Long	11	4	1.4	-1.2	1.20	11	0.7
UUD	Short	4	1	2.0	-0.3	6.76	8	1.6
UUU	Long	13	7	1.4	-1.0	1.38	11	0.6

Let us now consider the case when open is in the bottom range, i.e. in the bottom half of the previous day's range.

The pre-condition for entering the trade is that the previous day should have been an inside day. Entry is assumed at the day's open, which must be in the bottom range, and exit at the close (*see* Table 15.3).

Table 15.3

ID Open-to-Close Study When Open is in the Bottom Range

Pattern	*Action*	*Winning Trades*	*Losing Trades*	*Avg Profit*	*Avg Loss*	*W/L Ratio*	*Gross Profit*	*Profit per Trade*
DD	Short	9	9	2.5	-1.3	1.99	11	0.6
DU	Short	15	17	1.7	-1.0	1.59	7	0.2
UD	Short	9	9	1.4	-1.1	1.23	2	0.1
UU	Long	5	5	1.4	-1.2	1.18	1	0.1
DDD	Short	2	3	2.9	-1.2	2.43	2	0.4
DDU	Short	5	3	1.8	-0.9	1.98	6	0.8
DUD	Short	7	5	1.0	-1.4	0.73	0	0.0
DUU	Long	5	4	1.4	-1.2	1.13	2	0.2
UDD	Short	7	6	2.4	-1.3	1.86	9	0.7
UDU	Short	10	14	1.6	-1.1	1.48	1	0.0
UUD	Short	2	4	2.6	-0.7	3.48	2	0.4
UUU	Short	1	0	0.9	NA	NA	1	0.9

ID and High / Low as Entry Reference

ID Open-to-Close: High as Entry Reference

The pre-condition for entering the trade is that the previous day should have been an inside day. Entry is assumed above the previous day's high and exit at the close. Table 15.4 summarises the price movements on Nifty after an ID occurs.

Table 15.4

ID Performance with Yesterday's High as a Reference Entry

Pattern	*Action*	*Winning Trades*	*Losing Trades*	*Avg Profit*	*Avg Loss*	*W/L Ratio*	*Gross Profit*	*Profit per Trade*
DD	Short	4	5	0.9	-0.7	1.25	0	0.0
DU	Short	13	15	1.2	-1.0	1.21	1	0.0

(Contd . . .)

Table 15.4 (contd.)

ID Performance with Yesterday's High as a Reference Entry

Pattern	*Action*	*Winning Trades*	*Losing Trades*	*Avg Profit*	*Avg Loss*	*W/L Ratio*	*Gross Profit*	*Profit per Trade*
UD	Long	19	15	0.9	-0.7	1.33	7	0.2
UU	Long	46	33	1.0	-1.1	0.84	7	0.1
DDD	Short	2	0	0.2	NA	NA	0	0.2
DDU	Short	2	1	0.4	-0.6	0.60	0	0.0
DUD	Long	16	12	1.0	-0.7	1.35	7	0.2
DUU	Short	27	35	1.3	-0.8	1.50	5	0.1
UDD	Short	2	5	1.5	-0.7	2.17	0	0.1
UDU	Short	11	14	1.4	-1.0	1.33	1	0.0
UUD	Short	3	3	0.5	-0.5	1.06	0	0.0
UUU	Long	11	6	1.3	-0.5	2.39	11	0.7

ID Open-to-Close: Low as Entry Reference

The pre-condition for entering the trade is that the previous day should have been an inside day. Entry is assumed below the previous day's low and exit at the day's close. Table 15.5 summarises the price movements on Nifty after an ID occurs.

Table 15.5

ID Performance with Yesterday's Low as a Reference Entry

Pattern	*Action*	*Winning Trades*	*Losing Trades*	*Avg Profit*	*Avg Loss*	*W/L Ratio*	*Gross Profit*	*Profit per Trade*
DD	Short	12	3	1.7	-1.4	1.25	17	1.1
DU	Short	17	7	1.2	-1.1	1.10	13	0.6
UD	Short	17	8	1.2	-0.9	1.37	13	0.5
UU	Short	12	13	0.7	-0.7	1.06	0	0.0
DDD	Short	3	2	2.0	-1.4	1.44	3	0.6
DDU	Short	5	1	1.4	-1.1	1.22	6	0.9
DUD	Short	12	8	1.0	-0.9	1.10	5	0.2
DUU	Short	10	8	0.7	-0.8	0.91	1	0.1
UDD	Short	9	1	1.7	-1.5	1.13	14	1.4
UDU	Short	12	6	1.2	-1.1	1.06	8	0.4
UUD	Short	5	0	1.8	NA	NA	9	1.8
UUU	Long	5	2	0.5	-0.8	0.68	1	0.2

ID Close-to-Close

In this case, we enter the trade at an inside day's close and exit at the next day's close. Table 15.6 summarises the results.

Table 15.6

Close-to-Close Performance — Entry at ID's Close and Exit at the Next Day's Close

Pattern	*Action*	*Winning Trades*	*Losing Trades*	*Avg Profit*	*Avg Loss*	*W / L Ratio*	*Gross Profit*	*Profit per Trade*
DD	Short	8	7	2.0	-1.0	2.10	10	0.6
DU	Long	68	51	1.2	-1.3	0.93	15	0.1
UD	Short	25	32	1.6	-1.3	1.28	0	0.0
UU	Short	15	19	1.6	-1.1	1.37	2	0.1
DDD	Short	5	5	2.3	-1.0	2.29	7	0.7
DDU	Short	28	24	1.3	-1.5	0.86	0	0.0
DUD	Short	15	11	1.7	-1.3	1.34	12	0.4
DUU	Short	6	7	2.1	-1.0	2.08	6	0.4
UDD	Short	3	2	1.6	-0.9	1.80	3	0.6
UDU	Long	44	23	1.0	-1.3	0.80	16	0.2
UUD	Long	21	10	1.3	-1.5	0.86	12	0.4
UUU	Long	12	9	1.2	-1.2	1.02	4	0.2

ID Close-to-Close Modified

Now we would modify the above pattern and enter the trade the day after an ID is observed. Entry is assumed at the close of the day after an ID and we exit at the next day's close. Table 15.7 summarises the results.

Table 15.7

Close-to-Close Performance — Entry One Day After an ID

Pattern	*Action*	*Winning Trades*	*Losing Trades*	*Avg Profit*	*Avg Loss*	*W / L Ratio*	*Gross Profit*	*Profit per Trade*
DD	Short	17	17	2.2	-1.5	1.49	13	0.4
DU	Long	19	20	1.5	-1.2	1.30	5	0.1
UD	Short	29	35	1.7	-1.1	1.55	11	0.2
UU	Long	53	35	1.1	-1.0	1.05	21	0.2

(Contd . . .)

Table 15.7 (contd.)

Close-to-Close Performance — Entry One Day After an ID

Pattern	*Action*	*Winning Trades*	*Losing Trades*	*Avg Profit*	*Avg Loss*	*W / L Ratio*	*Gross Profit*	*Profit per Trade*
DDD	Short	4	5	4.0	-1.6	2.41	8	0.8
DDU	Short	5	5	2.2	-2.1	1.05	0	0.0
DUD	Long	29	19	1.1	-1.5	0.77	5	0.1
DUU	Long	42	25	1.0	-1.1	0.88	14	0.2
UDD	Short	13	12	1.7	-1.4	1.18	5	0.2
UDU	Long	14	15	1.3	-0.8	1.59	6	0.2
UUD	Short	10	6	2.1	-0.8	2.53	16	1.0
UUU	Long	11	10	1.2	-0.7	1.88	7	0.3

Application

An inside day is indecisive from supply and demand point of view. The logic is that when the market overcomes this indecision by penetrating either the high or the low, it is evidence of demand or supply and should lead to a profitable trade.

Inside days act as springboards for an immediate continuation in the direction of the run. One can conclude from the above patterns that there is a tendency to trend after an inside day. When combined with the information of open after the inside day, we can have clues to the direction for the day. A clear bias of short, almost in all rows in Table 15.5 ("ID Performance with Yesterday's Low as a Reference Entry"), does provide some trading edges. Going long can be considered after knowing the direction of the open and making sure that the open is in the top 50 % of the previous day's range, as mentioned in Table 15.2 ("ID Open-to-Close Study, Open in the Top Range"). Couple Table 15.2 with yesterday's high as an entry point and you would get some high win / loss ratios and high gross profit patterns. However, I leave that as an exercise for the readers.

On the other hand, close to close entries after an inside day don't seem to provide any profitable trade opportunities as the future direction is not as predictable at the time of the occurrence of an inside day.

Chapter 16

Doji

Definition

On a candlestick chart, a Doji day is defined as one when the open price and close price are the same (0% Doji), or the difference between the open and the close is very small. "Very small" is a relative term, so I have taken the range for the day as the reference. For example, if the range for the day is 100 points and if the difference between open and close is 10 points, I have called it 10% Doji. Similarly, if the difference between open and close is 20 points in a 100 points intraday range, I have called it 20% Doji, and so on.

Figure 16.1 shows what a Doji looks like on a candlestick chart.

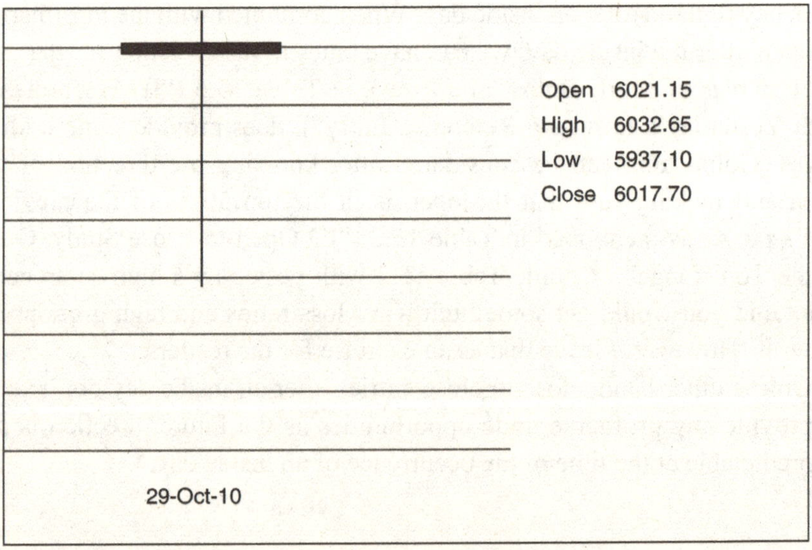

Figure 16.1: **Doji Formation**

A Doji indicates market indecision, and it is said that the Japanese believe Doji precedes market turning points. The strategy, then, is to look closely at the price movements that follow a Doji day, and be ready to enter the market once the direction of the market is known. Logically, it makes sense to study only the open-to-close price action after the Doji day. The reason being it would be difficult to calculate the Doji appearance at the time of close with confidence, as any move of approximately 5% of the range at the time of close (say from 3.15-3.30 p.m.) will give a room for a calculation error in identifying the Doji.

1-Point Doji Pattern

A 1-point Doji is, as you might have guessed, a day when the difference between open and close is less than 1 point. The pre-condition for entering the trade is that yesterday should have been a Doji day. Entry is assumed at today's open, and exit at the close. Table 16.1 summarises the results for this pattern on Nifty.

Table 16.1

1-Point Doji Performance of Nifty

Pattern	*Action*	*Winning Trades*	*Losing Trades*	*Avg Profit*	*Avg Loss*	*W/L Ratio*	*Gross Profit*	*Profit per Trade*
DD	Short	51	34	2.0	-1.3	1.52	58	0.7
DU	Long	68	49	1.4	-1.3	1.08	32	0.3
UD	Short	3	2	2.0	-1.0	2.03	4	0.8
UU	Long	3	1	1.2	-0.2	7.00	3	0.9
DDD	Short	31	28	2.2	-1.5	1.42	24	0.4
DDU	Long	34	32	1.6	-1.4	1.12	8	0.1
DUD	Long	1	0	1.2	NA	NA	1	1.2
DUU	Short	0	1	NA	-0.4	NA	0	0.4
UDD	Short	20	6	1.9	-0.5	3.67	34	1.3
UDU	Long	34	17	1.3	-1.2	1.08	24	0.5
UUD	Short	3	1	2.0	-0.8	2.57	5	1.3
UUU	Long	2	1	1.6	-0.2	9.42	3	1.0

Looking through Table 16.1 you can see a few profitable trading ideas, namely DD-Short and UDU-Long.

10% Doji Pattern

The pre-condition for entering the trade is that the previous day should have been a 10% Doji day. Entry is assumed at the day's open, and exit at the close. Table 16.2 summarises the results for this pattern.

Table 16.2

10% Doji Performance of Nifty

Pattern	*Action*	*Winning Trades*	*Losing Trades*	*Avg Profit*	*Avg Loss*	*W/L Ratio*	*Gross Profit*	*Profit per Trade*
DD	Short	13	11	1.4	-0.5	2.70	13	0.5
DU	Short	31	30	1.2	-1.1	1.06	3	0.1
UD	Short	28	19	1.7	-1.5	1.13	19	0.4
UU	Long	40	32	1.1	-0.9	1.24	16	0.2
DDD	Short	6	3	1.6	-0.5	3.00	8	0.9
DDU	Short	14	13	1.2	-1.2	1.01	1	0.0
DUD	Long	11	11	1.6	-1.1	1.46	6	0.3
DUU	Long	19	12	1.3	-1.2	1.06	10	0.3
UDD	Short	7	8	1.3	-0.5	2.44	5	0.3
UDU	Short	17	17	1.2	-1.1	1.09	2	0.1
UUD	Short	17	8	2.1	-1.4	1.52	24	1.0
UUU	Long	21	20	1.0	-0.7	1.36	6	0.2
DDDD	Short	2	1	0.8	-0.1	8.16	2	0.5
DDDU	Short	9	5	1.5	-1.7	0.92	5	0.4
DDUD	Long	5	7	1.9	-1.0	1.91	3	0.2
DDUU	Short	8	5	1.2	-1.9	0.62	0	0.0
DUDD	Short	5	3	1.6	-0.5	3.50	7	0.8
DUDU	Short	6	4	1.5	-1.6	0.92	2	0.2
DUUD	Short	6	4	2.7	-2.3	1.14	7	0.7
DUUU	Short	10	5	1.1	-0.3	3.36	9	0.6
UDDD	Short	3	1	2.2	-1.1	2.09	6	1.4
UDDU	Long	3	4	0.9	-0.3	2.73	1	0.2
UDUD	Long	5	4	1.4	-1.3	1.08	2	0.2
UDUU	Long	13	4	1.1	-1.2	0.89	9	0.5
UUDD	Long	5	2	0.6	-0.5	1.04	2	0.3
UUDU	Long	13	8	0.9	-1.2	0.76	2	0.1
UUUD	Short	9	4	1.6	-0.4	4.15	13	1.0
UUUU	Long	14	10	1.2	-0.4	2.88	12	0.5

From Table 16.2 it would appear that after a 10% Doji day the next day's open provides clues to the direction of the that day's close; namely if open is down, the close would also probably be down, and *vice versa.*

20% Doji Pattern

The pre-condition for entering the trade is that the previous day should have been a 20% Doji day. Entry is assumed at the open, and exit at the close. Table 16.3 summarises the results for this pattern:

Table 16.3

20% Doji Performance of Nifty

Pattern	*Action*	*Winning Trades*	*Losing Trades*	*Avg Profit*	*Avg Loss*	*W/L Ratio*	*Gross Profit*	*Profit per Trade*
DD	Short	36	33	1.4	-0.9	1.59	21	0.3
DU	Long	66	53	1.4	-1.2	1.13	26	0.2
UD	Short	52	38	1.6	-1.2	1.31	37	0.4
UU	Long	69	62	1.2	-1.1	1.07	13	0.1
DDD	Short	19	11	1.8	-1.0	1.80	23	0.8
DDU	Long	27	24	1.9	-1.2	1.58	23	0.4
DUD	Short	20	17	1.3	-1.5	0.89	1	0.0
DUU	Long	32	22	1.4	-1.1	1.24	20	0.4
UDD	Long	22	17	0.8	-1.0	0.83	1	0.0
UDU	Long	39	29	1.0	-1.2	0.80	3	0.0
UUD	Short	32	21	1.8	-1.0	1.77	35	0.7
UUU	Short	40	37	1.1	-1.0	1.09	7	0.1
DDDD	Short	8	3	1.5	-0.7	2.14	10	0.9
DDDU	Long	17	12	2.3	-1.7	1.38	19	0.7
DDUD	Short	13	8	1.4	-1.9	0.75	3	0.2
DDUU	Long	12	12	1.7	-1.4	1.16	3	0.1
DUDD	Short	7	6	1.2	-0.5	2.50	6	0.4
DUDU	Short	13	15	1.2	-1.1	1.09	1	0.0
DUUD	Short	12	9	2.3	-1.6	1.47	13	0.6
DUUU	Short	17	14	1.4	-1.1	1.30	9	0.3
UDDD	Short	11	8	1.9	-1.1	1.79	12	0.7
UDDU	Long	10	12	1.4	-0.8	1.70	4	0.2

(Contd . . .)

Table 16.3 (contd.)
20% Doji Performance of Nifty

Pattern	Action	Winning Trades	Losing Trades	Avg Profit	Avg Loss	W/L Ratio	Gross Profit	Profit per Trade
UDUD	Long	9	7	1.1	-1.1	0.98	2	0.1
UDUU	Long	20	10	1.2	-0.7	1.68	17	0.6
UUDD	Long	16	10	1.0	-0.9	1.11	7	0.3
UUDU	Long	24	16	0.8	-1.1	0.73	2	0.0
UUUD	Short	20	12	1.4	-0.6	2.52	22	0.7
UUUU	Long	23	23	1.0	-0.9	1.11	2	0.0

As you can observe in most of the above patterns, after a Doji appears the market eventually follows the direction of the Open, providing some trading patterns which offer us 0.5%+ profitable actions; 20% Doji might present us with many such trading opportunities.

Let us now see if segregating the Doji into a narrow range day (NR) or a wide spread day (WS) reveals any further information.

But why should we consider such a segregation? The market logic behind this is that on days when the range is large — say, more than 3% of the closing price — 20% of that range seems a little too high. So the next two patterns are about segregating the 20% Doji into either an NR or a WS.

20% Doji + NR Pattern

The pre-condition for entering the trade is that the previous day should have been both a Doji day and a narrow-range day (NR). Entry is assumed at the day's open, and exit at the close. Table 16.4 shows the results for this pattern.

Table 16.4

20% Doji +NR Performance of Nifty

Pattern	*Action*	*Winning Trades*	*Losing Trades*	*Avg Profit*	*Avg Loss*	*W/L Ratio*	*Gross Profit*	*Profit per Trade*
DD	Short	22	21	1.6	-0.9	1.81	16	0.4
DU	Long	42	35	1.5	-1.3	1.13	16	0.2
UD	Short	40	29	1.4	-1.4	1.07	19	0.3
UU	Short	52	48	1.1	-1.1	1.00	5	0.0
DDD	Short	11	9	1.9	-1.1	1.84	12	0.6
DDU	Long	18	18	2.1	-1.4	1.42	11	0.3
DUD	Short	18	13	1.4	-1.7	0.84	4	0.1
DUU	Long	20	20	1.4	-1.1	1.24	5	0.1
UDD	Short	11	12	1.2	-0.7	1.65	4	0.2
UDU	Long	24	17	1.0	-1.1	0.90	5	0.1
UUD	Short	22	16	1.5	-1.1	1.35	15	0.4
UUU	Short	32	28	1.1	-0.9	1.22	10	0.2
DDDD	Short	5	2	2.0	-0.5	3.85	9	1.3
DDDU	Long	12	12	2.3	-1.7	1.39	8	0.3
DDUD	Short	12	7	1.5	-2.2	0.71	3	0.2
DDUU	Short	12	6	1.4	-2.4	0.61	3	0.2
DUDD	Short	6	5	1.3	-0.3	3.81	6	0.6
DUDU	Long	10	7	1.0	-1.3	0.81	1	0.1
DUUD	Short	10	6	1.9	-1.8	1.02	8	0.5
DUUU	Short	15	9	1.5	-0.7	2.09	16	0.7
UDDD	Short	6	7	1.9	-1.2	1.54	3	0.2
UDDU	Long	6	6	1.5	-1.0	1.51	3	0.3
UDUD	Short	6	6	1.2	-1.1	1.04	0	0.0
UDUU	Long	14	8	1.0	-0.6	1.55	9	0.4
UUDD	Long	7	5	1.0	-1.0	0.99	2	0.2
UUDU	Long	14	10	1.0	-1.1	0.97	4	0.2
UUUD	Short	12	10	1.1	-0.6	1.77	7	0.3
UUUU	Long	19	17	1.0	-0.8	1.30	6	0.2

20% Doji + WS Pattern

The pre-condition for entering this trade is that the previous day should have been both a Doji day and a wide spread (WS) day. Entry is assumed at the day's open, and exit at the close. Table 16.5 summarises the results for this pattern.

Table 16.5

20% Doji +WS Performance of Nifty

Pattern	*Action*	*Winning Trades*	*Losing Trades*	*Avg Profit*	*Avg Loss*	*W/L Ratio*	*Gross Profit*	*Profit per Trade*
DD	Short	14	12	1.2	-0.9	1.26	5	0.2
DU	Long	24	18	1.2	-1.0	1.14	10	0.2
UD	Short	12	9	2.1	-0.8	2.69	18	0.9
UU	Long	21	10	1.4	-1.1	1.25	18	0.6
DDD	Short	8	2	1.5	-0.6	2.48	11	1.1
DDU	Long	9	6	1.7	-0.6	2.87	12	0.8
DUD	Long	4	2	0.9	-0.6	1.48	2	0.4
DUU	Long	12	2	1.3	-1.0	1.29	14	1.0
UDD	Long	10	6	1.0	-0.7	1.39	6	0.4
UDU	Short	12	15	1.2	-0.8	1.49	2	0.1
UUD	Short	10	5	2.4	-0.7	3.44	20	1.4
UUU	Long	9	8	1.4	-1.1	1.25	4	0.2
DDDD	Short	3	1	0.7	-1.1	0.66	1	0.3
DDDU	Long	5	0	2.2	NA	NA	11	2.2
DDUD	Short	1	1	0.4	-0.4	0.95	0	0.0
DDUU	Long	6	0	1.0	NA	NA	6	1.0
DUDD	Short	1	1	0.5	-1.2	0.41	1	0.3
DUDU	Short	6	5	1.2	-1.4	0.88	0	0.0
DUUD	Short	2	3	4.4	-1.0	4.28	6	1.2
DUUU	Long	5	2	1.8	-0.9	1.99	7	1.0
UDDD	Short	5	1	2.0	-0.1	18.7	10	1.6
UDDU	Short	6	4	0.6	-1.1	0.53	1	0.1
UDUD	Long	3	1	1.0	-0.8	1.28	2	0.6
UDUU	Long	6	2	1.7	-1.0	1.65	8	1.0
UUDD	Long	9	5	1.0	-0.8	1.28	5	0.4
UUDU	Short	6	10	1.3	-0.6	2.25	2	0.1
UUUD	Short	8	2	1.9	-0.2	10.38	15	1.5
UUUU	Short	6	4	1.2	-0.8	1.45	4	0.4

Comparing the percentage profits for days preceded by a Doji and narrow range with those of a Doji preceding a Wide Range day proves interesting. While NR+Doji presents us many trading opportunities, the profit per trade is lower compared to that of WS+Doji. NR+Doji patterns can be enhanced with range breakout techniques discussed in Chapter 14 (Opening Range Breakout) to find enhanced profitability patterns.

10% DBY Doji Pattern

Let's now try a little modification: What if the Doji occurred not yesterday but the day before yesterday? I have restricted this study to 10% Doji instead of running it for all the varied combinations as was done in the earlier cases.

The condition for entering the trade is that the day before yesterday should have been a Doji day. Entry is assumed at the open and exit is assumed at the trading day's close. Table 16.6 sums up the results for this pattern for Nifty.

Table 16.6

10% DBY Doji Open-to-Close Performance of Nifty

Pattern	*Action*	*Winning Trades*	*Losing Trades*	*Avg Profit*	*Avg Loss*	*W/L Ratio*	*Gross Profit*	*Profit per Trade*
DD	Short	24	19	1.9	-0.9	1.97	27	0.6
DU	Short	27	28	1.4	-1.3	1.06	1	0.0
UD	Long	24	17	1.3	-1.3	1.01	10	0.2
UU	Long	36	22	1.0	-0.9	1.12	17	0.3
DDD	Short	12	6	1.4	-0.6	2.59	14	0.8
DDU	Long	11	11	1.3	-0.9	1.46	4	0.2
DUD	Long	11	8	1.3	-0.9	1.51	7	0.4
DUU	Long	10	8	0.9	-0.9	1.03	2	0.1
UDD	Short	12	12	2.3	-1.1	2.09	14	0.6
UDU	Short	16	17	1.7	-1.3	1.32	5	0.2
UUD	Long	13	9	1.4	-1.7	0.79	2	0.1
UUU	Long	25	13	1.1	-1.0	1.09	14	0.4
DDDD	Short	5	4	0.9	-0.8	1.20	2	0.2
DDDU	Long	4	6	1.5	-0.7	2.16	2	0.2

(Contd . . .)

Table 16.6 (contd.)
10% DBY Doji Open-to-Close Performance of Nifty

Pattern	Action	Winning Trades	Losing Trades	Avg Profit	Avg Loss	W/L Ratio	Gross Profit	Profit per Trade
DDUD	Short	2	2	1.5	-0.9	1.56	1	0.3
DDUU	Short	4	2	1.2	-1.2	0.97	2	0.4
DUDD	Short	4	3	4.0	-0.6	6.40	14	2.0
DUDU	Long	8	7	1.3	-1.1	1.23	3	0.2
DUUD	Short	3	5	3.0	-1.3	2.27	2	0.3
DUUU	Long	15	7	1.2	-1.6	0.71	6	0.3
UDDD	Short	7	2	1.8	-0.2	11.53	12	1.4
UDDU	Long	7	5	1.2	-1.1	1.05	3	0.2
UDUD	Long	9	6	1.4	-0.7	2.10	8	0.6
UDUU	Long	8	4	0.8	-0.6	1.41	4	0.4
UUDD	Short	8	9	1.4	-1.3	1.13	0	0.0
UUDU	Short	9	9	2.2	-1.2	1.74	8	0.5
UUUD	Long	8	6	1.4	-1.1	1.28	5	0.3
UUUU	Long	10	6	1.0	-0.2	3.94	8	0.5

An important clue from the above table is that if a trade taken at the open, after a 10 % Doji two days earlier, is profitable, it may pay to continue the trade till next day open, and if we get the open direction right we can continue till the close. A row by row comparison of the above table with Table 16.2 — 10% Doji performance of Nifty — suggest this clue.

10% Doji Yesterday, Close-to-Close Pattern

This pattern extends the above concept to study price movements from close-to-close when a Doji occurred the previous day and the direction of the market is known at the time of today's close.

The pre-condition for entering the trade is that yesterday should have been a Doji day. Entry is assumed at today's close, and exit is at tomorrow's close. Table 16.7 summarises the results for this pattern.

Table 16.7
10% Doji Yesterday, Close-to-Close Performance of Nifty

Pattern	*Action*	*Winning Trades*	*Losing Trades*	*Avg Profit*	*Avg Loss*	*W / L Ratio*	*Gross Profit*	*Profit per Trade*
DD	Short	30	21	1.7	-2.5	0.69	1	0.0
DU	Long	28	21	1.2	-1.2	0.96	7	0.2
UD	Short	23	18	1.5	-1.1	1.31	13	0.3
UU	Long	39	25	1.1	-1.1	1.02	16	0.3
DDD	Long	12	12	2.1	-1.8	1.20	4	0.2
DDU	Long	10	8	1.1	-0.9	1.20	4	0.2
DUD	Short	10	8	1.9	-1.2	1.49	9	0.5
DUU	Long	14	8	0.7	-1.0	0.75	2	0.1
UDD	Short	18	9	1.7	-3.0	0.56	4	0.1
UDU	Long	18	12	1.3	-1.6	0.81	4	0.1
UUD	Short	13	10	1.1	-1.0	1.14	5	0.2
UUU	Long	24	16	1.4	-1.2	1.15	14	0.3
DDDD	Long	6	6	2.0	-1.2	1.64	5	0.4
DDDU	Short	5	3	1.1	-1.1	0.99	2	0.3
DDUD	Short	4	2	1.7	-1.4	1.21	4	0.7
DDUU	Short	3	2	0.9	-1.6	0.58	0	0.1
DUDD	Long	4	6	3.4	-1.5	2.20	4	0.4
DUDU	Long	8	4	1.5	-1.2	1.28	7	0.6
DUUD	Short	5	7	1.1	-0.8	1.43	0	0.0
DUUU	Long	12	8	1.6	-1.6	1.00	7	0.3
UDDD	Short	6	6	2.4	-2.3	1.02	0	0.0
UDDU	Long	7	3	1.0	-0.6	1.86	6	0.6
UDUD	Short	6	6	1.9	-1.2	1.65	5	0.4
UDUU	Long	12	5	0.6	-1.0	0.58	2	0.1
UUDD	Short	12	5	1.8	-2.7	0.65	8	0.5
UUDU	Short	8	10	1.7	-1.0	1.68	4	0.2
UUUD	Short	8	3	1.2	-1.6	0.76	5	0.4
UUUU	Long	12	8	1.1	-0.7	1.48	7	0.4

From the above table it appears that a trade taken at close for a holding period of one day, after a Doji is observed on the previous day, doesn't appear to be particularly profitable, it clearly indicates that the bulls and the bears are at equilibrium, a state of indecision. From my experience, much of the next day's trading moves after a Doji depend, and are predicated, upon knowing the direction of the Open.

Application

The Doji is one of the most revealing signals in trading. In an effort to find explosive moves, look for the direction of the open after a Doji occurrence. The Doji and narrow range day combinations offer excellent possibilities for finding such explosive moves. Doji formations reveal high probability of profitable trades and are a valid precursor for a highly explosive move. If you observe all the tables in this section, you will find a higher concentration of 0.5%+ profit per trade in this chapter than in any other.

Chapter 17

Pivot Points

Calculation of Pivot Points

A pivot point can be defined as the average of the high, low, and closing price. Pivot points are used to project support and resistance levels.

Here are the formulas for calculating pivot points:

Pivot Point (PP)	=	(High + Low + Close) / 3
Support Level 1 (S1)	=	(2 * PP) - High
Support Level 2 (S2)	=	PP - Range
Support Level 3 (S3)	=	S2 - Range
Resistance Level 1 (R1)	=	(2 * PP) - Low
Resistance Level 2 (R2)	=	PP + Range
Resistance Level 3 (R3)	=	R2 + Range

For example, assume the following values of OHLC for the Nifty:

Open: 4,523.15, High: 4,544.00, Low: 4,481.1 Close: 4,487.15.

The following calculations will make things clear:

PP = (4,544+4,481.1+4,487.15) / 3 = (13,512.25 / 3) = 4,504.08

Range = 4,454.00 – 4,481.1 = 62.9

S1 = (2*4,504.08) – 4,544.00 = 4,464.17

S2 = 4,504.08 - 62.9 = 4,441.18

S3 = 4,441.18 - 62.9 = 4,378.28

R1 = (2 * 4,504.08) – 4,481.18 = 9,008.16 – 4,481.18 = 4,527.06

R2 = 4,504.08 + 62.9 = 4,566.98

R3 = 4,566.98+62.9 = 4,629.88

Pivot Point Distributions

My intention is to find where the daily O, H, L, C values fall *vis-à-vis* the pivot-point values. Table 17.1 presents the number of instances and the break-up of the daily O, H, L, C values *vis-à-vis* the pivot points.

A couple of points need to be noted, however:

- One, although we could calculate the R4 and S4 values separately, for the sake of simplicity I have included them under R3 and S3, respectively.
- Two, even when the market traded above R2, I have counted such an instance under R2 only and have not it included under R1 and the same applies to R3, S2 and S3 as well.

Table 17.1
Nifty OHLC *vis-à-vis* Pivot-Point Distributions

	R3	*R2*	*R1*	*PP*	*S1*	*S2*	*S3*
Open	0	2	9	2,344	5	0	0
High	39	455	714	1,152	0	0	0
Low			1	1,400	518	364	77
Close	21	236	403	1,169	304	192	35

From Table 17.1 you would observe that rarely did the market open either above R1 or below S1. Also, you would observe that the day's high is never below S1, and the low is never above R1 (excluding one day in the data under review, 28 November 2005, when the previous day had a narrow range. However, the above observation needs to be taken with a pinch of salt, as the Nifty open tick is a slow moving one, when compared with that of Nifty futures.

Extending the study further, Table 17.2 presents data about where the market closed if it traded above R1. Unlike in the previous study, it also includes all the closes which are in the R1, R2, and R3 zones.

There were 1,208 instances of Nifty trading above its R1 level among a total 2,360 trading days.

Table 17.2
Nifty Closing Levels When Market Traded above R1, R2 & R3

	Traded Above R1 (1,208 instances)	*Traded Above R2 (494 instances)*	*Traded Above R3 (39 instances)*
Closed Above R3	21	21	21
Closed Above R2	257	257	37
Closed Above R1	660	409	38
Closed Around PP	453	67	1
Closed Below S1	95	18	0
Closed Below S2	35	10	0
Closed Below S3	3	2	0

Correspondingly, Table 17.3 presents data about where the market closed if it traded below S1. It includes all the closes at S1, S2 and S3. There were 959 such instances out of 2,360 where Nifty traded below S1.

Table 17.3
Nifty Close Possibilities if Market Traded above S1, S2 & S3

	Traded Below S1 (959 instances)	*Traded Below S2 (441 instances)*	*Traded Below S3 (77 instances)*
Closed Above R3	0	0	0
Closed Above R2	15	3	0
Closed Above R1	48	10	0
Closed Around PP	380	50	3
Closed Below S1	531	381	74
Closed Below S2	227	227	69
Closed Below S3	35	35	35

Application

It is evident from the two studies above that once Nifty starts trading either above R2 or below S2, the likely chances of reversal (that is, close in the opposite direction, i.e. expecting for a negative close when Nifty starts trading above R2 and *vice versa* — are slim. This information can be used for placing defensive stop losses, i.e. if we are in a long position above R1, then a stop loss below S2, and *vice versa*. I will be presenting some of my favourite patterns around pivot points in Section-4 (Chapter 26, Pivot Point Trading Secrets).

Chapter 18

Tri- and Penta-Section

This chapter focuses on the relationship of the previous day's open and close positions within the context of the previous day's range.

Let me introduce a new term here, tri-section. By tri-section what I mean is this: we divide a day's range into three segments. For example, assume yesterday's high and low were 4,150 and 4,000, respectively. If we were to divide the range between the high and the low into three segments, here is what we get:

- Segment 1: 4,000 – 4,050,
- Segment 2: 4,050 – 4,100. and
- Segment 3: 4,100 – 4,150.

Now, if yesterday's open was 4,125, then it falls under Segment 3; likewise, if yesterday's close was 4,090, then it falls under Segment 2.

Logically, it makes sense to take a trade once the open's direction is known, after tri-secting the previous day's range. Let us now study Nifty's price movements in this light.

Observing Tri-section

In the first column in Table 18.1 — labelled "Pattern" — you would see an entry such as O1C3, which means that yesterday's open was in Segment 1 and the close was in Segment 3. The second column indicates the direction of today's open. The other columns are the same as presented throughout this book.

Entry is assumed at today's open and exit at the close. Table 18.1 presents the results for this tri-section study.

Table 18.1
Tri-section Study

Pattern	*Open*	*Action*	*Wining Trades*	*Losing Trades*	*Avg profit*	*Avg Loss*	*W/L Ratio*	*Gross Profit*	*Profit per Trade*
O1C2	U	Long	81	54	1.1	-1.0	1.12	36	0.3
O1C3	U	Long	241	159	1.2	-0.9	1.28	138	0.3
O2C1	U	Long	68	71	1.4	-1.2	1.13	7	0.1
O2C2	U	Long	65	41	1.1	-1.3	0.87	21	0.2
O2C3	U	Short	65	68	1.3	-1.1	1.10	4	0.0
O3C1	U	Long	123	99	1.4	-1.3	1.06	41	0.2
O3C2	U	Long	60	43	1.4	-1.2	1.14	31	0.3
O3C3	U	Long	39	31	1.6	-1.3	1.23	23	0.3
O1C1	D	Short	40	28	1.2	-0.9	1.38	25	0.4
O1C2	D	Short	38	33	1.0	-1.1	0.95	3	0.0
O1C3	D	Long	152	86	1.1	-1.3	0.83	51	0.2
O2C1	D	Short	64	52	1.3	-1.2	1.13	23	0.2
O2C2	D	Short	28	27	1.6	-1.3	1.24	10	0.2
O2C3	D	Short	52	33	1.4	-0.9	1.50	42	0.5
O3C1	D	Short	142	104	1.9	-1.3	1.37	123	0.5
O3C2	D	Short	37	31	1.8	-1.1	1.72	35	0.5
O3C3	D	Short	15	19	1.9	-1.3	1.44	3	0.1

A few patterns in Table 18.1, such as an Up open after O1C3 , and a Down open after O3C1 do suggest the follow through effect; namely, that there are good chances of Nifty continuing in the same direction as the previous day's close , as can be seen under the gross profit column.

Penta-Section

This study is an extension of the tri-section study above, but the range here is divided into five segments. So, in the first column you would notice an entry such as O4C5, which means yesterday's open was in Segment 4 and the close was in Segment 5.

Entry is assumed at today's open and exit at the close. Table 18.2 and Table 18.3 show the results for the Penta-section study.

Table 18.2

Penta-Section Study after the Open is Up

Pattern	*Action*	*Wining Trades*	*Losing Trades*	*Avg Profit*	*Avg Loss*	*W/L Ratio*	*Gross Profit*	*Profit per Trade*
O1C1	Long	6	5	0.9	-0.9	1.09	1	0.1
O1C2	Long	23	18	0.9	-1.0	0.89	2	0.1
O1C3	Long	35	22	1.0	-0.9	1.17	17	0.3
O1C4	Long	61	45	1.1	-1.1	1.02	18	0.2
O1C5	Long	158	95	1.3	-0.9	1.43	116	0.5
O2C1	Long	14	10	0.8	-0.8	0.97	3	0.1
O2C2	Short	19	10	1.0	-1.3	0.76	6	0.2
O2C3	Long	21	9	0.8	-1.2	0.72	7	0.2
O2C4	Long	31	18	1.1	-0.9	1.21	18	0.4
O2C5	Long	39	33	1.2	-1.1	1.06	9	0.1
O3C1	Long	23	23	1.4	-1.1	1.22	6	0.1
O3C2	Long	31	25	1.3	-1.5	0.85	2	0.0
O3C3	Long	20	20	1.2	-1.0	1.21	4	0.1
O3C4	Long	22	15	1.3	-1.4	0.94	8	0.2
O3C5	Short	28	28	1.2	-1.1	1.02	1	0.0
O4C1	Long	37	27	1.2	-1.4	0.90	9	0.1
O4C2	Long	27	22	1.2	-1.2	1.02	6	0.1
O4C3	Long	19	16	1.2	-1.3	0.92	2	0.1
O4C4	Long	15	11	1.3	-1.2	1.09	6	0.2
O4C5	Long	14	13	1.5	-1.4	1.07	3	0.1
O5C1	Long	57	48	1.3	-1.4	0.95	9	0.1
O5C2	Long	33	32	1.9	-1.0	2.05	34	0.5
O5C3	Long	22	15	1.4	-1.5	0.92	8	0.2
O5C4	Long	22	14	1.4	-2.0	0.68	2	0.1
O5C5	Long	13	8	1.8	-0.8	2.35	17	0.8

Table 18.3
Penta-Section Study after the Open is Down

Pattern	*Action*	*Wining Trades*	*Losing Trades*	*Avg Profit*	*Avg Loss*	*W/L Ratio*	*Gross Profit*	*Profit per Trade*
O1C1	Short	13	5	1.7	-1.0	1.66	17	0.9
O1C2	Short	18	13	1.1	-1.1	0.99	5	0.2
O1C3	Long	18	19	1.4	-1.0	1.42	6	0.2
O1C4	Short	24	26	1.0	-0.8	1.24	3	0.1
O1C5	Long	102	48	1.0	-1.4	0.73	36	0.2
O2C1	Short	10	10	1.2	-1.1	1.18	2	0.1
O2C2	Short	16	17	1.3	-0.6	2.18	11	0.3
O2C3	Long	9	7	1.7	-0.8	2.16	10	0.6
O2C4	Short	15	6	0.7	-0.9	0.79	5	0.2
O2C5	Long	29	21	1.5	-1.6	0.91	9	0.2
O3C1	Short	23	22	1.2	-1.2	0.97	1	0.0
O3C2	Short	24	12	1.4	-1.2	1.14	19	0.5
O3C3	Short	8	11	2.0	-1.0	1.96	5	0.3
O3C4	Short	13	7	0.8	-0.7	1.10	5	0.3
O3C5	Short	18	15	1.5	-0.9	1.66	13	0.4
O4C1	Short	42	29	1.6	-1.1	1.41	34	0.5
O4C2	Short	26	20	1.3	-1.5	0.87	4	0.1
O4C3	Short	13	7	1.5	-1.0	1.45	12	0.6
O4C4	Short	8	9	2.6	-1.1	2.33	11	0.6
O4C5	Short	6	7	1.5	-1.0	1.59	2	0.2
O5C1	Short	73	47	1.9	-1.2	1.56	81	0.7
O5C2	Short	31	27	2.3	-1.6	1.39	26	0.5
O5C3	Short	10	13	2.0	-1.3	1.61	4	0.2
O5C4	Short	9	12	2.7	-0.7	3.79	16	0.8
O5C5	Long	7	6	1.8	-1.3	1.43	5	0.4

Application

A review of this study reveals that the win / loss ratio of some of the patterns, like O1C5, O5C1, O1C3, O3C1, is truly astonishing This suggests that the tri-section and penta-section patterns can be effectively used as a reference for trade entry.

Moreover, I am not aware of any measurement unit to quantify human emotions, but Влад* and I used to consider the penta-section tool as a unit reflecting the trading crowd's emotions. Let me explain the logic behind this thinking. Empirically. the trading volume constructed for various half-hour intervals is observed to be U-shaped for the day. In other words, the trading volume is high in the first half an hour and the last half an hour, and lower during the middle of the trading day, i.e. 5.30 hours (or 5.15 hours, to be precise if you remove the pre-open session recently introduced by both BSE and NSE). Under the assumption that Open is controlled by amateurs and the Close is controlled by the professionals, the penta-section tool is trying to quantify the trading day's range into the emotions of the amateurs and the professionals by giving them a rating on a scale of 1-5. It is often well documented that 90% of the amateurs lose money in stock market by trading.

The most revealing patterns in the above table are the follow-through effect of a trend day once the direction of the open is known. A trend day can be described as one wherein the open and close are in opposite extremes, that is, if open falls in Segment 1, the close should be in Segment 5 — and *vice versa*, namely if the open is in Segment 5, the close should be in Segment 1. The follow-through I'm talking about is the high profit per trade, especially for the O1C5 if the open is up, and for O5C1 if the open is down.

* That is Vlad, an even shorter name for Влади, usually after few vodkas; by the way, drinking vodka, or any alcohol for that matter, in excess is injurious to health.

Chapter 19

Hook Days

Definitions

- **Bear Hook:** A bear hook is defined as a day on which the open is below the previous day's low, and the close is above the previous day's close, along with a narrow range relative to the previous day's range. As implied by the name, there is a tendency for the price action following a bear hook to move to the downside.
- **Bull Hook:** A bull hook is defined as a day on which the open is above the previous day's high and the close is below the previous day's close. The bull hook has a narrow range relative to the previous day's range. As implied by the name, there is a tendency for the price action following a bull hook to move to the upside.

Hook Observations

Hook days are assumed to be valid precursors of reversal and explosive moves. Why? Take for example bull hook, an up open move which fails to lift today's close beyond yesterday's close. Upon such a reversal of the move from the open, short term traders might reverse their trades. Example: someone who is long upon seeing the close, and is in loss; might reverse the trade which was long at the open — and now go short. I wasn't able to confidently validate the theory and results behind the hook days on Nifty, as there were very few occurrences of these during the test period. On the other hand, the BSE Sensex provides quite a few hook day appearances, particularly of the bear hook, and validates the theory behind the bear hook days, but not for the bull hook days.

Well, we can go on and on about various logically possible permutations, such as what happens when ID and NR4 occur together, or what happens when a Doji and NR4 occur together . . . .all these logical permutations can be observed with several entry techniques that are presented in Chapter 14; for example Open+/- certain percentage point, previous day's high / low, various pivot point levels, etc. Combine these with "day of the week" techniques and you can develop your own trading patterns.

I want to make a small enthusiastic point before I close this section; Toby Crabel in his book, *Day Trading with Short Term Price Patterns and Opening Range Breakout* talks about Ayn Rand at length in a few pages, and grapevine is that the way he surgically dissected the market movements (be it NR4 or NR7 and three-day close movements before the NR4 day occurrence) is founded on the base of Ayn Rand's epistemology. Ayn Rand was Russian novelist and a philosopher who wrote a book called *Introduction to Objectivist Epistemology*, which was published in 1979.

The book deals with the mental processes of conceptualisation, the nature of definitions, how to distinguish legitimate concepts from "anti-concepts," the hierarchical nature of knowledge and what constitutes valid axiomatic knowledge.

Rand describes the role of concept formation as "The ability to regard entities as units is man's distinctive method of cognition." Rand defines a concept as "a mental integration of two or more units which are isolated according to a specific characteristic(s) and united by a specific definition". The formation of concepts requires not only abstraction — isolating certain attributes from others — but also integration, i.e. combining concretes into a larger category.

You need to see the world differently and you will also need to think differently, guided by principles, not just perceptions. Without a solid epistemological foundation, what assurance do we have that we're trading anything other than randomness? Such an epistemological undertaking transforms the knower by expanding the realm of the known.

I think by this juncture I have done at least a little justice in presenting you with various price patterns and a framework for you to start exploring them yourself. For your benefit, I have included a few more short term patterns, along with their pictorial representations, in this book's Glossary.

Now, it's time to put the theoretical learning into practice . . . .

Section - 3

Money and Risk Management

Chapter-20

Pyramids and Day Dreams

Chapter-21

The Risk of Ruin

Chapter-22

Drawdown: A Trader's Best Friend

Chapter-23

Performance Summary

Chapter-24

Trading Rules

Chapter 20

Pyramids and Day Dreams

Successful traders seem to keep winning and making profits. They seem to have an edge in the market; a cultivated or acquired edge they are able to put to good use day in and day out. It's all a numbers game, and some traders appear to get it right more often than others.

I should admit right away that this is the most foolish chapter that I have written in the entire book, and I would not hesitate to suggest that upon reading it, you could either tear it to shreds, or — hopefully . . . .

In the blockbuster movie *Ghajini*, the protagonist, Sanjay Singhania (Aamir Khan) suffers from anterograde amnesia (short term memory loss). There is a variant form of a theoretical memory concept to the above form of amnesia called "repressed memory". I would suggest you use those repressed memory techniques to automatically erase the word pyramiding from your brain.

Now, back to business. Take a look at the four scenarios in Table 20.1:

Table 20.1

Scenario	*1*	*2*	*3*	*4*
Average Win Points	20	10	20	10
Average Loss Points	10	5	10	5
Cost per trade	4	4	4	4
Average P/L per trade	1	1	6	3
%Winners	50	67	67	80
Number of trades	100	100	100	100
Expected Profit (in points)	100	100	600	300
Num contracts traded	1	1	1	1
Total expected profit	₹ 5,000	₹ 5,000	₹ 30,000	₹ 15,000

Under Scenario 1, our average winning trade gives us 20 points and the average losing trade gives us 10 points and the commissions are ₹ 200 per round trip per trade (₹ 50 * 4 points as mentioned in the above table). Given these figures, we end up with an average expected return of ₹ 5,000 from 100 trades.

I will now take up Scenario 3. You might well ask why Scenario 3? The reason is to build an eighth wonder of the modern world, a great pyramid from stock market earnings that is larger than the three pyramids in the Giza Necropolis, and construct it in less than 10 years whereas the Great Pyramid of Giza took more than 20 years, and try to create a situation that might well get your adrenalin levels surging. Unlike Scenario 1, we will end up with a profit of ₹ 30,000 after just 100 trades under Scenario 3.

How Long Does it Take to Make ₹ 10 Crore?

Incidentally, how long do you think it would take you to make ₹ 10 crore from trading Nifty futures contracts, on an investment of a mere ₹ 50,000? That leads to my take on pyramiding. I would define pyramiding as buying more and more contracts, driven by the motive of increasing profit on every trade.

Let's say you begin with a trading capital of ₹ 50,000. You start trading one Nifty future contract and make a profit of ₹ 50,000. That prompts you to trade another contract, and another, and another, as you continue to make profits. Let's assume the number of trading days in month as 20 (Table 20.2).

Table 20.2

Cumulative Profit	*# Contracts Traded*	*# Trades required to accumulate ₹50,000 Profit*	*Profit per Trade (₹)*	*# of Months required to achieve (₹) 50,000 Profit*	*Cumulative Months*
₹ 50,000	1	167	300	8.3	8.3
₹ 100,000	2	83	600	1.3	12.5
₹ 150,000	3	56	900	0.8	15.3
₹ 200,000	4	42	1,200	0.6	17.4
₹ 250,000	5	33	1,500	0.5	19.0
₹ 300,000	6	28	1,800	0.4	20.4
₹ 350,000	7	24	2,100	0.4	21.6
₹ 400,000	8	21	2,400	0.3	22.6
₹ 450,000	9	19	2,700	0.3	23.6
₹ 500,000	10	17	3,000	0.3	24.4
₹ 550,000	11	15	3,300	0.2	25.2
₹ 600,000	12	14	3,600	0.2	25.9
₹ 650,000	13	13	3,900	0.2	26.5
₹ 700,000	14	12	4,200	0.2	27.1
₹ 750,000	15	11	4,500	0.2	27.7
₹ 800,000	16	10	4,800	0.2	28.2
₹ 850,000	17	10	5,100	0.2	28.7
₹ 900,000	18	9	5,400	0.1	29.1
₹ 950,000	19	9	5,700	0.1	29.6
₹ 1,000,000	20	8	6,000	0.1	30.0

At the end of the 6th year you are probably trading 3,155 contracts. The money flowing in is so good that it's like having a mini mint running full steam at home; a mint equipped to turn out crisp currency notes worth over ₹ 9 lakh every trading day. That's a briefcase full of money a day. Phew! It looks like after six years, your cumulative profits would have swelled to ₹ 15 crore and small change of little more than ₹ 75 lakh! Continue for another few years, you may have to appeal to Indian treasury to print zillion rupee notes as it doesn't make any notes bigger than ₹ 1,000. Suddenly, you find you have all the money to indulge in the luxuries of life: the best villa in town, the fastest wheels, and a lifestyle that's the envy of your peers.

Are We Being Realistic?

Forget about maths, this is how your 10-bedroom dream villa looks:

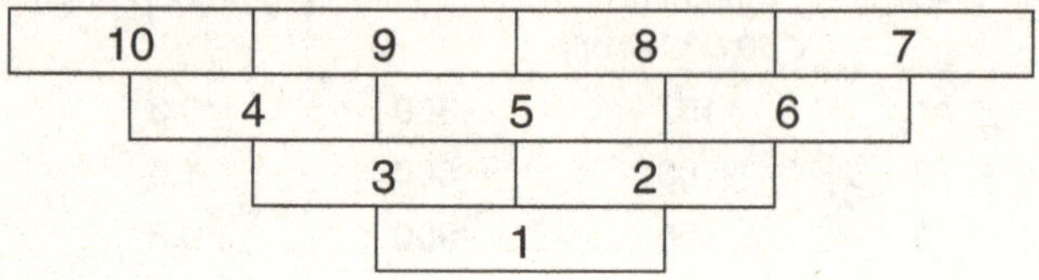

Ask any civil engineer how solid such a structure is? As you can see, it is a top heavy pyramid and not the bottom heavy pyramid that the Great Pyramid of Giza is. Well, let me quickly bring you back to earth. Don't be taken in by slick ads and sales spiel regularly trotted out by stock trading subscription services. Their sales talk is liberally spiced with terms such as pyramiding, systematic investment plan, and so on. They will have you believe that by employing pyramiding you would emerge a multi-millionaire in double quick time.

The reality is, of course, very different. Only a handful of professional traders in India have succeeded in making big money and that, too, after years and years in the trade. In fact, the only name in the trading billionaires bracket that comes to mind is that of Rakesh Jhunjhunwala, a man who ranks amongst the richest Indians and whose wealth has almost entirely been created from stock markets.

To conclude: I'm not saying that you should not aspire to be a member of the big league. I am not saying pyramiding is all bad. It has its virtues, no doubt. All I am saying is, and here I'm particularly addressing the novice trader — don't get carried away by the word pyramiding.

Chapter 21

The Risk of Ruin

Let me caution you that the tone and tenor of this chapter is going to be rather pessimistic. Yet, I consider it the most important chapter in the whole book. What I am going to attempt in this chapter is to show you how to calculate and take into consideration the risk of losing your entire trading capital. This happens to millions of people who start trading the stock markets without spending the time and effort needed to learn how to trade. Much of the distress, in terms of financial loss that such traders go through can be avoided if they were to take some time and effort to educate themselves first.

Risk or ruin revolves around the probability that at some point in your career as a trader you find yourself at a juncture where you believe it's impossible, or plainly unwise, to continue trading when you take stock of the current status of your trading account *vis-à-vis* what it was when you first began trading. You might not, of course, have gone bankrupt though in reality it's quite possible to get there. You may simply have arrived at a point where you are actively considering closing your trading account, or mulling how you are going to go about repaying the various loans you had taken when you embarked on a trading career.

If you pursue a trading career long enough, whether full time or part time, and if you execute a sufficiently large number of trades, you would most likely see both extended losing and winning periods. The longer you trade, the more likely you are to see such extreme events. Talking of losing streaks, it could, for instance, be as many as 20 consecutive losing streaks, or it could be 10. The point is, as a trader you need to be prepared to take in your stride spells of consecutive losing streaks. I would leave you to decide what is "long" for you.

Consecutive Losers

In one of the strategies — Momentum Aided Manic Monday strategy — presented in Chapter 27, you will note that at one point during the life of that particular trading pattern, your account would have stood at a loss of around 260 points (2 consecutive losers). I would consider this as a very good, real-life tradable pattern since it meets all the criteria that make a pattern approximate a real-world trading scenario.

Now, consider the same pattern in the context of the largest drawdown period. If you had started with a trading capital of ₹ 50,000 and were trading one Nifty contract, your account would be reduced to a 25% drawdown. How would you feel at this point? Devastated, no doubt. Do you rank yourself among those who still have the mental and emotional resolve to persevere with this strategy and continue trading?

Extending the same logic, how long do you think it would take to turn ₹ 50,000 into 0? The answer: about another two similar unlucky trades in a week's time, or a month's time, by using some other strategy — if you had started off at the wrong time. Granted there would still be ₹ 25,000 left in the account, but that's not much of a capital base to trade, is it? If Nifty were trading at 2,500-plus levels you wouldn't anyway have enough money to trade even a single contract. Still, we're looking at around a 50% loss in the account at this point.

Some Calculations

In the book, *Smarter Trading*, Perry Kaufman discusses the risk of ruin and provides us with a formula to work with. He considers the following two premises:

1. In real trading, once profits accumulate the chance of ruin reduces. The greatest risk is at the beginning.
2. If we plan to withdraw profits, thereby maintaining the same relative commitment to the market, the risk of ruin would be greater than if we accumulate profits and keep the trading position the same.

Kaufman gives us the following formula for calculating the risk of ruin:

Risk of Ruin = ((1 - Edge) / (1 + Edge)) ^ Capital_Units
Edge is the probability of a win.

I won't go into the complexities, but I present below the following hypothetical example whose import strikes you once you start trading. Note, I am not exactly applying Kaufman's formula. I won't be using the number of capital units in the above formula, as the brain subconsciously picks up the thought of pyramiding when your account size multiplies by a factor of 2 or 3. I dislike pyramiding like I dislike compounding — as presented in the Chapter 20 , Pyramids and Day Dreams.

Our Example

If we start with ₹ 50,000 as the initial capital in our account and we risk 20 Nifty points per trade, we are then risking ₹ 1,000 or ₹ 1,200 per trade, assuming a commission of ₹ 100 on each side of the trade; that is, entering the trade and exiting the trade. After 20 straight losing trades, we would have lost ₹ 24,000 and so would be compelled to cease trading as our capital would have come down to only ₹ 26,000, an amount not sufficient to trade even one Nifty futures contract.

Now, assume that our account had grown to ₹ 1 lakh before we hit a losing streak. Each losing trade now costs us the same ₹ 1,200. So, after 20 losing trades our capital drops by ₹ 24,000 and stands at ₹ 76,000. We are still well prepared to withstand another streak of 23 consecutive losses to come back to the point where we started from, ₹ 50,000.

Conclusion

By Kaufman's formula — as presented in his book — the risk of ruin is the greatest at the beginning. The risk of ruin also increases the longer you continue trading for the simple reason that the risk of experiencing a series of losses increases. To put all that into perspective, I would suggest that if you don't have at least four times the capital required to trade one contract, stay clear of trading Nifty futures.

Chapter 22

Drawdown: A Trader's Best Friend!

This chapter will be short and sweet. Though the topic may seem a bit unusual, it may end up being the most important chapter in the book for many of you. The information it contains is crucial.

All the set-ups and concepts in this book, or any book on trading for that matter, are completely worthless without following some general rules and proper money management principles. This approach can be best illustrated through the study of drawdown.

Drawdown

Drawdown can simply be defined as the amount of money you lose trading, expressed as a percentage of your total trading equity. Its calculation begins only with a losing trade and continues as long as the trading account keeps hitting new lows.

Maximum drawdown is the largest percentage drop in your account between equity peaks. To put it differently, it's how much money you lose until you get back to breakeven. If, say, you begin with ₹ 1,00,000 and lose ₹ 40,000 before getting back to breakeven, your maximum drawdown would be 40%. Keep in mind that no matter how much you are up in your account at any given time, a 100% drawdown will completely wipe out your trading account.

Recovering from a drawdown can be extremely difficult, which is why money management is so important. Those new to trading believe that if they lose 10% they will be back to breakeven on the first 10% gain thereafter. Unfortunately, this is not true. In order to make good a 10% loss, you must make at least 11.11% on your remaining equity. Even worse, as the drawdown becomes deeper, the recovery percentage begins to grow geometrically. For example, a 50% loss requires a 100% return just to get back to break even.

I'm sure you would have read such explanations in many of the trading books you might have come across. My attempt here, though, would be to present a more depressing scenario specific to maximum drawdown.

24 Wild Swings

Table 22.1 captures the 24 wildest swings, whether up or down, in our test period. Why have I chosen to dwell on 24 swings? Does the number 24 have any particular significance? Keep guessing for a moment.

I have taken the close-to-close as a reference, and have presented the wildest swings in an ascending order. The column captioned "Diff" is simply the difference between the current day's close and the previous day's close. The column captioned "Abs-Diff" is the absolute difference between the current day's close and the previous day's close.

Table 22.1
24 Wildest Swings of Nifty

Date	*Open*	*High*	*Low*	*Close*	*Diff*	*Abs-Diff*
18-May-09	3673.15	4384.30	3673.15	4323.15	652	652
21-Jan-08	5705.00	5705.00	4977.10	5208.80	-497	497
24-Oct-08	2936.25	2936.25	2525.05	2584.00	-359	359
25-Jan-08	5035.05	5399.25	5035.05	5383.35	350	350
22-Jan-08	5203.35	5203.35	4448.50	4899.30	-310	310
23-Jan-08	4903.05	5328.05	4891.60	5203.40	304	304
23-Oct-07	5185.30	5488.50	5176.85	5473.70	290	290
14-Feb-08	4944.65	5220.25	4944.65	5202.00	273	273
17-Dec-07	6037.95	6039.95	5740.60	5777.00	-271	271
3-Mar-08	5222.80	5222.80	4936.05	4953.00	-271	271
25-Mar-08	4616.80	4896.80	4616.80	4877.50	268	268
11-Feb-08	5120.55	5126.40	4803.60	4857.00	-263	263
13-Mar-08	4868.70	4868.80	4580.15	4623.60	-248	248
18-May-06	3636.45	3636.45	3365.90	3388.90	-246	246
17-Mar-08	4745.45	4745.45	4482.10	4503.10	-243	243

(Contd . . .)

Table 22.1 (contd.)
24 Wildest Swings of Nifty

Date	*Open*	*High*	*Low*	*Close*	*Diff*	*Abs-Diff*
14-Nov-07	5703.95	5950.20	5700.05	5937.90	243	243
15-Oct-07	5428.35	5682.65	5419.90	5670.40	242	242
9-Oct-07	5062.65	5348.70	5000.95	5327.25	242	242
23-Jul-08	4246.70	4491.55	4246.70	4476.80	237	237
10-Oct-08	3502.05	3502.05	3198.95	3279.95	-234	234
21-Nov-07	5778.80	5790.05	5530.85	5561.05	-220	220
24-Dec-07	5771.30	6001.05	5771.30	5985.10	219	219
6-Oct-08	3817.30	3820.85	3581.60	3602.35	-216	216
13-Oct-08	3272.90	3510.20	3272.90	3490.70	211	211

Got the answer to my earlier poser? No? Well, here it is.

As reported by NSDL, in 2009 there were more than 10 million demat holders in India. Let us assume that this figure represents the number of people who have traded online at least once. Now, 10 million is approximately 2 raised to the power 24. Employing simple probability formulas, one can easily figure out that something "bad" could well happen to at least one person in that group of 2 power 24 people. I'm sure none of us wants to be that "unlucky" person. What am I talking about? Ending up on the wrong side of the market on those 24 wild swings is what I am referring to. Now you know why I have chosen to focus on 24 wild swings!

Being caught on the wrong side would have cost you or me or that one unlucky soul, about 6,905 points. And that translates to a total loss of ₹ 3,45,000 rupees per one Nifty futures contract traded. So, my approach in terms of money management if I were to trade one Nifty contract would go somewhat like this: ₹ 50,000 — margin money required to trade one Nifty contract (assuming Nifty is around the 6,000 level), plus ₹ 3,45,000, making a total of around ₹ 4 lakh. As a trader, you would need this cushion to give you some degree of confidence.

You Win a Few, You Lose Many

Just like everything else in life, the market doesn't behave perfectly and precisely to any price pattern. The market is, nevertheless, always right

> "In this world nothing can be said to be certain except death and taxes"
>
> **— Benjamin Franklin**

and we are wrong. If we can be right every time, trading would be easy and the market would be our dream employer. There are times when the patterns don't perform exactly, which is frustrating but, then, such is life.

The above also holds true in the markets. Nothing works a hundred percent of the time, but with money management, discipline, and hard work, you can become a successful trader.

Please note, scared money never wins. Before becoming an active trader, you should be on sound financial footing; without that trading will be more about fear and less about confidence. This rule simply means you must be in a position to lose all your speculative capital without the loss materially affecting your life.

I'm not saying that if you begin your career as a trader with an initial capital of ₹ 4 lakh, make a debut with trading of one Nifty contract and religiously follow the best patterns presented in this book, you would then be assured of a steady and unfailing income. Real-life trading is a different ball game. Brace yourself; the best of patterns can fail. Consecutive losses can — and will — happen. Earnings from trading are never certain. You win a few, you may lose many. If you are looking for a steady and regular income, a monthly pay cheque, then trading, and more particularly day trading, is not for you.

Chapter 23

Performance Summary

Why test a trading pattern before using it? Here are quick answers to the question:

- To determine whether a theory or hypothetical construct is valid in historical testing; and
- To summarize the overall hypothetical performance of a system and to analyse its various aspects in order to isolate its strong and weak points.

The purpose of testing a pattern or a trading system is simply to find out what will work best on the basis of what had worked best in the past.

Backtesting

Backtesting is the process of evaluating a trading theory, or model by applying it to historical data .A thorough backtest of a trading system should include the following information:

Number of Years Analysed: Although it is desirable to test as much data as possible, the minimum should be 10 years of recent historical data. Often people test the previous bull market's data if they figure that the current market resembles a bull market, and *vice versa*. The most important data tranche is the most recent one as that is what the current market phase is, as you want your trades to work there.

Number of Trades Analysed: More important than the number of years analysed is the number of trades analysed. A typical pattern should generate at least 20 to 25 trades over the test period in order to support the statistical significance of backtesting results. It would be wrong to assume that a pattern that had formed only a couple of times in the past is a guide or reference to a good trading opportunity in the future.

You may perhaps have come across the term called accuracy while reading statistics. Accuracy usually increases as the number of samples becomes larger and the measurement of deviation or error becomes proportionately smaller. Accuracy is calculated as follows:

Accuracy = (1- (1/ Square root of the sample size))*100.

I have extended this concept to the number of trades analysed. For example, with a sample of four trades, the error is 50%. If a system has had only 4 trades, whether profitable or loss-making, it is very difficult to draw any conclusions about performance expectations. To reduce the error to 10%, the sample size has to be 100 trades. But this could be tricky in respect of a system that might generate only 3 or 4 trades in a year. To compensate for this, the identical pattern can be applied to other markets and the sample size thus increased. By keeping the sample error to no more than 20%, the risk of small sample size can be minimized.

Percentage Winning Trades: This is not as important as one might think. In reality, few patterns have more than 70 percent winning trades. Patterns that are correct as little as 35 percent of the time can still be good systems, whereas systems that are accurate as much as 90 percent of the time may be bad systems.

Average Profit per Trade: This measure tells you what the average profit per trade for all the trades has been, minus commission and slippage. The average profit per trade figure is important as it considers all profits and all losses. Some people might question — and legitimately, too — whether, say, a 40-point average profit would vary to a great degree from the underlying Nifty value. For example, a 40-point gain translates to less than 1 percentage gain when the Nifty is trading above 4,000 levels, as opposed to a 2 percentage gain when the Nifty is trading below 2,000 levels. So, it's important to view the trade details in percentage terms as well.

Maximum Drawdown: This is one of the most important aspects of a trading system. A very large drawdown is a negative factor. Maximum drawdown is the largest peak-to-valley loss of a trading system's historical profit curve. Maximum drawdown can be presented in absolute rupee terms.

Maximum Number of Consecutive Losers / Winners: The maximum number of consecutive winning and losing generated is, more often than not, purely psychological. Even using an excellent trading pattern is no guarantee that you will only have winning trades in succession all the time. In other words, there are bound to be a string of consecutive losing trades. But not many traders have the ability to maintain their discipline through four or more successive losing trading trades. Even at the third consecutive loss, you would find many traders ready to abandon their system. I would say, to be a winner one would need to weather such storms and be able to take ten or more consecutive losses in one's stride.

Largest Single Losing Trade: This measure indicates how much of the drawdown is the result of a single losing trade. In real-life trading, this helps you adjust the initial stop loss. For example, if the average losing trade was ₹ 1,000 and the largest single losing trade was ₹ 8,000, as you would readily guess, a good portion of the average losing trade is borne by the largest losing trade. If you had a better way of managing the largest loser, your overall system performance would be considerably better. You should investigate further the cause for the larger losing trades. In real life trading be prepared to encounter an even higher largest loss, than thrown up by back tested results and brace yourself to handle such situation.

Largest Single Winning Trade: This is more important than the largest single losing trade. Why? Suppose, for example, your total hypothetical profit was ₹ 50,000 for 50 trades, and ₹ 32,250 of this is attributed to only one trade (e.g., long at the close of 15 May 2009), then what you have is a distorted average trade figure. It's often a good idea to remove such an exceptional single trade from the overall results and re-compute the system performance in order to confirm whether the trading system is actually good enough to trade. In real life trading, be as realistic as possible and prepared that you may never encounter that largest winning trade derived from the backtested results.

Some Other Considerations

Profit Factor: Profit factor is the system's gross profit divided by gross loss. Look for systems that have a profit factor of 2, or higher.

Recovery Factor: Because maximum drawdown is measured by the actual amount, it makes little sense to compare it to a buy and hold strategy drawdown during the test period. However, we can compare the recovery factor, which is equal to the absolute value of net profit divided by maximum drawdown. It's desirable for a system to have a recovery factor greater than buy and hold.

Payoff Ratio: Payoff ratio is the system's average profit in rupee terms per winning trade, divided by the average loss in rupee terms per losing trade. Unless the system has a particularly high win / loss ratio, we look for high payoff ratios.

Maximum Drawdown (%): As discussed earlier, maximum drawdown is the largest peak-to-valley loss — in absolute rupee terms — of the trading system's historical profit. Now, suppose you would like to determine the efficiency of a trading strategy in terms of the overall returns it provided on your starting capital. In that case, we can calculate the maximum drawdown as a percentage of the starting capital.

Account Size Required: The account size required is calculated by considering the capital required (with the margin in consideration) at the highest value achieved in the overall testing period, plus the maximum drawdown. Throughout this book, 6,288 (Nifty's highest closing value during the test period) is considered as the base value for calculating the minimum capital requirement. Considering a margin of 16%, the minimum account size required works out to ₹ 50,304 (6,288*50*16/100 = 50,304) for all the patterns. The account size is arrived at by simply adding the maximum drawdown value to ₹ 50,304. Some backtesting system might consider the maximum drawdown as the account size required. The problem with this type of calculation is that the return on account (final equity value, expressed in percentage terms of the account size required) will be a hyper-inflated number, giving a wrong impression about possible real life trading results.

Luck Factor This measure shows how the largest trade compared with the average trade and is calculated by dividing the percentage profit of the largest winning trade by the average percentage profit of all winning trades. The larger the value of the luck factor, the greater portion of the system's results can be attributed to the largest winning trade, or, luck.

Outlier Adjusted Profit Factor: With any trading pattern, you are going to have one or two exceptional wins. The chances of these trades recurring in the future are very slim and shouldn't be considered in the overall performance summary. In this book while calculating the outlier adjusted profit factor I've removed the largest single winning trade. You might want to consider removing even the top 5% winners. For example, if the number of trades is 40, then remove top 2 largest winners, if number of trades is 60, then remove top 3 largest winners. Look for trading systems with an outlier adjusted profit factor of more than 2.

Percent Winning Months or Years: Depending on the time horizon, a trading pattern that averages only one winning month out of twelve, or two winning years out of ten years, is unattractive. You need to look for patterns with at least five profitable months in a year and five profitable years in a ten-year period.

Theory into Reality

Turning a theory into reality can be a daunting task. When one first reads about trading patterns, the question that probably immediately comes to mind is, "This all sounds great in theory, but can it be applied to real markets?" So what further number crunching would I do after finding a reasonably good pattern (say with a profit factor of 3), before going ahead and start trading it in the real world? Here are three other calculations that I run my pattern through to gather confidence to trade it in real life.

Sharpe Ratio

This is probably the most common measure used by large fund houses in comparing potential investments. The Sharpe Ratio was formulated by Nobel Laureate William F. Sharpe in 1966 as a measure for comparing the performance of mutual funds. This measure was introduced as a reward-to-variability ratio but subsequently came to be referred to simply as the Sharpe Ratio after its originator. Sharpe Ratio was one of the first statistical measures that factored both return and risk into a single formula, thereby giving us a single statistical measure of risk-adjusted return.

Sharpe Ratio = (APR - RFR)/ (StdDevAPR)

where:

APR = Annualised portfolio return

RFR = Annualised risk-free rate (90-day T-bills are typically used as a proxy)

Standard Deviation of APR (StdDevAPR) = Annualised standard deviation of the portfolio's returns.

For short-term trading as our holding period is only one day, I've set the RFR to zero.

Sharpe Ratio indicates the smoothness of the equity curve. The higher the ratio, the smoother the equity growth or decline. A Sharpe Ratio value of above 0.5 is considered good, while a value above 1.0 is excellent and a value above 2.0 is considered outstanding.

When choosing a pattern's reliability in real-life trading, I use Sharpe Ratio on the assumption of a zero risk-free rate of return and at least a Sharpe Ratio of 0.6 from the backtesting results.

Pessimistic Rate of Return

Pessimistic return on margin (PROM) is an annualised yield on margin that is adjusted in a way that pessimistically assumes that a trading strategy will win less and lose more in real-time trading than it did in its historical simulation.

PROM adjusts the gross profit by calculating a new, mathematically adjusted, pessimistic lower gross profit. The first step is to calculate the number of winning trades reduced by its square root or, in other words, adjusted by its standard error. This adjusted number of winning trades is then multiplied by the average winning trade to arrive at a new, adjusted lower gross profit.

PROM next adjusts the gross loss by calculating a new; mathematically adjusted, pessimistic higher gross loss. The first step is to calculate the number of losing trades increased by its square root or, in other words, adjusted by its standard error. This adjusted number of losing trades is then multiplied by the average losing trade to arrive at a new, adjusted larger gross loss.

A new adjusted gross profit, or loss, is then calculated using these adjusted pessimistic gross profit and gross loss values. This is then used to produce an annualised rate of return on margin.

The formula is:

PROM = {[AW x (#WT – Sqrt(#WT))] — [AL × (#LT – Sqrt(#LT))]} / Margin

#WT = Number of Wins

AW = Average Win

#LT = Number of Losses

AL = Average Loss
A#WT = Adjusted Number of Wins
A#LT = Adjusted Number of Losses
AAGP = Adjusted Annualised Gross Profit
AAGL = Adjusted Annualised Gross Loss
A#WT = #WT – Sqrt (#WT)
A#LT = #LT + Sqrt (#LT)
AAGP = A#WT × AW
AAGL = A#LT × AL
Sqrt = Square root.

Let us consider an example. Assume a ₹ 50,000 annualised gross profit, 50 wins, ₹ 20,000 annualised gross loss, 50 losses, and a starting capital of ₹ 1,00,000.

As a basis for comparison, let us first calculate an annualised rate of return on the starting capital. This would be a 30 percent annualised return on margin (50,000 – 20,000) /1,00,000 = 0.3 ×100 = 30%).

In contrast, let us look at the PROM of this strategy:

Adjusted Number of Wins = 50 – Sqrt (50) = 43
Adjusted Number of Losses = 50 + Sqrt (50) = 57
Adjusted Annual Gross Profit = (50,000/50) x 43 = 42,929
Adjusted Annual Gross Loss = (20,000/50 x 57 = 22,828
PROM = ₹ (42,929 – 22,828) / 1,00,000 = ₹ 20,101
PROM = 20.1 percent per year.

As you would note, I have rounded off to the nearest digit in the above calculations.

This example clearly demonstrates why this measure is termed pessimistic. It assumes that a trading system will never win as frequently in real life as it had in testing and also that the system will lose more frequently in real life than it did in its testing. PROM is a robust measure because it factors in a number of significant performance statistics, such as gross profit, average win, gross loss, average loss, number of wins, and number of losses. Also, PROM by nature of the square-root calculation, penalizes small trade samples; that is, the square root of 4 is 2 which 50%, whereas the square root of 100 is 10, which is 10%.

PROM is an excellent measure to compare the performance of different trading models; I would suggest a trading model's PROM be at least 50% of the historical returns.

Pattern Overlap

> "A man with a watch knows what time it is. A man with two watches is never sure" — **Segal's Law**

I don't have a simple formula for this parameter, but it is assumed that we will be trading multiple patterns in real life, and these will overlap at times. This is no problem so long as they both point to either long or short. But, clearly, there can be confusion if each points differently, one long and the other short. Simple ways to overcome this pattern overlap problem is by recording all the patterns individually, and see that they don't give conflicting signals more than 20% of the time, better still no more than 10% of the time.

Remember; even though there is a strong tendency for the market to behave the way it did the last time when a particular pattern occurred, this is not a hard and fast rule. It will not happen all the time. However, it will recur often enough and will provide enough trading opportunities if you do a rigorous job of thoroughly analysing the performance summary.

I hope I've shed some light on the various parameters that one needs to consider in the historical system performance summary. An in depth analysis of the track record is necessary to determine a pattern's practicability. An entire book could easily be filled with a discussion of performance summary and other metrics. (Please SMS me @ +91 98450 bkora*, if you have the money and time to be the co-author for that book!)

* bkora=25672 (try this when typing the number on your mobile phone)

Chapter 24

Trading Rules

Based on a study of numerous trading books, my trading experience and the trading advice that I have received from friends and experts who are into the hedge funds business, I've tried to summarize the rules that you need to adhere to when embarking on a trading career.

Rule # 1: Trading is a Business

No one would start a business without first ensuring everything — or almost everything — that's needed to keep it going is firmly in place. Yet, when it comes to trading people try to cut corners, be it with regard to the initial capital investment or the infrastructure. Let me be blunt: If your initial capital is less than ₹ 5 lakh, you'd probably be better off putting that money in a mutual fund rather than attempting to be a trader; that way at least you might get some income tax benefits. On the other hand, if you are serious about getting into trading on your own, make sure you have the basic infrastructure in place, in addition to the start-up capital. This would include a high-end computer dedicated for trading, high speed Internet connections (couple of them; if one goes down, you could use the other), subscription to the best trading platform, plus price charts, data, etc, that you would need.

Rule # 2: Have a Trading Plan

> "If you fail to plan, you plan to fail."

A trading plan is absolutely essential. It is vital to your trading success. A trading plan is your road map to success in the market, without it you will get lost. Developing a trading plan is essential for long term trading success. Consider the following simple steps in creating a trading plan.

- **Step 1:** The first step in making your trading plan is to create a trading strategy. The biggest mistake that new traders make is to trade on gut feeling, or someone else's trading tip. Even if you make some money in this manner, it is a trading sin because you can't possibly repeat the profits again unless your friend gives you another tip. You need to develop a trading strategy that you yourself understand inside out.
- **Step 2:** Step two is to consider risk management because knowing when to enter a trade is just as important as knowing when to exit it. Trading is just like surgery where you want your doctor to get both the first incision and the final stitch right — only in this case, you are the doctor.
- **Step 3:** Once you have created your trading strategy, it is time to test, re-test, and test. Everything needs to be tested backwards and forwards. You test drive a car before buying it; there is no reason why you shouldn't test your trading strategy before applying it.
- **Step 4:** Know your trading strategy like your best friend.

Rule # 3: Be Patient

Patience is an essential trait in trading. A majority of people who are new to trading, however, tend to err towards overtrading. Carried away by an adrenaline rush, they tend to become reckless. They trade more often than they should, and trade a larger number of contracts than they ought to. Sure, you experience more thrills when you trade often. It gives you a quick high. But this approach can ruin a trader's financial well-being, particular one who has just ventured into the business.

In the prevailing "I want it right now, right here" trading environment, traders have little patience. However, if you study the lives of successful traders, you will find that they have many things in common. The one important similarity among successful traders is patience. This formula has not changed since early 1800s, when US futures trading began. In fact, it can even be traced as far back as 1640, when trading took place in tulip bulb futures.

Rule # 4: Remain Consistent

Successful traders find a formula and stick to it. I would suggest a trader, particularly a novice trader, should adhere to one or two carefully selected trading patterns that work best for him / her. The need for a plan, a strategy and applying it in a consistent, methodical manner cannot be overemphasized.

When it comes to trading, rules are not made to be broken unless you want to end up broke. More importantly, rules exist to protect us from ourselves. Take the example of a few simple traffic rules, namely driving on the left side of the road, not over speeding, and not driving after consuming alcoholic drinks. Now consider breaking the three rules by speeding on the right side of the road after couple of alcoholic drinks; what do you think will happen? Do you think that the only risk is that the traffic police will catch you and fine you? Actually, you are likely to be added to the list of road accident victims. In India, 1.2 lakh people were killed in road mishaps in 2007. Why? Simply because most of them failed to obey simple traffic rules: The same goes for a trader; should you choose to speculate in an inconsistent fashion, trust me, the financial results might well be similar to your trading account.

Rule # 5: Let Winners Run, Not the Losers

This is the most important rule in trading simply not because Larry Williams has written so in many of his trading books. Losers do the opposite: they increase the size of their bets when losing, and trim their bets when winning! Winners look for positive streaks and press home their advantage. You can see that the combined pivot point trading secrets as a whole strategy presented in Chapter 26 had a string of 23 winning trades in a row. After 3 winning trades in a row, 75 percent of the traders would hesitate to take the next trade; after 6 winners in a row, I don't know how many of you can take the next trade!

In the current lot of Indian cricketers, and other than the cricket's almighty Sachin Ramesh Tendulkar, I like Virendar Sehwag. How often commentators repeat whenever Virendar Sehwag walks out to bat that he is highly unpredictable. Many of my friends even start counting the score as 0 runs for 1 wicket, discounting Sehwag in the belief that he is going to get out any moment. The fact is that Sehwag is the only Indian batsman with two Test triple centuries in the annals of cricket. Now consider this:

There are actually only a few records of Sir Donald George Bradman's that have been broken. Thus, while Sachin Tendulkar has scored more centuries than did the Don but Bradman scored his 29 centuries in 52 test matches, whereas Sachin had scored only 17 after his 52 tests. If you start looking at the records in this manner; you will find very few batting records of Don that have truly been broken. So which of Virendar Sehwag's batting records am I talking about? Do a survey of 150+ consecutive scores by both Sehwag and Bradman. It is probable that Sehwag's sequence of 150+ scores, or his tally of 100 to 150* conversions, will remain very high by the time he retires. Thus, the next time you are watching a test match, the odds are very high for Sehwag to get a 150+ score the moment he scores a hundred. Yes that's how unpredictable Virendar Sehwag is!

The moral of the story: "Press your winners and not the losers".

That reminds me: How many of us would have thought Australia would beat India in the ICC 2003 World Cup cricket final in South Africa, considering the statistical fact that Australia had already won 17 matches in a trot prior to that? The same statistical fact was in the headlines of many newspapers before the match started, many an SMS were exchanged between Indian cricket fans highlighting this statistical fact to generate a feel good atmosphere that India would win. Well, Australia won that match, beating India comprehensively by a margin of 125 runs.

The point is, the human mind cannot relate easily to an unbroken string of successes. All of us expect a failure to happen after a successful run. And once a good run has been broken, we again wait for success. In trading, though, if you are on a clear winning streak, press on. Don't allow the fear of loss to stop you in your winning tracks.

* This sequence was broken on 24 November 2009, after 11 such occurrences. Personally I believe it is going to start again.

Rule # 6: Never Average Down and Never Lie about Your Losses

The short point is only people with room-temperature IQ* double losses. Professionals average up, never down. They got to be professionals in the first place because they added to their winners, not their losers. For one, you shouldn't even be in a situation where you start thinking about averaging down. You should have exited the trade before it got to the point where averaging down became tempting

In fact, this rule is as old as trading itself. Dickson G. Watts , who was President of the New York Cotton Exchange between 1878 and 1880, wrote about it as early as the 1880s, in the book Speculation as a Fine Art and Thoughts on Life:

> "It is better to 'average up' than to 'average down'. This opinion is contrary to the one commonly held and acted upon; it being the practice to buy, and on a decline to buy more. This reduces the average. Probably four times out of five this method will result in striking a reaction in the market that will prevent loss, but the fifth time, meeting with a permanently declining market, the operator loses his head and closes out, making a heavy loss — a loss so great as to bring complete demoralization, often ruin."

Then, too, you will often hear traders boasting about their winning trades. In contrast, seldom will you hear traders admit about their losing trades. My unasked advice would be: never delude yourself by boasting about your winning trades; instead, be honest to yourself about your losing trades. Please make it a habit not to lie about your trading losses, at least to yourself and your spouse. By facing the truth when you do make losses, at least you won't be tempted to average down again.

Why should one never average down? Mathematically, it would take too long to explain. It's sufficient to know that that's how real life trading works. Almost all huge bankruptcies in trading companies worldwide hap-

* Room-temperature IQ /quant. / Used in describing the expected intelligence range of the user. Nominal room temperature is 72 degrees Fahrenheit, 22 degrees Celsius. This is a much more insulting phrase in countries like India that use Celsius degrees for measuring the temperature.

pened because the trades involved doubled up losing positions with excessive leverage or lied about the losses to themselves and to their bosses. Hoping to recover losses by averaging down through additional leverage hardly ever works unless someone is really very lucky.

Rule # 7: Follow the Pattern, Not the Price

Put your trust in your trading patterns, and do not be afraid when price reach historic highs or lows. Markets are where they are for a reason. Evaluate that reason on its own merits. Ignore the price, follow the signal. Thinking on the lines that "The Nifty is now at an all-time / five-year high and trading at 6,400 levels and my pattern is telling me to go long but I don't think it will go beyond 7,000, etc." is not very wise. Just go by the pattern. Likewise, if Nifty is trading at, say, 1,000 don't be afraid to go short if the pattern tells you to do so.

Rule # 8: Use Stop Loss

As soon as a trade is initiated, you should have a protective stop loss.

However, there is 99% chance that a very tight stop loss of 1 or 2 points will invariably get triggered and you would be stopped out of a perfectly good trade.

If, on the other hand, you use a very wide stop loss value of 755 it will never get triggered if you go by Nifty's historical data that we have. (The OHLC values on 23 January 2008 were 5,203.35, 5,203.35, 4,448.5, 4,899.3, and the difference between high and low was 754.85 giving that value of 755 as a stop loss figure.) The point is, you need to give your stop loss some breathing space to work, but not those extreme levels of 755 on every trade you initiate.

Well, that is the theory. Coming now to the practicality of stop loss.

The market loves stop losses. In real-life trading you will soon discover that the market has a way of "knowing" where your stop loss is. The market will periodically test your stop losses so as to take as much money as possible from you.

From the financial literature that I've read, and from a post-mortem of the trade log that I maintain, I have personally come to the following conclusion: The traditional stop loss neither reduces nor increases a trader's losses relative to the buy-and-hold strategy. This is, of course, in sharp contrast to the common belief that using stop loss strategies can improve investment returns.

While I may not be able to offer the nitty-gritty of stop-loss workings in detail in this book, here are my reasons why the stop loss strategy doesn't work in real life trading, as envisaged in the back-testing results:

1. Stop losses are not guaranteed to work because of full gap openings against one's positions. For example you are long with an overnight position with Nifty trading at 6,000 level, and your stop loss, let us say is at 5,900. Now suppose Nifty opens at 5,800 the next day, where do you think your stop loss level of 5,900 would have got executed?
2. During the intraday movements, it may look reasonably well that stop loss might get executed at our desired level but again because the data set only has OHLC figures for our back-testing purposes, it is impossible to tell if our entry or our stop loss is the one that occurred during the adverse movement happened during intraday (for example, consider OHLC levels of 6,000, 6,100, 5,900, 6,050, and assume we had gone long at Open+1%, i.e. at 6,060 level, by placing a stop loss level at open-1%, i.e. at 5,940. Now either of the following two would have happened on that day:

   (a) 6,060 is hit after 5,900 in the intraday movements, in which case the outcome is a 10-point loss if exited at close.

   (b) If 5,900 is hit, after 6100, in which case the outcome is a 60-point loss as our stop loss level of 5,940 is hit sometime during the course of the day.

3. It gets even more complex to design a stop loss if one is holding multiple trading contracts. For example, consider your stop is at 5,900 in the above OHLC case, and you are holding 20 contracts (or lots, as in futures contract terminology), whereas only five or fewer of them get executed at 5,900, how, then, would you treat the remaining lots?

So, what, then, is the solution?

- As a rule of thumb limit your losses with the use of stop losses as per your risk appetite (and no backtesting results are sure about your risk appetite, for example a 0.1 % loss of the trading capital might hurt someone, whereas even a 2% loss of the trading capital may not particularly bother someone else.). It hurts to take a stop loss, but it is much less painful than the ruin of the trading capital. Hence the old adage, "Bulls make money, bears make money, but pigs get slaughtered".

- On the other hand, since all our backtesting is done assuming we close out the positions as per fixed time, that is either next day at close, or at today's close, why do we need to bother about the stop losses. A proper alternative to the use of a stop loss strategy in such a situation is to trade with a low enough percentage of the trading capital, so that disaster won't knock us down
- As a rule of thumb, whether you follow stop losses or not, I would suggest a cap of 2% of your trading capital to risk on a single trade as your protective stop, which gives you room for 50 trades.

Rule # 9: Don't Be Obsessed by Minute-by-Minute Market Movements

> "One great mistake the man makes who watches the ticker all the time is that he trades too often" — **William D. Gann**

Watching the ticker can be fun. It can even be mesmerizing. Many people, though, enter a trade and then anxiously watch the tape with their eyes glued to the screen, almost as if their whole life depended on this one trade. Or, they go channel surfing, moving from one business TV channel to the next, their mind obsessed with the outcome of that one particular trade.

This kind of behaviour does no one any good. Rather, what it does is raise your blood pressure and add to your stress levels. Do your blood pressure a favour, enter the trade if all of your trading rules are met, put a stop loss, and go take a nap, or go to a movie, or play with your kid, or help your wife with the cooking . . . .

Rule # 10: Avoid Over-Reliance on Market Gurus

I'm spitting in my own rice bowl here, but you should not be letting some self-appointed market guru dictate or dominate your trading decisions. The most you should expect, or accept, from folks like me are a few trading patterns, and a bit of advice on how to make a trading plan. No one knows or cares as much about your personal circumstances as you yourself do: how much money you can invest, your tolerance for pain, your goals, your most suitable and comfortable time frame, etc. And note, your guru will not bother to part with a single penny if all his "great picks" you fall for come a cropper.

Rule # 11: Maintain a Trading Log

A trading diary or log is a great way to check and confirm your trading entries and exits. Consider what this can do for you as a trader. If it is followed properly, it can, and most likely will, help improve your level of self-discipline and ultimately lead to an increase in your self-confidence. How? If you execute when the signals call for action, you can validate whether you responded when called upon to do so. You can check your work. You will find out whether you hesitated when your methods called for you to exit and if you timed it as per the system or not.

Ask yourself the following questions in addition to working out your profit and loss account:

1. Did I follow my trading plan today?
2. Did I maintain discipline today?
3. Did I do the research required today?

The trading log will reinforce the validity of your trading strategy. By cataloguing your trades, you will gain more experience in identifying the patterns that drive your trading signals. It also keeps track of what went right or what went wrong with a trading plan. It will allow you to study and examine the results in black and white. On successful trading days, it will be good to capitalize on your successes so that it can be repeated. Of course, on bad days, provided you are not tempted to average down or tempted to hide from your spouse about your bad day, it can help you focus on what went wrong so that you can understand and improve on it and stop repeating the same mistakes over and over again.

Rule # 12: Don't Think "This Market Stuff" is Easy

It's not that hard to make money either in a roaring bull market or a raging bear market. Don't take yourself to be a genius when everything is going great for you. Equally, don't think of yourself to be dumb when nothing is going right. The market whips us all now and then. The whipping usually comes just when we think we've got it all figured out.

Here I would like to present an analogy with the possible moves in chess.

Just after the first move, there are 400 moves open for both players. Each player can move any of his 8 pawns 1 or 2 squares and the knights each have two squares they can go on to — and, hence 20 × 20 possibilities. After two moves apiece, there are 72,084 possible moves available, after three moves apiece, there are 9+ million moves possible, and after the four moves apiece, there are 318,979,564,000, or about 319 billion possibilities.

If the calculations that I made are correct, there are 169,518,829,100,544,000,000,000,000,000 ways to play the first ten moves of a game of chess. That is about 169 octillion possibilities! I would be happy to be corrected if I am wrong.

Well those are the numbers of possibilities in a game of chess which is played between only 2 players. In contrast, the trading game has hundreds of thousands of players and, therefore, practically infinite number of possible moves available!

So, you must learn to put your ego aside when dealing with the market. Remember, the market, and only the market, is always right, and it's we who could be wrong.

> "Don't be a hero. Don't have an ego. Always question yourself and your ability. Don't ever feel that you are very good. The second you do, you are dead." — **Paul Tudor Jones**

And the Rule # 13: Live by the Rules

If you follow the rules you have made, then you have a better chance of succeeding. This applies to any aspect of life. As Leonardo da Vinci stated, "Simplicity breeds elegance."

Keep things simple and follow the rules. Ignore the rules and you'll have no money.

To my mind, the definition of successful trader is one who has his or her trading plan written down, who also applies risk and money management rules, and the one who then lives by those rules.

One final take on rules: take some time off to work out a set of trading rules that you believe work for you. Take a printout of the rules in large font and paste one copy on the top of your trading terminal and another — in an even larger type font — at a prominent spot in your trading room.

Section - 4

High Profit Trading Secrets

"There is only one side to the stock market; and it is not the bull side or the bear side, but the right side."
— Jesse Livermore

Chapter-25
Minute and Mega Market Clock

Chapter-26
Greed is Good

Chapter-27
Pivot Point Trading Secrets

Chapter-28
Gap Trading Secrets

Chapter-29
Walk Forward

Chapter-30
Sayonara

Chapter 25

Minute and Mega Market Clock

In Chapter 5, we concluded that the market moves in natural cycles. In this chapter, I have tried to extend the same concept, albeit in a brief manner, to the market structure applicable to various time periods, ranging from mere hours to fifty-plus years.

Weekly

Monday, Bloody Monday

The first trading day of the week sets the tone for the rest of the week. What happens on Monday is, typically, an indication of things to come over the rest of the week. It's not a day you would want to miss trading on — and then scramble to catch up with the trend later in the week.

In a bull market, Monday often happens to be the best trending day, the day on which you would want to be on long side at the open and out at the close.

In a bear market, Monday is the day to be on the short side on the open and out on the close.

Not surprisingly, both the highest-ever Nifty up move and down move — in terms of points — occurred on Mondays.

Turnaround Tuesday

In a bull market, if Mondays are characterized by strength from the opening, Tuesdays need time to digest Monday's strength before resuming the climb to higher prices. Tuesday tends to be the choppiest day of the week.

Tuesdays are, by far, the least desirable day to trade during the week. Turnaround Tuesday describes a well-known time bias. Trends that begin on Friday and persist through Monday frequently reverse during Tuesday. New trends that start at this time may trigger sharp price expansion for the next two days.

Wednesday, a Late Surge Day

Wednesday has a choppy price action during the open and later in the afternoon; however, prices tend to move in the same direction as the open.

In a bull market, if Wednesday's open is up, it's the right time to be long at open and out on the close. In bear markets, you might consider to be on the short side but not with same degree of predictability as with bull markets.

Along with Tuesdays, Wednesdays also indicate a possible reversal of the trend that can occur on Thursdays. The strongest correlation between market sentiment and the day of the week occurs on either Tuesdays or Wednesdays when the price action gets reversed.

Thursday, the Weakest Day

If there is a one good day to sell in a bull market, it is Thursday. This is clearly the short-sell day with the high made first earlier in the day and a subsequent sell-off occurring late in the afternoon

In a bull market, with a higher Monday, Tuesday and Wednesday, you will almost always see some profit taking by Thursday, the weakest day of the week. But if you are witnessing steadily lower prices, with weakness on Monday, Tuesday and Wednesday, then Thursday will be the counter-trend day and rally higher. This is an important distinction to make when deciding on how to trade on a Thursday.

Friday, End of the Week

By Thursday, the uninformed Johnny-come-lately traders who have been following the bull market all week are finally ready to take the plunge. They want to get in on a "sure thing", but have been cautious earlier in the week when, in fact, they should have been bold. They finally take the plunge by buying the top! You could make the same argument that stock investors are finally willing to sell their shares at the bottom, after being hammered on the prior three days. That's the day, of course, when the market will rally — right after the uninformed abandon their positions. When you think about this, you might conclude it is all only human psychology. Most people are wrong at the significant market turns.

This brings us to Friday when the weekly cycle is setting up again. If the market has been weak, traders will use the excuse to drive the market lower, and if the market has been strong, they drive the market higher. Whatever happens on Friday will be discussed over the next two off days, and a psychological bias will develop in the minds of traders who are resting and catching up with the news, and there is a high degree of certainty that the effect will continue into the coming Monday. That is, If Friday has a down close, Monday tends to be a down close. And the cycle goes on.

Fridays have other major forces to contend with. Fresh options series will start on the last Friday of each month. That option expiry week often generates unusual volatility which peaks on expiration day. Market action during this period can be highly unpredictable.

Some of the day-of-the-week behaviour discussed above has shown a high probability of repetition over many years. I would strongly advise you to combine the day-of-week, and any other seasonal behaviour, to time the market. I have deliberately repeated and added to what I had already covered in the earlier Chapter 9, "Day of the week" because the patterns I am going to discuss in Section 4 are based heavily on the market's day-of-the-week behaviour.

Intraday Characteristics

Natural cycles drive the daily market momentum. The nature of the trading crowd changes dramatically as the day progresses. The first and last market hours favour strong directional price movement. The day can be broken into three time segments and each of these time segments contains predictable price characteristics.

Amateurs Control the Open

The general belief is that amateurs, namely the individual traders and investors, tend to make emotional, uninformed decisions before the market starts trading. Some of the reasons for this are obvious, and some may be less obvious. The obvious reasons are that most people get up early and go to work. Therefore, if they have an opinion about the market direction, whether informed or uninformed, they act on that opinion in the morning, or at the time of the market open. The less obvious reasons are emotional. People are generally more positive in the morning after a night's sleep. With that fresh dash of positive feeling, many people who are new to trading feel compelled to open the trade.

Never, ever, do that. It's like jumping into an alligator-infested lake while you are bleeding; you will be eaten for breakfast. Instead, think like a professional and sit out the first 15 minutes or so after the market opens. Let the market clean up and settle down a bit.

Midday Markets

A new type of trading crowd emerges after the first hour. While public participation dominates the open, the balance of the day belongs to institutions and professional traders. The resolution of opening orders, driven by overnight supply demand imbalance, creates an upward, downward, or a sideways bias that will likely persist for the entire day.

One can execute longer-term positions in the middle of the day as trade fills during this quieter time benefit from the slippage. Traders can make better decisions after observing the bull-bear struggle during the opening.

Traders take their cues from whatever the markets offer and choose long, short, or wait-and-watch strategies. This often requires waiting for counter-trend weakness after the first hour before entering long positions or counter-trend strength to sell short. An unexpected shift from the day's trending direction can occur around 1 p.m. to 2 p.m. These important times correspond with trading that surrounds lunch time and the opening of the European markets. A rally or sell-off can begin right after lunch in these trending conditions. But erratic activity becomes much more likely if the market direction is not clear.

Last Hour — The Closing Bell

The last phase of the market day displays unique characteristics that can enhance or undermine profits. Intraday traders seek to exit all positions prior to the closing bell. Both retail and institutions contribute to the last hour's volatility through active trading. Classic buy-sell programs strike throughout the last 60 minutes, while mutual fund activity surges during the last 20 minutes of the day. This dramatic increase in institutional participation heightens price movement that leads into the close. The professionals represent the smart money and control the last hour of trading.

In fact, there is a technical indicator called smart money index which comprises of the net change in the market for the first hour *versus* the net change in the market for the last hour. The smart money index is appropriate in a trading book if only to heighten a trader's awareness of weak hands ("dumb", retail money.) *versus* strong hands (smart, informed institutional money).

Monthly Characteristics

Well-defined seasonal variations can signal opportunity. Some periods of a month generate a special bias that can affect trade alignment. Understand these cyclical quirks before taking a position that falls under their influence.

Table 25.1 has been compiled with the total data that www.nseindia.com offered from January 1997 till June 2009. The average gain column indicates what the gains from Nifty could have been by entering a trade on open of the first day of trading in the month and exiting at the close of the last trading day of the month.

Table 25.1
Month-wise Gains by Nifty (1997 to 2009)

Month	*Total Months*	*Average Gain*	*Months Profitable*	*% Months Profitable*
January	13	0.004%	7	53.8%
February	13	1.752%	9	69.2%
March	13	-1.532%	5	38.5%
April	13	1.688%	7	53.8%
May	13	1.055%	6	46.2%
June	13	1.050%	9	69.2%
July	12	1.537%	8	66.7%
August	12	1.979%	8	66.7%
September	12	0.745%	8	66.7%
October	12	-1.855%	5	41.7%
November	12	4.089%	8	66.7%
December	12	5.663%	10	83.3%

There's Always a Santa Claus Rally

The Santa Claus Rally marks a psychological end to tax loss selling as investors jump the gun on next year's bargains. The last few weeks before the Christmas holidays carry a positive bias that often triggers a substantial rally. Although investors can sell losing positions through 31 December , most of their negative impact eases by mid-month. Market players then concentrate on rebuilding portfolios with cash directed toward broad sectors. This combines with natural holiday bullishness to favour a pleasant end to the trading year. I would attribute the Santa Claus Rally to the heavy involvement of the foreign institutional investors (FII) in Nifty, even though the number of people celebrating Christmas in India is not more than 2.4% of the country's population.*

Avoid the October Surprise

October presents market players with the most dangerous period in the entire year. It represents the month that has generated the highest average monthly decline in value over Nifty's 13-year history. Remember that this month also witnessed the Black October events of 1929 and 1987 in the US markets, and several such in India too.

Tax Loss Selling

Tax loss selling infects market activity in India in March. Investors reduce their year-end tax burden by taking capital losses on non-performing positions. This selling often limits broad rallies in March. Mutual funds face their own major reallocations towards the end of March as they prepare for end-of-year reporting. This can trigger ferocious volatility with broad strategies that dump old losers and chase new winners.

Finally, a consistent, foolproof, let's-all-make money approach is just never going to happen because there will always be investors who try to make more money by taking advantage of the rigid schedule it follows. That very act messes up the schedule.

---

* Source; http://www.censusindia.gov.in/Census_Data_2001/Census_Data_Online/Social_and_cultural/Religion.aspx.

Yet, no fixed rule can be expected to last for ever. Too many smart people are around to anticipate and dissipate the effect. The cycles, as we often remind ourselves, are always changing.

Yearly

Time bias does not end with monthly cycles. Clearly defined cycles appear through yearly periods as well. Here are some of the mega market cycles that I have come across.

4-Year Cycle (Kitchin Wave)

In 1923, Joseph Kitchin found that there existed a 40-month cycle in a variety of economic and financial factors in both Great Britain and the United States between 1890 and 1922. The four-year cycle was later found to have an extremely strong presence in the stock market between 1868 and 1945. Although it is called a four-year cycle, the cycle length has actually been found to vary between 40 and 53 months.

9.2-Year Cycle (Juglar Wave)

In 1860, Clemant Juglar found that a cycle lasting approximately 9 years existed in many areas of economic activity. Subsequent research found this cycle to have had a strong presence during the period from 1840 to 1940.

54-Year Cycle (Kondratieff Wave)

Named after a Russian economist, the Kondratieff Wave is a long-term, 54-year cycle identified in prices and economic activity. Since the cycle is extremely long-term, it has only repeated itself three times in the stock market so far.

Please refer to the book *The Master Swing Trader* by Alan Farley for a more detailed explanation of the market clock. But remember that market timing cannot turn a bad trade into a good one. It can only make a good one better. By the way I being, a very short-term trader do not believe in the yearly cycles as there is no way to test such long cycle's existence and their helpfulness for the short trading.

Chapter 26

Greed is Good

"Greed, for lack of a better word, is good".
— Gordon Gekko (Michael Douglas), in the movie, *Wall Street*

Table 26.1 shows the Open, High, Low, Close values of Nifty on the first trading day of the year. The sixth column in the table shows what would have been the year-wise returns, in terms of points, for a buy-and-hold strategy, i.e. simply buying at the start of the year and exiting at the start of the next year. And the seventh column shows the returns in terms of percentage. This simple strategy, which almost all mutual fund managers use in their media advertisements to show their fund's returns *vis-à-vis* the Nifty, would have yielded a holding period return of 189%,

Table 26.1
Returns from Buying and Holding Nifty from January 2000 to June 2009

Year	*Open*	*High*	*Low*	*Close*	*Returns*	*% Returns*
3-Jan-00	1,482.15	1,592.90	1,482.15	1,592.20	-337.90	-21.2%
1-Jan-01	1,263.50	1,276.15	1,250.65	1,254.30	-199.00	-15.9%
1-Jan-02	1,058.85	1,071.15	1,052.05	1,055.30	44.85	4.2%
1-Jan-03	1,093.60	1,102.10	1,093.60	1,100.15	812.10	73.8%
1-Jan-04	1,880.35	1,917.05	1,880.35	1,912.25	202.75	10.6%
3-Jan-05	2,080.00	2,118.60	2,080.00	2,115.00	720.95	34.1%
2-Jan-06	2,836.80	2,849.45	2,825.40	2,835.95	1,171.45	41.3%
2-Jan-07	3,966.25	4,016.65	3,964.95	4,007.40	2,136.95	53.3%
1-Jan-08	6,136.75	6,165.35	6,109.85	6,144.35	-3,110.90	-50.6%
1-Jan-09	2,963.30	3,039.25	2,963.30	3,033.45	1,257.65	41.5%
30-Jun-09	4,391.50	4,426.75	4,267.35	4,291.10		

and an average annual return of 18.9% (I've used 10 years instead of 9.5 years to arrive at this average to keep things simple). Well that is one of the mistake most of the people do while calculating the average returns over long periods , the returns needs to be calculated in terms of Compound Annual Growth Rate. The Compound Annual Growth Rate is calculated by taking the nth root of the total percentage growth rate, where n is the number of years in the period being considered. So our 18.9% in turn becomes 11.2% . Even that 11.2% annual growth rate is, indeed, very good if you compare it with any of the other passive investments, where you invest and forget for some time; examples include typical savings bank account, government bonds, post office savings, provident fund accounts, and so on. In fact, more than 70% of equity mutual fund managers struggle to consistently beat a return of 12 % over a 10-year time span.

Buy and Hold Strategy

Well, some of the compounding enthusiasts might ask why not calculate the compounded annual returns for the above case? That is reinvesting each year's returns back into the market, In that case it would have been a 170% return, or a compounded annualised yield of 11.1%. Table 26.2 presents the performance summary for the Nifty buy and hold strategy.

I have a little story to share with you here on compound interest. But before that let's see what John Bollinger, the developer of Bollinger Bands, which is a well-known technical indicator, had to say on compound interest in his book *Bollinger on Bollinger Bands*. According to him while the simplest system, compound interest, was truly the eighth wonder of the world but not even this approach could be relied upon to grow and stay rich:

> Taxes interfere; banks collapse; capital is confiscated; wars intervene; governments change; jail looms; the public objects; socialism arrives. . . . It is no accident that the annual tabulation of the world's richest people is composed mostly of people who made their fortunes, not those who inherited.

Table 26.2
Buy and Hold Nifty Strategy Performance Summary

Total net profit	₹ 134,945		
Gross profit	₹ 317,335	Gross loss	₹ -182,390
Total # of trades	10	Percent profitable	70%
Number of winning trades	7	Number of losing trades	3
Largest winning trade	₹ 106,848	Largest losing trade	₹ -155,545
Largest winning trade %	73.80%	Largest losing trade %	-50.60%
Average winning trade	₹ 45,334	Average losing trade	₹ -60,797
Average winning trade %	37.00%	Average losing trade %	-29.20%
Ratio avg win/avg loss	0.7		
Ratio avg win/avg loss %	1.3		
Average profit per trade	₹ 13,495		
Average profit per trade %	17.10%		
Max consecutive winners	6	Max consecutive losers	2
Max drawdown	₹ 155,545	Max drawdown %	-57.90%
Profit factor	1.7		
Account size required	₹ 205,849	Return on account	65.60%
Luck factor	4.3		
Recovery factor	0.9		
Pessimistic Rate of Return	4.3		
Sharpe ratio	0.4		
Accuracy	68%		

Compounding

Taking the passive, compound interest route is a big no-no to creating wealth as can easily be seen from the following, partly hypothetical, story.

The Nizam of Hyderabad, Nawab Mir Osman Ali Khan Asaf Jhah VII, was, at one time, the richest man alive. In the 1940s, his wealth was estimated at US $2 billion. *Time* magazine (issue of 22 February 1937) even featured him on its cover as the "richest man in the world". As per the list of the wealthiest historical figures of 2008 is based on research done around the world by *Forbes* magazine in 2007 and other sources of information, adjusted for 2007 US dollars, Nizam is acknowledged as the fifth richest man ever. Basing its assessment on modified calculations, including adjusting for inflation, etc., it is reckoned that in 2010 terms, his wealth would have been around US$ 225 billion, i.e. more than ₹ 9 lakh crore if one were to convert the dollar at a modest rate of ₹ 40.

I don't have a historian friend, so pardon me for any mistakes as regards The Nizam's family tree. The Nizam had four sons and a daughter from his five wives. Now, if each of his heirs had chosen to park their inheritance — let's say a modest US$ 10 million each, a pittance, considering his total wealth was $2 billion in the 1940s — even in a bank savings account paying 10% annual interest, they would all have ended up with a staggering wealth of more than US$ 3 billion each. But not one of the Nizam's heirs in the last ten years figured among the list of India's richest people! The reason is simple: passive compound interest — which is what money deposited in a bank savings account would earn — can take you only so far, and no further.

Perfect Prediction

Coming back to our analysis, let's go a step further from the Nifty buy-and-hold strategy and construct a "perfect" strategy. I call it "perfect", as this is an ideal situation and everyone would love such a trade. What if we could correctly call the direction of the market, that is, simply whether Nifty will go up or down in the next year, all ten times (an absolutely rare probability of 1 in 1,024!) and then, accordingly, either go long or short?

Table 26.3 is similar to the earlier Table 26.1 but with one additional column on the extreme right which shows whether we went long or short — and the kind of returns one could have expected.

Table 26.3

Perfectly Predicted Nifty Performance, January 2000 till June 2009

Year	*Open*	*High*	*Low*	*Close*	*Returns*	*% Returns*	*Long / Short*
3-Jan-00	1,482.15	1,592.90	1,482.15	1,592.20	337.90	21.2%	Short
1-Jan-01	1,263.50	1,276.15	1,250.65	1,254.30	199.00	15.9%	Short
1-Jan-02	1,058.85	1,071.15	1,052.05	1,055.30	44.85	4.2%	Long
1-Jan-03	1,093.60	1,102.10	1,093.60	1,100.15	812.10	73.8%	Long
1-Jan-04	1,880.35	1,917.05	1,880.35	1,912.25	202.75	10.6%	Long
3-Jan-05	2,080.00	2,118.60	2,080.00	2,115.00	720.95	34.1%	Long
2-Jan-06	2,836.80	2,849.45	2,825.40	2,835.95	1,171.45	41.3%	Long
2-Jan-07	3,966.25	4,016.65	3,964.95	4,007.40	2,136.95	53.3%	Long
1-Jan-08	6,136.75	6,165.35	6,109.85	6,144.35	3,110.90	50.6%	Short
1-Jan-09	2,963.30	3,039.25	2,963.30	3,033.45	1,257.65	41.5%	Long
30-Jun-09	4,391.50	4,426.75	4,267.35	4,291.10			

Hold your breath for a second — this strategy would have given a whopping holding period return of 993% (on a margined investment on one Nifty contract) over a 10-year-period! And that means around 100% arithmetic average return every year, or about 26 % compounded annual growth per year.

Table 26.4 presents the performance summery for the perfectly predicted Nifty strategy.

Table 26.4

Performance Summary — Perfectly Predicted Nifty Strategy

Total net profit	₹ 499,725		
Gross profit	₹ 499,725	Gross loss	₹ 0
Total # of trades	10	Percent profitable	100%
Number of winning trades	10	Number of losing trades	0
Largest winning trade	₹ 155,545	Largest losing trade	₹ 0
Largest winning trade %	73.80%	Largest losing trade %	0.00%
Average winning trade	₹ 49,973	Average losing trade	NA
Average winning trade %	34.70%	Average losing trade %	NA
Ratio avg win/avg loss	NA		
Ratio avg win/avg loss %	NA		
Average profit per trade	₹ 49,973		
Average profit per trade %	34.70%		
Max consecutive winners	10	Max consecutive losers	0
Max drawdown	₹ 0	Max drawdown %	0.00%
Profit factor	NA		
Account size required	₹ 50,304	Return on account	993.40%
Luck factor	2.1		
Recovery factor	NA		
Pessimistic Rate of Return	679.30%		
Sharpe ratio	1.6		
Accuracy	68%		

As you would have gathered from Table 26.3, with a perfect strategy we could generate just a little less than ₹ 5,00,000 by trading one single Nifty futures contract. Or, roughly 10,000 points of Nifty gain in 10 years. And to achieve that kind of returns, you and me, surely have to be greedy — and therefore the title of this chapter.

Chapter 27

Pivot Point Trading Secrets

We had considered pivot points in detail in Chapter 17. Now, in this chapter we shall look at some robust Nifty trading patterns based on simple classic pivot points. These are patterns traded by entering the trade before close of the market and exiting at the next day's close. In other words; our trade holding period will be just one trading day.

As an example, Table 27.1 (overleaf) presents how I have marked pivot points for each day, based on the previous day's Open, High, Low, Close (OHLC), covering a period of 10 days.

A few points need to be made specific to the way I have constructed Table 27.1:

- As stated earlier, pivots points have been calculated based on the previous day's OHLC values.
- I have only marked up to R3 and S3; thus, if the Nifty traded at R4 or S4 levels, they are nevertheless marked only as R3 or S3.
- If, for example, the open is marked as PP, it means that the open is neither below the S1 levels nor above the R1 levels . This can be observed in all the days considered for this example. The same applies to highs, lows and closes as well.
- If, for example, low is marked as S2, it means the low for that day is below S2; and in some of the patterns, it could be considered as below S1 as well. Observe this for 30 June 2009.
- If, for example, the high is marked as R1, it means the high for that day was above R1, but below R2. Observe this for 26 June 2009.

Table 27.1

Pivot Point Construction Against Yesterday's OHLC Values

Date	*Open*	*High*	*Low*	*Close*	*R3*	*R2*	*R1*	*PP*	*S1*	*S2*	*S3*	*Open*	*High*	*Low*	*Close*
30 Jun 09	4391.50	4426.75	4267.35	4291.10	4572.03	4482.98	4436.97	4393.93	4347.92	4304.88	4215.83	PP	PP	S2	S2
29 Jun 09	4375.40	4439.95	4350.90	4390.95	4614.00	4474.20	4424.85	4334.40	4285.05	4194.60	4054.80	PP	R1	PP	PP
26 Jun 09	4243.95	4383.75	4243.95	4375.50	4500.58	4383.78	4312.82	4266.98	4196.02	4150.18	4033.38	PP	R1	PP	R1
25 Jun 09	4293.85	4337.95	4221.15	4241.85	4450.23	4361.48	4327.22	4272.73	4238.47	4183.98	4095.23	PP	R1	S1	PP
24 Jun 09	4247.30	4307.00	4218.25	4292.95	4467.63	4343.43	4295.22	4219.23	4171.02	4095.03	3970.83	PP	R1	PP	PP
23 Jun 09	4223.30	4267.45	4143.25	4247.00	4530.50	440015	4317.70	4269.80	4187.35	4139.45	4009.10	PP	PP	S1	PP
22 Jun 09	4314.20	4352.25	4221.90	4235.25	4521.17	4401.57	4357.63	4282.17	4238.13	4162.67	4043.17	PP	PP	S1	S1
19 Jun 09	4251.10	4326.20	4206.70	4313.60	4589.25	4436.10	4343.75	4282.95	4190.60	4129.80	3976.65	PP	PP	PP	PP
18 Jun 09	4352.95	4375.30	4222.15	4251.40	4772.25	4587.25	4471.70	4402.25	4286.70	4217.25	4032.25	PP	PP	S1	S1

What makes a good trade? Obviously, most traders would say a nice profit makes a good trade. But when you're entering a trade, the outcome is unpredictable. We'd all love to know in advance if a trade will turn out well but, alas, the markets are not so accommodating. What you look for therefore when you're getting into a trade is a good entry point where the odds of a move in your favour are better than average. Then, by having a plan that determines when you'll exit — whether it be at a loss or at a profit — you try to structure a trade where the potential reward is greater than the known risk.

By using daily pattern analysis to determine short term trades, we accomplish several worthwhile goals:

- First, our trading performance reflects the quality of our statistical research and not just the trend of the market.
- Second, we create a diversified portfolio of trading methods which, when combined, create a lower risk profile than any single method can yield. To trade one method alone is to base our results on some random factors and elements beyond our control.
- Finally, by entering and exiting our positions rapidly, we create an environment that will tolerate our missing a move.

What we will also do is to use multiple conditions for arriving at a trade entry. The added advantage of the requirement that multiple conditions be met before entering a trade is that we are placing more demands on the market. It would mean you are unlikely to trade every day. This will automatically lead you to trade less frequently, not more. We want it our way, or we don't want it at all. We don't care if the trade we missed goes on to make a million, if it didn't happen the way we wanted it to happen, then we just miss that one. We miss plenty of good trades, but at least we're still alive to talk about them. We want, and will take, only those trades that develop our way.

Here, I must also share with you one of the two rebukes which I received from my fund manager that is still fresh in my mind even after a decade. In this case it was Влад who fumed at me with this one liner "нуль ватт членом клуба"*. Want to know what I had told him to earn the reprimand? — "Влад, I ran extensive computer searches and found that on this particular commodity future when the 17-day moving average crosses above the 29-day moving average, and if the range expands by 134 %, but less than 146 % of the last three days, and if today's date is either 9, 16,18, or 24, we have a killer trade with a profit factor of more than 3.7, that is to go long at a buy-stop above day before yesterday's high".** After that above one liner insult, and after 15 minutes of nonstop blustering, he patiently and passionately told me for about couple of hours, and over more than a couple of vodkas, that unless it reflects the market behaviour in a logical way, no matter the profit factor, a pattern cannot be traded in real world.

Every quant trader has a bunch of pet patterns to use each time certain conditions are met. Without further comments, I am giving you a sample library of my pet patterns. I have included only those patterns which any grown up with a basic, school-level knowledge of mathematics can confirm using just a pencil and paper whether the pattern occurred or not.

Let me now present you with a collection of daily Nifty trading patterns that I found through extensive computerized searches of historical price. Please note that while doing the computerized searches, I took care not turn it into a mindless exercise in data mining. I have only included only those patterns that also conform to inherent commonsense reasons for their effectiveness.

For all the trades, the entry is set at the day's close and exit is at the next day's close; no stops are used. For all the trades the test period considered is from 1st January 2000 till 30th June 2009.

Pattern 1: Manic Monday

Have you ever experienced the sensation of chill running down your spine when the market plummets on a Friday? Most of us wonder what on earth

* Translated into English, it means zero watt club member, an insulting way of describing a person's intelligence.

** Those may not be the exact numbers, but my presentation to Влад was even more brainless.

might happen on Monday when the public has had time to read about the sharp drop. This pattern capitalizes on that "weekend fear" effect.

Here are the rules for trade entry:

- Today is Friday;
- Today and yesterday were down closes;
- Today's open was up;
- Today's high was always below R1 throughout the day (We want to ensure those buyers who entered based on positive opening are wrong and find themselves trapped. Once they realise their mistake, they start pulling out creating a selling pressure.);
- If all the above rules met, we add fuel to the fire by going short today, i.e. at the end of Friday and covering the next trading day at close.

Table 27.2

Manic Monday Performance Summary

Total net profit	₹ 59,788		
Gross profit	₹ 66,503	Gross loss	₹ -6,715
Total # of trades	38	Percent profitable	74%
Number of winning trades	28	Number of losing trades	10
Largest winning trade	₹ 8,278	Largest losing trade	₹ -2,993
Largest winning trade %	5.7%	Largest losing trade %	-2.0%
Average winning trade	₹ 2,375	Average losing trade	-₹ 671
Average winning trade %	2.2%	Average losing trade %	-0.7%
Ratio avg win/avg loss	3.5		
Ratio avg win/avg loss %	3.1		
Average profit per trade	₹ 1,573		
Average profit per trade %	1.4%		
Max consecutive winners	8	Max consecutive losers	2
Max drawdown	₹ -3,030	Max drawdown %	-3.8%
Profit factor	9.9		
Account size required	₹ 53,334	Return on account	112.1%
Luck factor	3.9		
Recovery factor	19.7		
Pessimistic Rate of Return	84.6%		
Sharpe ratio	1.1		

Pattern 2: Momentum-Aided Manic Monday

The act of pushing to new low is an evidence of strong momentum and suggests the market has the potential to continue going further down. This trading pattern is an extension of Pattern 1 above. Have you ever switched on the TV over the weekends when the market trades at a 20-day low? With all those post-mortem discussions and prognostications on what's likely to happen on Monday, I wouldn't be surprised if you had sleepless nights over the weekend. Well, with the aid of this pattern, you can sleep easy!

Here are the trade entry rules:

- Today is Friday;
- Today's High was always below R1 throughout the day;
- Today's close is the lowest in the past 20 days (counting today);
- Today's close is below S1;
- Automagically* short today at close and cover the next trading day at close.

Table 27.3 gives the performance summary.

Table 27.3

Momentum-aided Manic Monday Performance Summary

Total net profit	₹ 71,323		
Gross profit	₹ 98,995	Gross loss	₹ -27,672
Total # of trades	36	Percent profitable	67%
Number of winning trades	24	Number of losing trades	12
Largest winning trade	₹ 24,825	Largest losing trade	₹ -10,538
Largest winning trade %	12.2%	Largest losing trade %	-6.4%
Average winning trade	₹ 4,125	Average losing trade	₹ -2,306
Average winning trade %	3.0%	Average losing trade %	-1.7%

(Contd . . .)

* Automagically /aw-toh-maj'i-klee//adv. / Automatically, but in a way that, for some reason (typically because it is too complicated, or too ugly, or perhaps even too trivial), the speaker doesn't feel like explaining to you. This term is quite old, going back at least to the mid-70s and probably much earlier. The word `automagic' occurred in advertising (for a shirt-ironing gadget) as far back as the late 1940s.

Table 27.3 (contd.)
Momentum-aided Manic Monday Performance Summary

Ratio avg win/avg loss	1.8		
Ratio avg win/avg loss %	1.8		
Average profit per trade	₹ 1,981		
Average profit per trade %	1.5%		
Max consecutive winners	6	Max consecutive losers	2
Max drawdown	₹ -12,960	Max drawdown %	-7.3%
Profit factor	3.6		
Account size required	₹ 63,264	Return on account	112.7%
Luck factor	8.3		
Recovery factor	5.5		
Pessimistic Rate of Return	68.2%		
Sharpe ratio	0.9		

Pattern 3: Buy When There is a Blood on the Street

This is a strategy that flatters the trader. While everyone else is panicking or ruined, the trader — of the intrepid kind — heroically strides into the battlefield, looting from the foolish dead. The saying, "Buy when there is blood on the street" is attributed to the legendary investor Lord Rothschild, who uttered these famous words on the eve of the Battle of Waterloo when Napoleon's forces met their end at the hands of the English General, Wellington.

Here are the rules for trade entry:

- Today is a Tuesday, a Wednesday, or a Thursday (Why only these three days? Because these are the possible days when the direction of the current market trend might reverse.);
- Today's close is the lowest in the past 20 days (counting today).
- Today, yesterday*, and the day before yesterday are down days.

* PS- Yesterday is the previous trading day and the same convention is used throughout the book.

- Go long today at close and exit tomorrow at close; no pivots are used — the rules are that simple.

Table 27.4 contains the performance summary

Table 27.4
Performance Summary — When there's Blood on the Street

Total net profit	₹ 85,795		
Gross profit	₹ 117,988	Gross loss	₹ -32,193
Total # of trades	63	Percent profitable	62%
Number of winning trades	39	Number of losing trades	24
Largest winning trade	₹ 15,205	Largest losing trade	₹ -6,805
Largest winning trade %	6.3%	Largest losing trade %	-5.4%
Average winning trade	₹ 3,025	Average losing trade	₹ -1,341
Average winning trade %	2.4%	Average losing trade %	-1.7%
Ratio avg win/avg loss	2.3		
Ratio avg win/avg loss %	1.4		
Average profit per trade	₹ 1,362		
Average profit per trade %	0.8%		
Max consecutive winners	8	Max consecutive losers	4
Max drawdown	₹ 6,805	Max drawdown %	-8.7%
Profit factor	3.7		
Account size required	₹ 57,109	Return on account	150.2%
Luck factor	7.6		
Recovery factor	12.6		
Pessimistic Rate of Return	105.6%		
Sharpe ratio	0.7		
Accuracy	87%		

Pattern 4: Buy When There is a Blood on the Street (Tuesday)

Let me now place an additional condition in Pattern 3 above: What if I limit my trades to Tuesdays?

Here are the rules for trade entry:

- Today is Tuesday.
- Today's close is the lowest in the past 20 days (including today).
- Today, yesterday, and the day before yesterday are down days.
- Go long today at close and exit at the next trading day's close.

Take a close look at the improvements in the profit factor achieved in Table 27.5.

Table 27.5

Blood on the Street (Tuesday) Performance Summary

Total net profit	₹ 52,262		
Gross profit	₹ 60,720	Gross loss	₹ -8,458
Total # of trades	28	Percent profitable	71%
Number of winning trades	20	Number of losing trades	8
Largest winning trade	₹ 15,205	Largest losing trade	₹ -2,220
Largest winning trade %	6.2%	Largest losing trade %	-4.0%
Average winning trade	₹ 3,036	Average losing trade	₹ -1,057
Average winning trade %	2.1%	Average losing trade %	-1.4%
Ratio avg win/avg loss	2.9		
Ratio avg win/avg loss %	1.5		
Average profit per trade	₹ 1,867		
Average profit per trade %	1.1%		
Max consecutive winners	9	Max consecutive losers	2
Max drawdown	₹ 2,220	Max drawdown %	-3.5%
Profit factor	7.2		
Account size required	₹ 52,524	Return on account	99.5%
Luck factor	5.6		
Recovery factor	23.5		
Pessimistic Rate of Return	68.0%		
Sharpe ratio	0.6		
Accuracy	81%		

Pattern 5: Buy When There is a Blood on the Street (Tuesday — Modified)

I am hesitant to give this pattern away but here goes the cat out of my bag:

- Today is Tuesday.
- Today's close is the lowest in the last 20 days (including today).
- Today, yesterday and the day before yesterday were down days.
- Not only down, but each of the three days' close was lower than the previous day's low; i.e. today's close was below yesterday's low, yesterday's close was lower than the day before yesterday's low, and the day before yesterday's close was lower than the low of the day before that.
- Go long today at close and exit at the next trading day's close.

Table 27.6

Blood on the Street (Tuesday — Modified) Performance Summary

Total net profit	₹ 48,275		
Gross profit	₹ 48,275	Gross loss	₹ 0
Total # of trades	15	Percent profitable	100%
Number of winning trades	15	Number of losing trades	0
Largest winning trade	₹ 15,205	Largest losing trade	₹ 0
Largest winning trade %	6.2%	Largest losing trade %	0.0%
Average winning trade	₹ 3,218	Average losing trade	NA
Average winning trade %	2.5%	Average losing trade %	NA
Ratio avg win/avg loss	NA		
Ratio avg win/avg loss %	NA		
Average profit per trade	₹ 3,218		
Average profit per trade %	2.5%		
Max consecutive winners	15	Max consecutive losers	0
Max drawdown	₹ 0	Max drawdown %	0.0%
Profit factor	NA		
Account size required	₹ 50,304	Return on account	96.0%
Luck factor	2.5		
Recovery factor	NA		
Pessimistic Rate of Return	71.2%		
Sharpe ratio	0.8		
Accuracy	74%		

Pattern 6: Buying "Monday"

During up trends, Monday sets the tone for the week and provides us with some large moves on the upside. How can we distinguish such special Mondays from the other Mondays?

The psychology is similar to the "weekend-fear" effect, but it's the other way around, that is, the market is entering a buying frenzy and will experience explosive moves on the upside on Mondays.

Here are the conditions and rules for trade entry:

- Today is Friday.
- Today's Open is in the PP zone.

Table 27.7

Buying Monday Performance Summary

Total net profit	₹ 108,400		
Gross profit	₹ 135,060	Gross loss	₹ -26,660
Total # of trades	87	Percent profitable	76%
Number of winning trades	66	Number of losing trades	21
Largest winning trade	₹ 32,575	Largest losing trade	₹ -10,375
Largest winning trade %	17.7%	Largest losing trade %	-4.2%
Average winning trade	₹ 2,046	Average losing trade	₹ -1,270
Average winning trade %	1.5%	Average losing trade %	-1.0%
Ratio avg win/avg loss	1.6		
Ratio avg win/avg loss %	1.4		
Average profit per trade	₹ 1,246		
Average profit per trade %	0.9%		
Max consecutive winners	17	Max consecutive losers	3
Max drawdown	₹ 11,478	Max drawdown %	-7.8%
Profit factor	5.1		
Account size required	₹ 61,782	Return on account	175.5%
Luck factor	20.7		
Recovery factor	9.4		
Pessimistic Rate of Return	139.1%		
Sharpe ratio	1.2		
Accuracy	89%		

- Today's High for the day was above R2.
- Today's Low was never below S1.
- Today's Close is above R1.
- Go long today at close and exit the next trading day at close.

I have a confession to make here, your honour! This pattern "fired" on the day when results of General Elections were announced (18 May 2009); a day which gives the performance summary a very high largest winner and a very high luck factor. If we eliminate this trading day from the pattern, it would still give a profit factor of 3.8 and a return on account of 122.7%.

Pattern 7: Buying "Thursday"

If, in the above pattern, Friday's behaviour is pushing the buying frenzy to Monday, something should have been happening on Thursday to lead to those up moves on Friday — right?

Here are the rules for trade entry for going long on Thursdays:

- Today is Thursday.
- Today's open was positive; that is, open was higher than yesterday's close.
- Today's close was up, and above R1.
- Today's low was never below S1.
- Go long today at close and exit the next trading day at close.

Table 27.8 provides the performance summary.

Table 27.8
Buying Thursday Performance Summary

Total net profit	₹ 80,580		
Gross profit	₹ 103,633	Gross loss	₹ -23,052
Total # of trades	98	Percent profitable	72%
Number of winning trades	71	Number of losing trades	27
Largest winning trade	₹ 7,253	Largest losing trade	₹ -3,903
Largest winning trade %	3.9%	Largest losing trade %	-2.6%

(Contd . . .)

Table 27.8 (contd.)
Buying Thursday Performance Summary

Average winning trade	₹ 1,460	Average losing trade	₹ -854
Average winning trade %	1.2%	Average losing trade %	-0.7%
Ratio avg win/avg loss	1.7		
Ratio avg win/avg loss %	1.7		
Average profit per trade	₹ 822		
Average profit per trade %	0.7%		
Max consecutive winners	10	Max consecutive losers	3
Max drawdown	₹ 4,353	Max drawdown %	-4.2%
Profit factor	4.5		
Account size required	₹ 54,657	Return on account	147.4%
Luck factor	5.7		
Recovery factor	18.5		
Pessimistic Rate of Return	116.8%		
Sharpe ratio	2.6		
Accuracy	90%		

Pattern 8: Buying "Thursday" — Modified

Let's place an additional demand on Pattern 7, namely we want a down close two days earlier than today (Thursday), that is on Tuesday — or Monday, if Tuesday were to be a holiday. Why? Because we're looking for a pullback that occurred two days before the current uptrend started, or resumed. By the way, this pattern is the least risky of all patterns presented in this chapter; have a look at its Sharpe Ratio.

Here are the rules for trade entry:

- Today is Thursday.
- Today's open was positive, i.e. it was above yesterday's close.
- Today's close is up and also above R1.
- Today's low was never below S1.
- Tuesday's (or Monday's if Tuesday happens to be a holiday) close was down.
- Go long today at close and exit at the next trading day's close.

Table 27.9 gives the performance summary.

Table 27.9
Buying Thursday — Modified — Performance Summary

Total net profit	₹ 58,435		
Gross profit	₹ 72,330	Gross loss	₹ -13,895
Total # of trades	52	Percent profitable	81%
Number of winning trades	42	Number of losing trades	10
Largest winning trade	₹ 7,253	Largest losing trade	₹ -3,903
Largest winning trade %	3.7%	Largest losing trade %	-2.6%
Average winning trade	₹ 1,722	Average losing trade	₹ -1,390
Average winning trade %	1.4%	Average losing trade %	-1.0%
Ratio avg win/avg loss	1.2		
Ratio avg win/avg loss %	1.4		
Average profit per trade	₹ 1,124		
Average profit per trade %	0.9%		
Max consecutive winners	12	Max consecutive losers	2
Max drawdown	₹ 4,353	Max drawdown %	-4.5%
Profit factor	5.2		
Account size required	₹ 54,657	Return on account	106.9%
Luck factor	3.9		
Recovery factor	13.4		
Pessimistic Rate of Return	78.5%		
Sharpe ratio	2.8		
Accuracy	90%		

Pattern 9: "Dip Buyer's Advantage" Monday

A dip buy right at the start of the week, that is Monday, if is profitable at the close, in which case our trade will be on the long side. I must also tell you that everyday's close minus that day's intraday's low will always be profitable if not zero at the minimum . So we will be tightening our criteria of profitable dip buy with the following rules within our pivot point trading framework.

Here are the rules for such trade entries:

- Today is Monday.
- Today's Open was down.
- Yesterday's close was down.
- Today's High is never above R1.
- Today's Low is below S1
- Today's Close is in the PP zone (indicating dip buyers are profitable at the close).
- Go long today at close and exit the next trading day at close.

Table 27.10 gives the performance summary.

Table 27.10
Dip Buyer's Advantage Monday Performance Summary

Total net profit	₹ 40,280		
Gross profit	₹ 48,105	Gross loss	₹ -7,825
Total # of trades	26	Percent profitable	65%
Number of winning trades	17	Number of losing trades	9
Largest winning trade	₹ 14,485	Largest losing trade	₹ -2,742
Largest winning trade %	6.4%	Largest losing trade %	-1.1%
Average winning trade	₹ 2,830	Average losing trade	₹ -869
Average winning trade %	1.7%	Average losing trade %	-0.7%
Ratio avg win/avg loss	3.3		
Ratio avg win/avg loss %	2.5		
Average profit per trade	₹ 1,549		
Average profit per trade %	0.9%		
Max consecutive winners	5	Max consecutive losers	2
Max drawdown	₹ 3,982	Max drawdown %	-3.0%
Profit factor	6.1		
Account size required	₹ 54,287	Return on account	74.2%
Luck factor	7.2		
Recovery factor	10.1		
Pessimistic Rate of Return	47.9%		
Sharpe ratio	0.7		
Accuracy	80%		

Pivot Patterns Combined

I'm now presenting what is probably one of the bigger tables that you have ever seen in a book, with results of all the pivot point patterns discussed in this chapter till now combined.

This table (Table 27.11) has a column — Pattern — which has details in an abbreviated form.

Here is what the abbreviations stand for:

- LONGBM is Pattern 4, i.e. Buying Monday
- LONGBOS is Pattern 3, i.e. Buy When There is Blood on the Street
- LONGBTHU is Pattern 8, i.e. Modified Buying Thursday
- LONGDBAM is Pattern 9, i.e. Dip buyer's advantage Monday
- SHORTMM is Pattern 1, i.e., Manic Monday
- SHORTMMM is Pattern 2, i.e. Momentum Aided Manic Monday
- SHORTMMMMM are those occurrences when both SHORTMM and SHORTMMM are matched.

Figures in the column labelled "Profit" indicate the difference between tomorrow's and today's closes, multiplied by 50. For long patterns, it is tomorrow's minus today's close; for short patterns it is the other way around.

The column "Cumulative Profit" indicates what the result would be if we were to accumulate the profits.

Table 27.11
Results of Pivot Patterns Combined

Date	*Day of the Week*	*Profit/ Loss (Points)*	*Pattern*	*Profit / Loss (₹)*	*Cumulative Profit*
11-Feb-00	FRIDAY	-11.50	LONGBM	-575	
10-Mar-00	FRIDAY	-42.05	SHORTMM	2,103	1,528
7-Apr-00	FRIDAY	55.85	LONGBM	2,793	4,320
18-Apr-00	TUESDAY	-9.85	LONGBOS	-492	3,828
19-Apr-00	WEDNESDAY	10.70	LONGBOS	535	4,363
28-Apr-00	FRIDAY	-73.10	SHORTMM	3,655	8,018
2-May-00	TUESDAY	-17.40	LONGBOS	-870	7,147
3-May-00	WEDNESDAY	64.50	LONGBOS	3,225	10,373
4-May-00	THURSDAY	41.85	LONGBTHU	2,093	12,465

(Contd . . .)

Table 27.11 (contd.)
Results of Pivot Patterns Combined

Date	*Day of the Week*	*Profit/ Loss (Points)*	*Pattern*	*Profit / Loss (₹)*	*Cumulative Profit*
5-May-00	FRIDAY	-57.35	LONGBM	-2,868	9,597
12-May-00	FRIDAY	16.45	SHORTMM	-823	8,775
15-May-00	MONDAY	7.60	LONGDBAM	380	9,155
19-May-00	FRIDAY	-35.00	SHORTMMMMM	1,750	10,905
23-May-00	TUESDAY	11.50	LONGBOS	575	11,480
2-Jun-00	FRIDAY	15.35	LONGBM	767	12,248
16-Jun-00	FRIDAY	21.45	LONGBM	1,073	13,320
19-Jul-00	WEDNESDAY	-11.60	LONGBOS	-580	12,740
20-Jul-00	THURSDAY	-26.95	LONGBOS	-1,348	11,393
21-Jul-00	FRIDAY	-79.50	SHORTMMMMM	3,975	15,368
31-Jul-00	MONDAY	-6.00	LONGDBAM	-300	15,068
11-Aug-00	FRIDAY	7.15	SHORTMMMMM	-358	14,710
31-Aug-00	THURSDAY	33.65	LONGBTHU	1,683	16,393
19-Sep-00	TUESDAY	25.90	LONGBOS	1,295	17,688
22-Sep-00	FRIDAY	26.10	SHORTMMM	-1,305	16,383
11-Oct-00	WEDNESDAY	4.35	LONGBOS	217	16,600
13-Oct-00	FRIDAY	-1.30	SHORTMMM	65	16,665
17-Oct-00	TUESDAY	-22.05	LONGBOS	-1,103	15,563
18-Oct-00	WEDNESDAY	30.15	LONGBOS	1,508	17,070
3-Nov-00	FRIDAY	-1.80	LONGBM	-90	16,980
24-Nov-00	FRIDAY	27.70	LONGBM	1,385	18,365
8-Dec-00	FRIDAY	18.45	LONGBM	923	19,288
18-Dec-00	MONDAY	-7.10	LONGDBAM	-355	18,933
22-Dec-00	FRIDAY	-30.00	SHORTMM	1,500	20,433
26-Dec-00	TUESDAY	16.30	LONGBOS	815	21,248
28-Dec-00	THURSDAY	14.60	LONGBTHU	730	21,978
19-Jan-01	FRIDAY	18.90	LONGBM	945	22,923
23-Feb-01	FRIDAY	-8.05	SHORTMMM	402	23,325
27-Feb-01	TUESDAY	55.85	LONGBOS	2,793	26,118
9-Mar-01	FRIDAY	-56.80	SHORTMMM	2,840	28,958
13-Mar-01	TUESDAY	69.50	LONGBOS	3,475	32,433
23-Mar-01	FRIDAY	0.20	SHORTMM	-10	32,423

(Contd . . .)

Table 27.11 (contd.)
Results of Pivot Patterns Combined

Date	*Day of the Week*	*Profit/ Loss (Points)*	*Pattern*	*Profit / Loss (₹)*	*Cumulative Profit*
2-Apr-01	MONDAY	11.15	LONGDBAM	558	32,980
11-Apr-01	WEDNESDAY	-41.90	LONGBOS	-2,095	30,885
12-Apr-01	THURSDAY	19.70	LONGBOS	985	31,870
1-Jun-01	FRIDAY	-20.85	SHORTMM	1,043	32,913
5-Jun-01	TUESDAY	0.10	LONGBOS	5	32,918
8-Jun-01	FRIDAY	4.50	LONGBM	225	33,143
15-Jun-01	FRIDAY	-9.45	SHORTMMM	473	33,615
18-Jun-01	MONDAY	18.35	LONGDBAM	918	34,533
22-Jun-01	FRIDAY	-20.65	SHORTMM	1,033	35,565
29-Jun-01	FRIDAY	-7.15	LONGBM	-358	35,208
20-Jul-01	FRIDAY	-7.05	SHORTMM	352	35,560
23-Jul-01	MONDAY	1.90	LONGDBAM	95	35,655
3-Aug-01	FRIDAY	0.65	LONGBM	33	35,688
31-Aug-01	FRIDAY	-5.70	SHORTMMM	285	35,973
7-Sep-01	FRIDAY	-1.80	SHORTMM	90	36,063
11-Sep-01	TUESDAY	-41.20	LONGBOS	-2,060	34,003
12-Sep-01	WEDNESDAY	-10.50	LONGBOS	-525	33,478
13-Sep-01	THURSDAY	-52.00	LONGBOS	-2,600	30,878
14-Sep-01	FRIDAY	-47.45	SHORTMMMMM	2,373	33,250
21-Sep-01	FRIDAY	14.85	SHORTMMMMM	-742	32,508
28-Sep-01	FRIDAY	-3.75	LONGBM	-188	32,320
1-Nov-01	THURSDAY	3.60	LONGBTHU	180	32,500
15-Nov-01	THURSDAY	32.45	LONGBTHU	1,623	34,123
21-Dec-01	FRIDAY	-2.35	SHORTMMM	117	34,240
26-Dec-01	WEDNESDAY	-14.25	LONGBOS	-713	33,528
27-Dec-01	THURSDAY	13.80	LONGBOS	690	34,218
3-Jan-02	THURSDAY	23.95	LONGBTHU	1,198	35,415
4-Jan-02	FRIDAY	3.95	LONGBM	198	35,613
25-Jan-02	FRIDAY	-8.75	SHORTMM	438	36,050
14-Feb-02	THURSDAY	9.95	LONGBTHU	498	36,548
15-Feb-02	FRIDAY	12.90	LONGBM	645	37,193
22-Feb-02	FRIDAY	1.95	LONGBM	98	37,290

(Contd . . .)

Table 27.11 (contd.)
Results of Pivot Patterns Combined

Date	*Day of the Week*	*Profit/ Loss (Points)*	*Pattern*	*Profit / Loss (₹)*	*Cumulative Profit*
15-Mar-02	FRIDAY	-0.45	LONGBM	-23	37,268
22-Mar-02	FRIDAY	-15.40	SHORTMM	770	38,038
26-Mar-02	TUESDAY	0.30	LONGBOS	15	38,053
4-Apr-02	THURSDAY	-3.95	LONGBTHU	-198	37,855
19-Apr-02	FRIDAY	3.85	SHORTMMM	-193	37,663
2-May-02	THURSDAY	3.65	LONGBTHU	183	37,845
21-May-02	TUESDAY	-3.90	LONGBOS	-195	37,650
22-May-02	WEDNESDAY	-18.55	LONGBOS	-928	36,723
23-May-02	THURSDAY	40.25	LONGBOS	2,013	38,735
24-May-02	FRIDAY	-4.30	LONGBM	-215	38,520
31-May-02	FRIDAY	10.95	SHORTMM	-548	37,973
28-Jun-02	FRIDAY	11.15	LONGBM	558	38,530
17-Jul-02	WEDNESDAY	8.75	LONGBOS	438	38,968
26-Jul-02	FRIDAY	-1.85	SHORTMMM	93	39,060
29-Jul-02	MONDAY	-11.00	LONGDBAM	-550	38,510
30-Jul-02	TUESDAY	-1.75	LONGBOS	-88	38,423
31-Jul-02	WEDNESDAY	-1.20	LONGBOS	-60	38,363
1-Aug-02	THURSDAY	-2.95	LONGBOS	-148	38,215
16-Aug-02	FRIDAY	0.60	LONGBM	30	38,245
30-Aug-02	FRIDAY	2.90	LONGBM	145	38,390
3-Oct-02	THURSDAY	0	LONGBOS	0	38,390
11-Oct-02	FRIDAY	1.40	LONGBM	70	38,460
24-Oct-02	THURSDAY	-14.70	LONGBOS	-735	37,725
25-Oct-02	FRIDAY	-9.50	SHORTMMM	475	38,200
15-Nov-02	FRIDAY	6.50	LONGBM	325	38,525
22-Nov-02	FRIDAY	6.05	LONGBM	303	38,828
6-Dec-02	FRIDAY	-11.15	LONGBM	-557	38,270
13-Dec-02	FRIDAY	-7.75	LONGBM	-388	37,883
26-Dec-02	THURSDAY	3.60	LONGBTHU	180	38,063
3-Jan-03	FRIDAY	-5.25	SHORTMM	263	38,325
9-Jan-03	THURSDAY	-17.10	LONGBTHU	-855	37,470
24-Jan-03	FRIDAY	-18.40	SHORTMMM	920	38,390

(Contd . . .)

Table 27.11 (contd.)

Results of Pivot Patterns Combined

Date	*Day of the Week*	*Profit/ Loss (Points)*	*Pattern*	*Profit / Loss (₹)*	*Cumulative Profit*
28-Feb-03	FRIDAY	-4.55	LONGBM	-228	38,163
6-Mar-03	THURSDAY	-14.15	LONGBOS	-708	37,455
7-Mar-03	FRIDAY	-10.40	SHORTMMM	520	37,975
28-Mar-03	FRIDAY	-22.40	SHORTMM	1,120	39,095
4-Apr-03	FRIDAY	14.55	LONGBM	728	39,823
10-Apr-03	THURSDAY	-12.40	LONGBOS	-620	39,203
24-Apr-03	THURSDAY	-5.40	LONGBOS	-270	38,933
2-May-03	FRIDAY	7.10	LONGBM	355	39,288
9-May-03	FRIDAY	-1.85	SHORTMM	93	39,380
16-May-03	FRIDAY	-6.55	LONGBM	-328	39,053
5-Jun-03	THURSDAY	11.35	LONGBTHU	568	39,620
6-Jun-03	FRIDAY	5.70	LONGBM	285	39,905
12-Jun-03	THURSDAY	4.90	LONGBTHU	245	40,150
13-Jun-03	FRIDAY	-4.40	LONGBM	-220	39,930
26-Jun-03	THURSDAY	9.20	LONGBTHU	460	40,390
27-Jun-03	FRIDAY	8.60	LONGBM	430	40,820
24-Jul-03	THURSDAY	23.30	LONGBTHU	1,165	41,985
25-Jul-03	FRIDAY	6.45	LONGBM	323	42,308
8-Aug-03	FRIDAY	10.20	LONGBM	510	42,818
21-Aug-03	THURSDAY	10.20	LONGBTHU	510	43,328
22-Aug-03	FRIDAY	-40.05	LONGBM	-2,003	41,325
29-Aug-03	FRIDAY	19.40	LONGBM	970	42,295
5-Sep-03	FRIDAY	18.95	LONGBM	947	43,243
12-Sep-03	FRIDAY	-42.85	SHORTMM	2,143	45,385
26-Sep-03	FRIDAY	13.00	LONGBM	650	46,035
3-Oct-03	FRIDAY	29.60	LONGBM	1,480	47,515
9-Oct-03	THURSDAY	21.00	LONGBTHU	1,050	48,565
10-Oct-03	FRIDAY	23.65	LONGBM	1,183	49,748
16-Oct-03	THURSDAY	13.75	LONGBTHU	688	50,435
30-Oct-03	THURSDAY	39.05	LONGBTHU	1,953	52,388
31-Oct-03	FRIDAY	45.75	LONGBM	2,288	54,675
19-Dec-03	FRIDAY	10.60	LONGBM	530	55,205

(Contd . . .)

Table 27.11 (contd.)
Results of Pivot Patterns Combined

Date	*Day of the Week*	*Profit/ Loss (Points)*	*Pattern*	*Profit / Loss (₹)*	*Cumulative Profit*
26-Dec-03	FRIDAY	37.00	LONGBM	1,850	57,055
1-Jan-04	THURSDAY	33.80	LONGBTHU	1,690	58,745
2-Jan-04	FRIDAY	8.95	LONGBM	448	59,193
8-Jan-04	THURSDAY	3.35	LONGBTHU	168	59,360
22-Jan-04	THURSDAY	77.05	LONGBOS	3,853	63,213
30-Jan-04	FRIDAY	-40.75	SHORTMM	2,038	65,250
3-Feb-04	TUESDAY	53.20	LONGBOS	2,660	67,910
26-Mar-04	FRIDAY	14.55	LONGBM	728	68,638
11-May-04	TUESDAY	11.65	LONGBOS	582	69,220
14-May-04	FRIDAY	-193.65	SHORTMMM	9,683	78,903
31-May-04	MONDAY	24.30	LONGDBAM	1,215	80,118
11-Jun-04	FRIDAY	-27.10	SHORTMM	1,355	81,473
21-Jun-04	MONDAY	-7.30	LONGDBAM	-365	81,108
22-Jun-04	TUESDAY	-28.60	LONGBOS	-1,430	79,678
23-Jun-04	WEDNESDAY	24.65	LONGBOS	1,233	80,910
16-Jul-04	FRIDAY	12.80	LONGBM	640	81,550
29-Jul-04	THURSDAY	13.60	LONGBTHU	680	82,230
9-Aug-04	MONDAY	9.55	LONGDBAM	478	82,708
16-Aug-04	MONDAY	5.20	LONGDBAM	260	82,968
17-Sep-04	FRIDAY	-4.85	LONGBM	-243	82,725
27-Sep-04	MONDAY	-17.25	LONGDBAM	-863	81,863
30-Sep-04	THURSDAY	29.65	LONGBTHU	1,483	83,345
1-Oct-04	FRIDAY	30.5	LONGBM	1,525	84,870
24-Dec-04	FRIDAY	-0.10	LONGBM	-5	84,865
12-Jan-05	WEDNESDAY	40.95	LONGBOS	2,048	86,913
13-Jan-05	THURSDAY	-23.45	LONGBTHU	-1,173	85,740
24-Jan-05	MONDAY	22.85	LONGDBAM	1,143	86,883
27-Jan-05	THURSDAY	53.30	LONGBTHU	2,665	89,548
28-Jan-05	FRIDAY	49.30	LONGBM	2,465	92,013
3-Mar-05	THURSDAY	19.30	LONGBTHU	965	92,978
14-Mar-05	MONDAY	-17.40	LONGDBAM	-870	92,108
23-Mar-05	WEDNESDAY	-11.00	LONGBOS	-550	91,558

(Contd . . .)

Table 27.11 (contd.)

Results of Pivot Patterns Combined

Date	*Day of the Week*	*Profit/ Loss (Points)*	*Pattern*	*Profit / Loss (₹)*	*Cumulative Profit*
24-Mar-05	THURSDAY	14.05	LONGBOS	703	92,260
31-Mar-05	THURSDAY	32.00	LONGBTHU	1,600	93,860
8-Apr-05	FRIDAY	-23.00	SHORTMM	1,150	95,010
15-Apr-05	FRIDAY	-28.50	SHORTMMM	1,425	96,435
19-Apr-05	TUESDAY	20.30	LONGBOS	1,015	97,450
21-Apr-05	THURSDAY	18.80	LONGBTHU	940	98,390
29-Apr-05	FRIDAY	14.25	SHORTMMM	-713	97,678
22-Jul-05	FRIDAY	26.15	LONGBM	1,308	98,985
19-Aug-05	FRIDAY	-15.60	SHORTMM	780	99,765
25-Aug-05	THURSDAY	2.50	LONGBTHU	125	99,890
16-Sep-05	FRIDAY	14.75	LONGBM	738	1,00,628
14-Oct-05	FRIDAY	0.75	SHORTMM	-38	1,00,590
20-Oct-05	THURSDAY	48.30	LONGBOS	2,415	1,03,005
28-Oct-05	FRIDAY	54.90	SHORTMMM	-2,745	1,00,260
11-Nov-05	FRIDAY	10.05	LONGBM	502	1,00,763
24-Nov-05	THURSDAY	29.30	LONGBTHU	1,465	1,02,228
25-Nov-05	FRIDAY	47.70	LONGBM	2,385	1,04,613
9-Dec-05	FRIDAY	19.75	LONGBM	988	1,05,600
19-Jan-06	THURSDAY	30.10	LONGBTHU	1,505	1,07,105
3-Feb-06	FRIDAY	59.85	SHORTMM	-2,993	1,04,113
10-Mar-06	FRIDAY	18.75	LONGBM	938	1,05,050
12-May-06	FRIDAY	-147.10	SHORTMM	7,355	1,12,405
19-May-06	FRIDAY	-165.55	SHORTMMMMM	8,278	1,20,683
1-Jun-06	THURSDAY	129.10	LONGBOS	6,455	1,27,138
7-Jun-06	WEDNESDAY	-136.10	LONGBOS	-6,805	1,20,333
8-Jun-06	THURSDAY	141.95	LONGBOS	7,098	1,27,430
14-Jun-06	WEDNESDAY	166.00	LONGBOS	8,300	1,35,730
15-Jun-06	THURSDAY	91.55	LONGBTHU	4,577	1,40,308
16-Jun-06	FRIDAY	26.55	LONGBM	1,328	1,41,635
22-Jun-06	THURSDAY	47.95	LONGBTHU	2,397	1,44,033
30-Jun-06	FRIDAY	22.75	LONGBM	1,138	1,45,170
20-Jul-06	THURSDAY	-78.05	LONGBTHU	-3,903	1,41,268

(Contd . . .)

Table 27.11 (contd.)
Results of Pivot Patterns Combined

Date	*Day of the Week*	*Profit/ Loss (Points)*	*Pattern*	*Profit / Loss (₹)*	*Cumulative Profit*
24-Jul-06	MONDAY	54.65	LONGDBAM	2,733	1,44,000
7-Aug-06	MONDAY	61.30	LONGDBAM	3,065	1,47,065
21-Sep-06	THURSDAY	-9.00	LONGBTHU	-450	1,46,615
5-Oct-06	THURSDAY	4.80	LONGBTHU	240	1,46,855
13-Oct-06	FRIDAY	47.90	LONGBM	2,395	1,49,250
20-Oct-06	FRIDAY	-19.55	SHORTMM	977	1,50,228
27-Oct-06	FRIDAY	29.75	LONGBM	1,488	1,51,715
2-Nov-06	THURSDAY	14.15	LONGBTHU	708	1,52,423
10-Nov-06	FRIDAY	24.00	LONGBM	1,200	1,53,623
20-Nov-06	MONDAY	62.10	LONGDBAM	3,105	1,56,728
30-Nov-06	THURSDAY	43.10	LONGBTHU	2,155	1,58,883
1-Dec-06	FRIDAY	3.40	LONGBM	170	1,59,053
12-Dec-06	TUESDAY	48.30	LONGBOS	2,415	1,61,468
14-Dec-06	THURSDAY	45.60	LONGBTHU	2,280	1,63,748
5-Jan-07	FRIDAY	-50.00	SHORTMM	2,500	1,66,248
11-Jan-07	THURSDAY	110.20	LONGBTHU	5,510	1,71,758
12-Jan-07	FRIDAY	25.95	LONGBM	1,298	1,73,055
25-Jan-07	THURSDAY	-23.25	LONGBTHU	-1,163	1,71,893
1-Feb-07	THURSDAY	46.30	LONGBTHU	2,315	1,74,208
2-Feb-07	FRIDAY	31.85	LONGBM	1,593	1,75,800
9-Feb-07	FRIDAY	-129.10	SHORTMM	6,455	1,82,255
13-Feb-07	TUESDAY	2.55	LONGBOS	127	1,82,383
22-Feb-07	THURSDAY	-101.05	LONGBOS	-5,053	1,77,330
23-Feb-07	FRIDAY	3.05	SHORTMMMMM	-153	1,77,178
2-Mar-07	FRIDAY	-150.25	SHORTMMM	7,513	1,84,690
13-Apr-07	FRIDAY	96.00	LONGBM	4,800	1,89,490
20-Apr-07	FRIDAY	1.55	LONGBM	77	1,89,568
30-Apr-07	MONDAY	62.95	LONGDBAM	3,148	1,92,715
3-May-07	THURSDAY	-33.50	LONGBTHU	-1,675	1,91,040
17-May-07	THURSDAY	-5.05	LONGBTHU	-253	1,90,788
25-Jun-07	MONDAY	26.30	LONGDBAM	1,315	1,92,103
29-Jun-07	FRIDAY	-4.55	LONGBM	-228	1,91,875

(Contd . . .)

Table 27.11 (contd.)

Results of Pivot Patterns Combined

Date	*Day of the Week*	*Profit/ Loss (Points)*	*Pattern*	*Profit / Loss (₹)*	*Cumulative Profit*
12-Jul-07	THURSDAY	58.40	LONGBTHU	2,920	1,94,795
13-Jul-07	FRIDAY	7.60	LONGBM	380	1,95,175
19-Jul-07	THURSDAY	3.95	LONGBTHU	197	1,95,373
10-Aug-07	FRIDAY	40.30	SHORTMMM	-2,015	1,93,358
17-Aug-07	FRIDAY	101.00	SHORTMMM	-5,050	1,88,308
31-Aug-07	FRIDAY	10.75	LONGBM	538	1,88,845
10-Sep-07	MONDAY	-10.80	LONGDBAM	-540	1,88,305
13-Sep-07	THURSDAY	-10.95	LONGBTHU	-547	1,87,758
21-Sep-07	FRIDAY	94.65	LONGBM	4,732	1,92,490
19-Oct-07	FRIDAY	-31.30	SHORTMM	1,565	1,94,055
22-Oct-07	MONDAY	289.70	LONGDBAM	14,485	2,08,540
26-Oct-07	FRIDAY	203.60	LONGBM	10,180	2,18,720
12-Nov-07	MONDAY	78.30	LONGDBAM	3,915	2,22,635
16-Nov-07	FRIDAY	0.80	SHORTMM	-40	2,22,595
22-Nov-07	THURSDAY	89.25	LONGBOS	4,463	2,27,058
30-Nov-07	FRIDAY	102.25	LONGBM	5,113	2,32,170
4-Jan-08	FRIDAY	4.80	LONGBM	240	2,32,410
18-Jan-08	FRIDAY	-496.50	SHORTMMM	24,825	2,57,235
22-Jan-08	TUESDAY	304.10	LONGBOS	15,205	2,72,440
1-Feb-08	FRIDAY	146.25	LONGBM	7,313	2,79,753
12-Feb-08	TUESDAY	91.20	LONGBOS	4,560	2,84,313
14-Feb-08	THURSDAY	100.90	LONGBTHU	5,045	2,89,358
7-Mar-08	FRIDAY	28.80	SHORTMMM	-1,440	2,87,918
10-Mar-08	MONDAY	65.50	LONGDBAM	3,275	2,91,193
28-Mar-08	FRIDAY	-207.50	LONGBM	-10,375	2,80,818
25-Apr-08	FRIDAY	-22.05	LONGBM	-1,103	2,79,715
12-May-08	MONDAY	-54.85	LONGDBAM	-2,742	2,76,973
23-May-08	FRIDAY	-71.50	SHORTMMMMM	3,575	2,80,548
27-May-08	TUESDAY	58.55	LONGBOS	2,928	2,83,475
4-Jun-08	WEDNESDAY	91.35	LONGBOS	4,567	2,88,043
10-Jun-08	TUESDAY	73.80	LONGBOS	3,690	2,91,733
20-Jun-08	FRIDAY	-81.15	SHORTMMM	4,058	2,95,790

(Contd . . .)

Table 27.11 (contd.)
Results of Pivot Patterns Combined

Date	*Day of the Week*	*Profit/ Loss (Points)*	*Pattern*	*Profit / Loss (₹)*	*Cumulative Profit*
24-Jun-08	TUESDAY	61.55	LONGBOS	3,077	2,98,868
27-Jun-08	FRIDAY	-96.10	SHORTMMM	4,805	3,03,673
1-Jul-08	TUESDAY	196.60	LONGBOS	9,830	3,13,503
15-Jul-08	TUESDAY	-44.40	LONGBOS	-2,220	3,11,283
16-Jul-08	WEDNESDAY	130.50	LONGBOS	6,525	3,17,808
17-Jul-08	THURSDAY	145.05	LONGBTHU	7,253	3,25,060
18-Jul-08	FRIDAY	67.25	LONGBM	3,363	3,28,423
25-Jul-08	FRIDAY	20.25	SHORTMM	-1,013	3,27,410
18-Aug-08	MONDAY	-24.80	LONGDBAM	-1,240	3,26,170
29-Aug-08	FRIDAY	-11.35	LONGBM	-568	3,25,603
12-Sep-08	FRIDAY	-155.55	SHORTMM	7,778	3,33,380
19-Sep-08	FRIDAY	-22.20	LONGBM	-1,110	3,32,270
26-Sep-08	FRIDAY	-135.20	SHORTMMM	6,760	3,39,030
3-Oct-08	FRIDAY	-215.95	SHORTMMM	10,798	3,49,828
10-Oct-08	FRIDAY	210.75	SHORTMMM	-10,538	3,39,290
17-Oct-08	FRIDAY	48.45	SHORTMMM	-2,423	3,36,868
24-Oct-08	FRIDAY	-59.80	SHORTMMM	2,990	3,39,858
27-Oct-08	MONDAY	160.40	LONGDBAM	8,020	3,47,878
31-Oct-08	FRIDAY	158.25	LONGBM	7,913	3,55,790
21-Nov-08	FRIDAY	14.80	LONGBM	740	3,56,530
4-Dec-08	THURSDAY	-73.60	LONGBTHU	-3,680	3,52,850
13-Jan-09	TUESDAY	90.35	LONGBOS	4,518	3,57,368
6-Feb-09	FRIDAY	76.80	LONGBM	3,840	3,61,208
13-Feb-09	FRIDAY	-99.85	LONGBM	-4,993	3,56,215
3-Mar-09	TUESDAY	22.80	LONGBOS	1,140	3,57,355
13-Mar-09	FRIDAY	58.00	LONGBM	2,900	3,60,255
23-Apr-09	THURSDAY	57.05	LONGBTHU	2,853	3,63,108
15-May-09	FRIDAY	651.50	LONGBM	32,575	3,95,683
28-May-09	THURSDAY	111.85	LONGBTHU	5,592	4,01,275
29-May-09	FRIDAY	80.95	LONGBM	4,047	4,05,323

Table 27.12 shows what the performance summary looks like for all the pivot point patterns combined together.

Table 27.12
Performance Summary for Combined Pivot Patterns

Total net profit	₹ 405,323		
Gross profit	₹ 519,030	Gross loss	₹ -113,708
Total # of trades	294	Percent profitable	72%
Number of winning trades	211	Number of losing trades	83
Largest winning trade	₹ 32,575	Largest losing trade	₹ -10,538
Largest winning trade %	17.7%	Largest losing trade %	-6.4%
Average winning trade	₹ 2,460	Average losing trade	₹ -1,370
Average winning trade %	1.9%	Average losing trade %	-1.3%
Ratio avg win/avg loss	1.8		
Ratio avg win/avg loss %	1.5		
Average profit per trade	₹ 1,379		
Average profit per trade %	1.0%		
Max consecutive winners	23	Max consecutive losers	4
Max drawdown	₹ 14,220	Max drawdown %	-8.1%
Profit factor	4.6		
Account size required	₹ 64,524	Return on account	628.2%
Luck factor	18.0		
Recovery factor	28.5		
Pessimistic Rate of Return	553.5%		
Sharpe ratio	2.2		
Accuracy	94%		

Table 27.13 gives what the year-wise break-up of returns would have been for all the combined patterns:

Table 27.13

Year-wise Performance for Combined Pivot Patterns

Year	*Profit (₹)*	*NIFTY points Gain / Loss*	*No of Trades*
2009	52,472	1,049	9
2008	1,20,680	2,413	37
2007	68,422	1,368	34
2006	58,147	1,162	28
2005	20,735	414	26
2004	27,810	556	23
2003	18,992	379	36
2002	3,845	76	35
2001	12,240	244	32
2000	21,977	439	35

To summarise, as you would have seen we would have been in the market for about 294 days, which is roughly 12.5% of trading days. I can be excused for feeling a little pleased; irrespective of any particular year's market direction, we managed to remain profitable during 9 out of 10* years of our test period. We made a profit even in the worst year — that is, 2008 — when not only in India but investors around the world went through traumatic times as the financial crisis hit stock markets. The reason, of course, for my sense of complete satisfaction should be obvious: the patterns we used worked — and worked great!

Astutely, you would have noticed that in 2009, when a supposed bull rally started leading to a gain of 1,258 Nifty points from the first trading day of January till 30 June 2009, our patterns could only manage to catch a gain of 1,049 points. Well, my take on that is simple:

* 2002 is actually a loss, as we could not even recoup the brokerage charges at INR 200 per round trip.

It is not the number of trades you do that makes you a successful trader, but the quality of your trades. It is the ability to separate wheat from the chaff that separates the best from the rest. Why trade a high number of questionable patterns when you can trade fewer patterns but which have a high degree of success?

An equity curve, which is a graphical representation of the change in value of a trading account over a time period, reveals more to the eye than do tabular reports. A trading system that looks decent in reports can sometimes look horrible as an equity curve. It is easier to interpret drawdown, the longest flat period, smoothness and growth of the equity curve in a visual format. Figure 27.1 visually represents the performance summary for all the pivot point patterns combined.

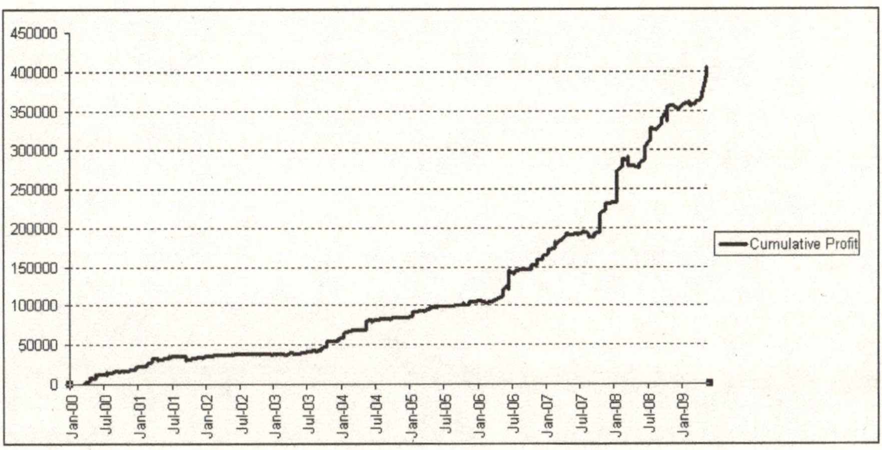

Figure 27.1: **Equity Curve for Combined Pivot Points**

The return on account, in net profit terms, by combining the pivot point combined strategies is close to the pessimistic rate of return for the perfectly predicted Nifty strategy performance summary, as presented in this chapter. This is excellent in itself but there is a small problem: these strategies imply open overnight positions. Accordingly, you may be beset with doubts and a sleepless night filled with apprehension about having exposed yourself to potential loss as a consequence of some market-affecting news that might surface overnight; news that could impact the Nifty movement on the wrong side. In short, if your overnight trading positions are keeping you awake at night, let us look for patterns that can be traded between the market's open and close. That naturally leads me to my next chapter.

Chapter 28

Gap Trading Secrets

First things first; for most of the patterns presented in this chapter I have used the direction of the Open, hence the name of this chapter. Another important point is that instead of ignoring cases where the open was the same as the previous day's close, I have considered these as gap downs.

Pattern 1: Turtle Short

This trading pattern is based on Richard Donchian's trend following Turtle Strategy; if the price made a new 20-day low, one would sell. We restrict ourselves to either Mondays or Fridays aided by the crowd reaction to the "weekend fear" factor.

Here are the rules for trade entry:

1. Today is either Friday or Monday;
2. Yesterday's close was the lowest in the preceding 20 days, including yesterday;
3. Today is gap down opening;
4. We go short at open minus 0.5%.
5. Exit is set at the close of today.

As you would note from Table 28.1, the Sharpe Ratio is on the lower side. This is because this pattern tends to work best during bear markets. Hence, the reason for a low Sharpe Ratio. It is a mistake to segregate the past years in to bear or bull markets by looking back at the returns. My take on the patterns where the bias is towards the Short, tends to fire heavily in years where the market returns are negative in that year and *vice versa*.

Table 28.1
Turtle Short Performance Summary

Total net profit	₹ 86,104		
Gross profit	₹ 100,946	Gross loss	₹ -14,842
Total # of trades	36	Percent profitable	72%
Number of winning trades	26	Number of losing trades	10
Largest winning trade	₹ 23,384	Largest losing trade	₹ -7,233
Largest winning trade %	11.6%	Largest losing trade %	-4.9%
Average winning trade	₹ 3,883	Average losing trade	₹ -1,484
Average winning trade %	2.7%	Average losing trade %	-1.4%
Ratio avg win/avg loss	2.6		
Ratio avg win/avg loss %	1.9		
Average profit per trade	₹ 2,392		
Average profit per trade %	1.6%		
Max consecutive winners	7	Max consecutive losers	2
Max drawdown	₹ -7,233	Max drawdown %	-10.4%
Profit factor	6.8		
Account size required	₹ 57,537	Return on account	149.6%
Luck factor	7.3		
Recovery factor	11.9		
Pessimistic Rate of Return	107.1%		
Sharpe ratio	0.5		
Accuracy	83%		

Pattern 2: Turtle Short on a Gap Up

Would we trade on days when all the rules presented in the turtle short pattern (Pattern 1) are met but if there is a gap up opening? Yes, we still go short, but at open minus 1%. So here are the rules:

1. Today is either a Friday or a Monday;
2. Yesterday's close was the lowest in the preceding 20 days, including yesterday;

3. Today is gap up opening;
4. Go short at Open minus 1% .
5. Exit is set at the close of the same day.

Table 28.2
Turtle Short on Gap-up Performance Summary

Total net profit	₹ 27,127		
Gross profit	₹ 38,523	Gross loss	₹ -11,396
Total # of trades	22	Percent profitable	59%
Number of winning trades	13	Number of losing trades	9
Largest winning trade	₹ 8,896	Largest losing trade	₹ -3,458
Largest winning trade %	11.4%	Largest losing trade %	-2.7%
Average winning trade	₹ 2,963	Average losing trade	₹ -1,266
Average winning trade %	2.6%	Average losing trade %	-1.2%
Ratio avg win/avg loss	2.3		
Ratio avg win/avg loss %	2.1		
Average profit per trade	₹ 1,233		
Average profit per trade %	1.0%		
Max consecutive winners	4	Max consecutive losers	2
Max drawdown	₹ -5,742	Max drawdown %	-4.0%
Profit factor	3.4		
Account size required	₹ 56,046	Return on account	48.4%
Luck factor	11.0		
Recovery factor	4.7		
Pessimistic Rate of Return	22.6%		
Sharpe ratio	0.5		
Accuracy	79%		

Pattern 3: Three Steps and a Stumble

If the market rises three days in a row and hits a 20-day high, there is strong probability that the market will then fall. As presented earlier in Chapter 27, the likelihood of reversal or turnaround is higher on Tuesdays.

Here are the rules for the trade:

1. Today is Tuesday;
2. Yesterday's close was the highest in the preceding 20 days, including yesterday;
3. Yesterday, the day before yesterday, and the day three days ago were all up closes;
4. Today is gap up opening;
5. Go short at open plus 0.5%.
6. Exit is set at today's close.

Table 28.3

Three Steps and a Stumble Performance Summary

Total net profit	₹ 27,704		
Gross profit	₹ 29,857	Gross loss	₹ -2,154
Total # of trades	31	Percent profitable	81%
Number of winning trades	25	Number of losing trades	6
Largest winning trade	₹ 4,590	Largest losing trade	₹ -1,081
Largest winning trade %	2.3%	Largest losing trade %	-0.8%
Average winning trade	₹ 1,194	Average losing trade	₹ -359
Average winning trade %	0.9%	Average losing trade %	-0.3%
Ratio avg win/avg loss	3.3		
Ratio avg win/avg loss %	2.9		
Average profit per trade	₹ 894		
Average profit per trade %	0.7%		
Max consecutive winners	12	Max consecutive losers	2
Max drawdown	₹ -1,452	Max drawdown %	-1.8%
Profit factor	13.9		
Account size required	₹ 51,756	Return on account	53.5%
Luck factor	3.5		
Recovery factor	19.1		
Pessimistic Rate of Return	40.3%		
Sharpe ratio	0.7		
Accuracy	82%		

Pattern 4: Two Tumbles and a Jump

This is a simple long strategy, but we don't use it on Mondays. The reason for avoiding Mondays is that Mondays tend to have a follow through from Fridays.

Here are the rules for the trade:

1. Today is not a Monday;
2. Yesterday and the day before yesterday were down closes;
3. Today is gap up opening (an indication of reversal);
4. Go long at Open plus 2%.
5. Exit is set at today's close.

Table 28.4

Two Tumbles and a Jump Performance Summary

Total net profit	₹ 60,846		
Gross profit	₹ 78,076	Gross loss	₹ -17,230
Total # of trades	52	Percent profitable	60%
Number of winning trades	31	Number of losing trades	21
Largest winning trade	₹ 10,114	Largest losing trade	₹ -4,278
Largest winning trade %	5.9%	Largest losing trade %	-3.1%
Average winning trade	₹ 2,519	Average losing trade	-₹ 820
Average winning trade %	1.9%	Average losing trade %	-0.7%
Ratio avg win/avg loss	3.1		
Ratio avg win/avg loss %	2.5		
Average profit per trade	₹ 1,170		
Average profit per trade %	0.8%		
Max consecutive winners	5	Max consecutive losers	4
Max drawdown	₹ 5,251	Max drawdown %	-6.6%
Profit factor	4.5		
Account size required	₹ 55,555	Return on account	109.5%
Luck factor	7.1		
Recovery factor	11.6		
Pessimistic Rate of Return	77.5%		
Sharpe ratio	0.8		
Accuracy	86%		

Pattern 5: Three Tumbles and a Jump

Same rules as in the above pattern (Pattern 4), except that in this case we are looking for three down closes.

Here are the rules for this trade:

1. Today is not a Monday;
2. The last three trading days were down closes.
3. Today is gap up opening.
4. Go long at Open plus 2%
5. Exit is set at today's close.

Table 28.5

Three Tumbles and a Jump Performance Summary

Total net profit	₹ 49,712		
Gross profit	₹ 54,340	Gross loss	₹ -4,628
Total # of trades	27	Percent profitable	70%
Number of winning trades	19	Number of losing trades	8
Largest winning trade	₹ 10,114	Largest losing trade	₹ -2,058
Largest winning trade %	4.2%	Largest losing trade %	-2.8%
Average winning trade	₹ 2,860	Average losing trade	₹ -579
Average winning trade %	2.1%	Average losing trade %	-0.6%
Ratio avg win/avg loss	4.9		
Ratio avg win/avg loss %	3.4		
Average profit per trade	₹ 1,841		
Average profit per trade %	1.3%		
Max consecutive winners	6	Max consecutive losers	3
Max drawdown	₹ 2,058	Max drawdown %	-3.9%
Profit factor	11.7		
Account size required	₹ 52,362	Return on account	94.9%
Luck factor	3.3		
Recovery factor	24.2		
Pessimistic Rate of Return	68.0%		
Sharpe ratio	0.7		
Accuracy	81%		

Pattern 6: Modified Three Tumbles and a Jump

What if we placed an additional condition, i.e. add a rule that yesterday's close be the lowest in the last 20 days? This is similar to the "Buy When There is Blood on the Street" pattern presented in Chapter 27.

Here are the rules for this trade:

- Today is not a Monday;
- Yesterday's close was the lowest in the last 20 days;
- Automagically, yesterday's close was also down;
- The previous three trading days were down closes;
- No need to look at the open direction.
- Go long at Open plus 1%.
- Exit is set at today's close.

Take a good look at Table 28.6 and note the improvement in the profit per trade both in rupee terms and percentage terms.

Table 28.6

Modified Three Tumbles and a Jump Performance Summary

Total net profit	₹ 72,571		
Gross profit	₹ 90,753	Gross loss	₹ -18,183
Total # of trades	57	Percent profitable	72%
Number of winning trades	41	Number of losing trades	16
Largest winning trade	₹ 12,566	Largest losing trade	₹ -4,419
Largest winning trade %	5.2%	Largest losing trade %	-2.2%
Average winning trade	₹ 2,213	Average losing trade	₹ -1,136
Average winning trade %	1.8%	Average losing trade %	-1.0%
Ratio avg win/avg loss	1.9		
Ratio avg win/avg loss %	1.8		
Average profit per trade	₹ 1,273		

(Contd . . .)

Table 28.6 (contd.)

Modified Three Tumbles and a Jump Performance Summary

Average profit per trade %	1.0%		
Max consecutive winners	12	Max consecutive losers	3
Max drawdown	₹ 4,419	Max drawdown %	-4.1%
Profit factor	5.0		
Account size required	₹ 54,723	Return on account	132.6%
Luck factor	5.2		
Recovery factor	16.4		
Pessimistic Rate of Return	98.4%		
Sharpe ratio	0.9		
Accuracy	87%		

Pattern 7: Two Tumbles, and Another Tumble

This trading pattern highlights the reasons why I said not to expect a jump on a Monday. The strategy is very similar to one of the strategies presented in the earlier chapter on pivot trading secrets (Chapter 27).

Here are the rules for this trade:

1. Today is a Monday;
2. Yesterday and the day before yesterday were down closes;
3. No need to look at the direction of the open.
4. Go short at open minus 0.5%;
5. Exit is set at today's close.

Table 28.7

Two Tumbles and Another Tumble Performance Summary

Total net profit	₹ 122,141		
Gross profit	₹ 143,942	Gross loss	₹ -21,801
Total # of trades	79	Percent profitable	71%
Number of winning trades	56	Number of losing trades	23
Largest winning trade	₹ 23,384	Largest losing trade	₹ -3,967
Largest winning trade %	8.2%	Largest losing trade %	-2.8%
Average winning trade	₹ 2,570	Average losing trade	₹ -948
Average winning trade %	1.7%	Average losing trade %	-0.9%
Ratio avg win/avg loss	2.7		
Ratio avg win/avg loss %	1.9		
Average profit per trade	₹ 1,546		
Average profit per trade %	1.0%		
Max consecutive winners	9	Max consecutive losers	2
Max drawdown	₹ -3,978	Max drawdown %	-3.0%
Profit factor	6.6		
Account size required	₹ 54,282	Return on account	225.0%
Luck factor	8.5		
Recovery factor	30.7		
Pessimistic Rate of Return	181.2%		
Sharpe ratio	1.3		
Accuracy	89%		

Pattern 8: Outside Day

An outside day is one where the day's high is higher than the previous day's high and the day's low is lower than the low of the previous day's low.

The outside day usually represents a one-day change to aggressive demand from supply, or *vice versa*. The theory is that one should go with the latest indication of demand or supply. It is very effective as an entry filter for testing the demand.

Rules for this trade are:

1. Yesterday was an outside day;
2. Today is gap up opening;
3. Yesterday was not a WS7 day (the reason: there is very little probability that two consecutive WS7 days will provide a long entry; you can check this for yourself with all possible permutations).
4. Go long at Open plus 1%.
5. Exit is set at today's close.

Table 28.8

Outside Day Performance Summary

Total net profit	₹ 46,715		
Gross profit	₹ 58,311	Gross loss	₹ -11,596
Total # of trades	38	Percent profitable	63%
Number of winning trades	24	Number of losing trades	14
Largest winning trade	₹ 9,388	Largest losing trade	₹ -1,976
Largest winning trade %	6.1%	Largest losing trade %	-2.2%
Average winning trade	₹ 2,430	Average losing trade	₹ -828
Average winning trade %	1.6%	Average losing trade %	-0.7%
Ratio avg win/avg loss	2.9		
Ratio avg win/avg loss %	2.3		
Average profit per trade	₹ 1,229		
Average profit per trade %	0.8%		
Max consecutive winners	8	Max consecutive losers	4
Max drawdown	₹ 2,699	Max drawdown %	-3.6%
Profit factor	5.0		
Account size required	₹ 53,003	Return on account	88.1%
Luck factor	7.9		
Recovery factor	17.3		
Pessimistic Rate of Return	59.8%		
Sharpe ratio	0.9		
Accuracy	84%		

Pattern 9: Inside Day

An inside day is indecisive from the supply and demand point of view. The theory is that when the market overcomes this indecision by penetrating the previous day's low, it is evidence of supply dominating the demand and might lead to a profitable trade. The strategy creates a short-term selling surge in the market.

Here are the rules for this trade:

1. Yesterday was an inside day;
2. Yesterday was also an NR4 day;
3. Today is gap down opening;
4. Go short at Open minus 0.5%.
5. Exit is set at today's close.

Table 28.9

Inside Day Performance Summary

Total net profit	₹ 51,851		
Gross profit	₹ 61,678	Gross loss	₹ -9,827
Total # of trades	33	Percent profitable	64%
Number of winning trades	21	Number of losing trades	12
Largest winning trade	₹ 10,931	Largest losing trade	₹ -3,177
Largest winning trade %	4.6%	Largest losing trade %	-2.4%
Average winning trade	₹ 2,937	Average losing trade	₹ -819
Average winning trade %	2.0%	Average losing trade %	-1.0%
Ratio avg win/avg loss	3.6		
Ratio avg win/avg loss %	2.1		
Average profit per trade	₹ 1,571		
Average profit per trade %	0.9%		
Max consecutive winners	6	Max consecutive losers	2
Max drawdown	₹ -3,177	Max drawdown %	-3.3%
Profit factor	6.3		

(Contd . . .)

Table 28.9 (contd.)
Inside Day Performance Summary

Account size required	₹ 53,481	Return on account	97.0%
Luck factor	5.0		
Recovery factor	16.3		
Pessimistic Rate of Return	66.5%		
Sharpe ratio	0.9		
Accuracy	83%		

Pattern 10: Short Bias Doji

This is a somewhat complicated pattern. Doji indicates indecision among buyers and sellers and it takes conviction on the part of buyers to sustain an upward move.

Here are the rules for trading this pattern:

1. Yesterday was a Doji day (open and close were within 10% of the range for the day);
2. Three days ago was a down close. This is our requirement to ensure that the market is in a short term down trend.
3. Yesterday was neither a 20-day highest nor a 20-day lowest closing.
4. The day before yesterday was neither a 20-day highest nor a 20-day lowest closing.

   (Avoiding the Doji occurrences at the market's major highs and lows, as they indicate a reversal in the trend, as per the chartists, and I am not sure about the trading edge of Doji appearance around either 20 day high or low)
5. No need to look at the direction of the open;
6. Go short at Open minus 1%
7. Exit is set at today's close.

Table 28.10
Short Bias Doji Performance Summary

Total net profit	₹ 46,304		
Gross profit	₹ 51,441	Gross loss	₹ -5,137
Total # of trades	28	Percent profitable	68%
Number of winning trades	19	Number of losing trades	9
Largest winning trade	₹ 10,617	Largest losing trade	₹ -1,150
Largest winning trade %	6.9%	Largest losing trade %	-1.6%
Average winning trade	₹ 2,707	Average losing trade	₹ -571
Average winning trade %	1.6%	Average losing trade %	-0.6%
Ratio avg win/avg loss	4.7		
Ratio avg win/avg loss %	2.8		
Average profit per trade	₹ 1,654		
Average profit per trade %	0.9%		
Max consecutive winners	7	Max consecutive losers	2
Max drawdown	₹ -1,150	Max drawdown %	-2.2%
Profit factor	10.0		
Account size required	₹ 51,454	Return on account	90.0%
Luck factor	7.4		
Recovery factor	40.3		
Pessimistic Rate of Return	63.7%		
Sharpe ratio	0.7		
Accuracy	81%		

Pattern 11: Buying Mondays and Fridays

In creating a set of trading patterns, there are two ways to proceed. The first method is to observe the markets and investigate market behaviour. Occasionally, useful trading patterns will be detected by using this method. Logically, a more efficient method of pattern research is to simply test all possible parameters and to see if any of the results look statistically valid. My additional intention here is to show you step-by-step methods that one could employ in developing a pattern.

Mondays and Fridays share some characteristics in trading patterns. To some extent, the fact that the close of the week could look like the week's opening should not come as a surprise. This pattern calls upon us to buy at open plus 1% on a Friday or on a Monday under the same circumstances.

Here are the rules for trade entry:

1. Today is either a Monday or a Friday;
2. Yesterday was both a gap up and an up close;
3. Today is a gap up opening;
4. Go long at open plus 1%.
5. Exit is set at today's close.

Table 28.11

Buying Mondays and Fridays Performance Summary

Total net profit	₹ 73,198		
Gross profit	₹ 120,236	Gross loss	₹ -47,037
Total # of trades	117	Percent profitable	55%
Number of winning trades	64	Number of losing trades	53
Largest winning trade	₹ 30,663	Largest losing trade	₹ -4,978
Largest winning trade %	16.5%	Largest losing trade %	-4.9%
Average winning trade	₹ 1,879	Average losing trade	₹ -887
Average winning trade %	1.4%	Average losing trade %	-0.9%
Ratio avg win/avg loss	2.1		
Ratio avg win/avg loss %	1.5		
Average profit per trade	₹ 626		
Average profit per trade %	0.3%		
Max consecutive winners	8	Max consecutive losers	10
Max drawdown	₹ 8,046	Max drawdown %	-5.8%
Profit factor	2.6		
Account size required	₹ 58,350	Return on account	125.4%
Luck factor	49.7		
Recovery factor	9.1		
Pessimistic Rate of Return	88.6%		
Sharpe ratio	0.4		
Accuracy	91%		

A first look at the performance summary might show that this is not a tradable pattern given that it has such a high luck factor, such a low average profit per trade (both in terms of percentages and points), and a low Sharpe Ratio.

Pattern 12: Buying Mondays and Fridays — Modification 1

So we've got to tweak some rules of the Buying Mondays and Fridays Pattern 8 to optimise it in a meaningful way. What if we are to enter at open plus 2%?

Here are the rules for this trade.

1. Today is either a Monday or a Friday.
2. Yesterday was both a gap up and an up close day;
3. Today is a gap up opening;
4. Go long at Open plus 2%
5. Exit is set at today's close

Check how the quality improves in Table 28.12 which provides the performance summary.

Table 28.12

Buying Mondays and Fridays — Modification 1:Performance Summary

Total net profit	₹ 58,570		
Gross profit	₹ 65,911	Gross loss	₹ -7,341
Total # of trades	41	Percent profitable	76%
Number of winning trades	31	Number of losing trades	10
Largest winning trade	₹ 28,827	Largest losing trade	₹ -2,219
Largest winning trade %	15.4%	Largest losing trade %	-2.7%
Average winning trade	₹ 2,126	Average losing trade	₹ -734
Average winning trade %	1.4%	Average losing trade %	-0.7%
Ratio avg win/avg loss	2.9		
Ratio avg win/avg loss %	2.0		

(Contd . . .)

Table 28.12 (contd.)

Buying Mondays and Fridays — Modification 1: Performance Summary

Average profit per trade	₹ 1,429		
Average profit per trade %	0.9%		
Max consecutive winners	5	Max consecutive losers	1
Max drawdown	₹ 2,219	Max drawdown %	-4.2%
Profit factor	9.0		
Account size required	₹ 52,523	Return on account	111.5%
Luck factor	17.2		
Recovery factor	26.4		
Pessimistic Rate of Return	84.6%		
Sharpe ratio	0.7		
Accuracy	84%		

Pattern 13: Buying Mondays and Fridays — Modification 2

The same old rules as in Pattern 8-a above, but with an additional condition, What if we were to avoid those days when the previous day was the highest close in the last 20 days? Successful traders need to know how much a market can move after reaching such a major high; it is a little difficult for the market to move another 2% after making a major high. Note the technique of altering the various parameters, in this case how we are tightening the parameters of the previous day's close and our entry stop.

So here are the rules for this trade:

1. Today is either a Monday or a Friday;
2. Yesterday was both a gap up and an up close;
3. Yesterday's was not the highest close in the last 20 days; and Day before yesterday was a down close
4. Today is a gap up opening;
5. Go long at Open plus 1%.
6. Exit is set at today's close

Table 28.13

Buying Mondays and Fridays Modification 2: Performance Summary

Total net profit	₹ 59,484		
Gross profit	₹ 63,054	Gross loss	₹ -3,570
Total # of trades	32	Percent profitable	81%
Number of winning trades	26	Number of losing trades	6
Largest winning trade	₹ 28,827	Largest losing trade	₹ -2,219
Largest winning trade %	15.4%	Largest losing trade %	-2.7%
Average winning trade	₹ 2,425	Average losing trade	-₹ 595
Average winning trade %	1.6%	Average losing trade %	-0.7%
Ratio avg win/avg loss	4.1		
Ratio avg win/avg loss %	2.2		
Average profit per trade	₹ 1,859		
Average profit per trade %	1.2%		
Max consecutive winners	9	Max consecutive losers	1
Max drawdown	₹ 2,219	Max drawdown %	-4.2%
Profit factor	17.7		
Account size required	₹ 52,523	Return on account	113.3%
Luck factor	13.2		
Recovery factor	26.8		
Pessimistic Rate of Return	86.9%		
Sharpe ratio	0.7		
Accuracy	82%		

Gap Patterns Combined

As in Chapter 27, we now present you that big table with the details of all the gap patterns combined occurrences (Table 28.14). This table has a column called "Pattern", which contains the following abbreviated forms:

- TURSHRT is Pattern-1, i.e. Turtle Short;
- GUTRTSHRT is Pattern-2, namely Turtle Short on a Gap-Up;
- FALTURTSHRT is Pattern-3, i.e. Three Steps and a Stumble;
- TTAJLNG is Pattern-6, namely Modified Three Tumbles and a Jump;
- TTATSHRT is Pattern-7, i.e. Two Tumbles and Another Tumble;
- ODLNG is Pattern-8, namely Outside Day;
- IDNR4SHRT is Pattern 9, i.e. Inside Day;
- DOJISHRT is Pattern-10, namely Short Bias Doji; and
- BMFLNG is Pattern 13, i.e. Buying Monday and Friday.

Figures in the column "Profit" indicate the difference between tomorrow's and today's closes, multiplied by 50. For long patterns, it is tomorrow's minus today's close; for short patterns it is the other way around. The column "Cumulative Profit" indicates what the result would be if we had accumulated the profits.

A couple of points need to be noted in cases when some patterns clashed:

1. If more than two patterns point in the same direction, the one with the highest profit is considered.
2. If more than two patterns point in different directions, the one with the highest loss is considered.

I think the above strategy gives a realistic result when all the patterns are combined together.

Table 28.14
Results for All Gap Patterns Combined

Date	*Open*	*High*	*Low*	*Close*	*Pattern*	*Profit / Loss (Points)*	*Profit/ Loss (₹)*	*Cumulative Profit*
17-Jan-00	1,623.50	1,668.45	1,604.65	1,611.60	BMFLNG	-44.37	-2,219	-2,219
7-Feb-00	1,599.80	1,645.90	1,599.80	1,636.60	BMFLNG	4.80	240	-1,978
9-Mar-00	1,667.45	1,692.25	1,595.45	1,646.25	ODLNG	-37.87	-1,894	-3,872
10-Mar-00	1,647.85	1,680.45	1,588.20	1,602.75	GUTRTSHRT	28.62	1,431	-2,441
13-Mar-00	1,601,.40	1,645.00	1,553.45	1,560.70	TURSHRT	0.00		-2,441
13-Mar-00	1,601.40	1,645.00	1,553.45	1,560.70	TTATSHRT	32.70	1,635	-806
24-Mar-00	1,554.20	1,579.40	1,540.45	1,569.55	ODLNG	-0.19	-10	-816
31-Mar-00	1,545.55	1,545.55	1,493.90	1,528.45	TURSHRT	9.37	469	-347
3-Apr-00	1,528.70	1,555.50	1,510.75	1,534.75	GUTRTSHRT	0.00		-347
3-Apr-00	1,528.70	1,555.50	1,510.75	1,534.75	TTATSHRT	-13.70	-685	-1,032
7-Apr-00	1,453.30	1,558.05	1,453.30	1,557.15	BMFLNG	0.00		-1,032
7-Apr-00	1,453.30	1,558.05	1,453.30	1,557.15	ODLNG	89.30	4,466	3,434
10-Apr-00	1,557.55	1,636.95	1,557.55	1,613.00	BMFLNG	24.30	1,215	4,649
13-Apr-00	1,587.95	1,587.95	1,502.70	1,518.65	IDNR4SHRT	61.36	3,068	7,717
17-Apr-00	1,518.55	1,518.55	1,412.45	1,443.55	TTATSHRT	67.41	3,370	11,087
19-Apr-00	1,417.75	1,469.05	1,375.05	1,404.95	TTAJLNG	-26.98	-1,349	9,738
20-Apr-00	1,405.70	1,425.55	1,339.75	1,415.65	TTAJLNG	-4.11	-205	9,533
4-May-00	1,317.95	1,385.15	1,317.95	1,380.55	TTAJLNG	49.42	2,471	12,004
5-May-00	1,381.90	1,428.60	1,381.90	1,422.40	BMFLNG	12.86	643	12,647
12-May-00	1,305.30	1,326.30	1,276.40	1,282.80	GUTRTSHRT	9.45	472	13,119
15-May-00	1,281.30	1,311.70	1,220.70	1,299.25	TURSHRT	0.00		13,119
15-May-00	1,281.30	1,311.70	1,220.70	1,299.25	TTATSHRT	-24.40	-1,218	11,902
22-May-00	1,267.85	1,267.85	1,228.40	1,233.00	TURSHRT	0.00		11,902
22-May-00	1,267.85	1,267.85	1,228.40	1,233.00	TTATSHRT	28.50	1,426	13,327
24-May-00	1,224.50	1,246.25	1,201.50	1,235.90	TTAJLNG	-0.85	-42	13,285
5-Jun-00	1,390.95	1,461.05	1,390.95	1,404.60	BMFLNG	-14.17	-708	12,576
28-Jun-00	1,453.70	1,474.70	1,445.60	1,470.00	IDNR4SHRT	-23.57	-1178	11,398
29-Jun-00	1,471.35	1,505.75	1,471.35	1,492.35	ODLNG	6.29	314	11,712

(Contd . . .)

Table 28.14 (contd.)

Results for All Gap Patterns Combined

Date	Open	High	Low	Close	Pattern	Profit / Loss (Points)	Profit/ Loss (₹)	Cumulative Profit
17-Jul-00	1,509.25	1,512.25	1,475.15	1,479.65	TTATSHRT	22.05	1,103	12,815
21-Jul-00	1,424.90	1,435.20	1,394.30	1,397.25	GUTRTSHRT	13.40	670	13,485
24-Jul-00	1,397.05	1,397.05	1,310.85	1,317.75	TURSHRT	0.00		13,485
24-Jul-00	1,397.05	1,397.05	1,310.85	1,317.75	TTATSHRT	72.30	3,616	17,101
25-Jul-00	1,317.35	1,363.45	1,269.25	1,348.90	TTAJLNG	18.38	919	18,020
7-Aug-00	1,319.70	1,321.70	1,299.90	1,310.80	TTATSHRT	2.30	115	18,135
8-Aug-00	1,312.10	1,348.25	1,311.15	1,345.60	TTAJLNG	20.38	1,019	19,154
14-Aug-00	1,312.25	1,321.55	1,295.45	1,317.90	GUTRTSHRT	0.00		19,154
14-Aug-00	1,312.25	1,321.55	1,295.45	1,317.90	TTATSHRT	-12.20	-611	18,543
12-Sep-00	1,457.10	1,470.55	1,447.80	1,467.65	FALTURTSHRT	-3.26	-163	18,380
18-Sep-00	1,416.05	1,416.05	1,352.10	1,354.35	TTATSHRT	54.62	2,731	21,111
20-Sep-00	1,317.80	1,351.10	1,311.10	1,342.90	TTAJLNG	11.92	596	21,707
22-Sep-00	1,329.10	1,329.10	1,261.20	1,266.45	IDNR4SHRT	56.00	2,800	24,507
3-Oct-00	1,270.75	1,288.15	1,254.35	1,282.00	IDNR4SHRT	-17.60	-880	23,627
12-Oct-00	1,201.30	1,214.35	1,185.10	1,206.25	TTAJLNG	-7.06	-353	23,274
19-Oct-00	1,135.65	1,171.50	1,108.20	1,166.15	TTAJLNG	19.14	957	24,231
27-Nov-00	1,225.40	1,254.45	1,225.35	1,252.90	BMFLNG	2.99	150	24,381
1-Dec-00	1,268.10	1,280.50	1,255.20	1,276.20	IDNR4SHRT	-14.44	-722	23,659
4-Dec-00	1,276.25	1,290.00	1,273.65	1,275.60	ODLNG	-13.41	-671	22,988
12-Dec-00	1,332.20	1,341.75	1,327.60	1,333.35	FALTURTSHRT	5.51	276	23,264
18-Dec-00	1,310.15	1,321.65	1,297.20	1,317.60	TTATSHRT	-14.00	-700	22,564
27-Dec-00	1,212.15	1,239.00	1,208.75	1,228.30	TTAJLNG	4.03	201	22,765
10-Jan-01	1,311.65	1,324.35	1,285.30	1,287.30	IDNR4SHRT	17.79	890	23,655
19-Jan-01	1,306.00	1,333.50	1,306.00	1,329.10	BMFLNG	-3.02	-151	23,504
9-Feb-01	1,395.55	1,416.30	1,395.55	1,405.70	ODLNG	-3.81	-190	23,313
26-Feb-01	1,320.90	1,325.20	1,299.05	1,312.40	GUTRTSHRT	0.00		23,313
26-Feb-01	1,320.90	1,325.20	1,299.05	1,312.40	TTATSHRT	1.90	95	23,408
28-Feb-01	1,295.30	1,362.25	1,294.60	1,351.40	TTAJLNG	43.15	2,157	25,565
9-Mar-01	1,292.70	1,292.70	1,219.35	1,254.75	IDNR4SHRT	0.00		25,565
9-Mar-01	1,292.70	1,292.70	1,219.35	1,254.75	DOJISHRT	31.50	1,574	27,140

(Contd . . .)

Table 28.14 (contd.)

Results for All Gap Patterns Combined

Date	*Open*	*High*	*Low*	*Close*	*Pattern*	*Profit / Loss (Points)*	*Profit/ Loss (₹)*	*Cumulative Profit*
12-Mar-01	1,253.25	1,253.25	1,193.95	1,197.95	TURSHRT	49.03	2,452	29,591
14-Mar-01	1,125.15	1,200.25	1,114.60	1,194.20	TTAJLNG	57.80	2,890	32,481
26-Mar-01	1,159.85	1,165.65	1,147.50	1,161.50	TTATSHRT	-7.45	-372	32,109
2-Apr-01	1,148.10	1,148.10	1,094.35	1,138.10	TTATSHRT	4.26	213	32,322
16-Apr-01	1,024.00	1,049.40	1,000.10	1,044.60	TURSHRT	0.00		32,322
16-Apr-01	1,024.00	1,049.40	1,000.10	1,044.60	TTATSHRT	-25.70	-1286	31,036
14-May-01	1,140.45	1,146.25	1,134.05	1,140.80	TTATSHRT	-6.05	-303	30,733
15-May-01	1,140.75	1,147.75	1,096.25	1,145.30	DOJISHRT	-15.96	-798	29,935
4-Jun-01	1,148.00	1,154.45	1,125.35	1,127.20	TTATSHRT	15.06	753	30,688
6-Jun-01	1,117.50	1,132.95	1,114.00	1,115.70	TTAJLNG	-12.97	-649	30,040
14-Jun-01	1,128.95	1,128.95	1,110.15	1,112.75	IDNR4SHRT	10.56	528	30,567
18-Jun-01	1,087.75	1,087.75	1,064.40	1,078.30	TURSHRT	0.00		30,567
18-Jun-01	1,087.75	1,087.75	1,064.40	1,078.30	TTATSHRT	4.00	201	30,768
19-Jun-01	1,078.25	1,099.70	1,075.45	1,096.65	TTAJLNG	7.62	381	31,149
25-Jun-01	1,087.10	1,087.10	1,064.40	1,067.00	TTATSHRT	14.66	733	31,882
26-Jun-01	1,066.40	1,099.80	1,060.05	1,096.60	TTAJLNG	19.54	977	32,859
9-Jul-01	1,064.80	1,064.80	1,052.10	1,059.50	TURSHRT	-0.02	-1	32,858
23-Jul-01	1,076.15	1,076.15	1,063.40	1,070.65	TTATSHRT	0.12	6	32,864
25-Jul-01	1,072.45	1,073.95	1,062.15	1,064.20	IDNR4SHRT	2.89	144	33,008
27-Jul-01	1,053.20	1,061.20	1,046.90	1,051.70	TURSHRT	-3.77	-188	32,820
3-Sep-01	1,054.65	1,059.90	1,046.35	1,048.05	TTATSHRT	1.33	66	32,886
13-Sep-01	982.20	993.05	969.00	971.70	TTAJLNG	-20.32	-1,016	31,870
14-Sep-01	972.05	974.50	902.70	919.70	GUTRTSHRT	42.63	2,131	34,001
17-Sep-01	916.15	916.15	861.05	872.25	TURSHRT	0.00		34,001
17-Sep-01	916.15	916.15	861.05	872.25	TTATSHRT	39.30	1,966	35,967
18-Sep-01	872.15	910.35	868.50	900.20	TTAJLNG	19.33	966	36,934
27-Sep-01	873.15	893.05	868.30	890.00	IDNR4SHRT	-21.22	-1,061	35,873
3-Oct-01	910.05	915.05	896.25	899.65	IDNR4SHRT	5.85	292	36,165
29-Oct-01	983.15	996.60	974.05	977.45	TTATSHRT	0.78	39	36,205
21-Dec-01	1,061.80	1,061.80	1,043.65	1,050.85	DOJISHRT	0.33	17	36,221
24-Dec-01	1,051.00	1,055.00	1,032.60	1,048.50	GUTRTSHRT	-8.01	-401	35,821

(Contd . . .)

Table 28.14 (contd.)

Results for All Gap Patterns Combined

Date	*Open*	*High*	*Low*	*Close*	*Pattern*	*Profit / Loss (Points)*	*Profit / Loss (₹)*	*Cumulative Profit*
28-Dec-01	1,019.90	1,036.35	1,010.45	1,033.80	TTAJLNG	-19.00	-950	34,871
28-Dec-01	1,019.90	1,036.35	1,010.45	1,033.80	TURSHRT	0.00		34,871
4-Jan-02	1,072.40	1,099.25	1,072.40	1,096.20	BMFLNG	2.35	118	34,988
28-Jan-02	1,083.25	1,088.75	1,068.70	1,071.35	TTATSHRT	6.48	324	35,313
30-Jan-02	1,072.85	1,072.85	1,058.80	1,067.45	DOJISHRT	-5.33	-266	35,046
6-Mar-02	1,176.55	1,182.65	1,162.75	1,172.60	IDNR4SHRT	-1.93	-97	34,950
19-Apr-02	1,125.55	1,127.05	1,097.60	1,100.30	IDNR4SHRT	19.62	981	35,931
22-Apr-02	1,100.50	1,107.20	1,088.05	1,104.15	GUTRTSHRT	-14.66	-733	35,198
20-May-02	1,091.70	1,097.95	1,071.35	1,074.35	TTATSHRT	11.89	595	35,792
23-May-02	1,045.20	1,045.35	1,024.30	1,026.75	IDNR4SHRT	13.22	661	36,454
24-May-02	1,026.90	1,069.20	1,026.90	1,067.00	TTAJLNG	29.83	1,492	37,945
18-Jul-02	1,032.55	1,044.00	1,032.55	1,041.30	TTAJLNG	-1.58	-79	37,866
26-Jul-02	1,001.05	1,001.05	972.55	973.50	TURSHRT	22.54	1,127	38,994
29-Jul-02	973.00	977.95	953.15	971.65	TURSHRT	0.00		38,994
29-Jul-02	973.00	977.95	953.15	971.65	TTATSHRT	-3.50	-176	38,818
30-Jul-02	973.00	987.50	956.80	960.65	TTAJLNG	-22.08	-1,104	37,714
1-Aug-02	959.20	972.05	954.15	957.70	TTAJLNG	-11.09	-555	37,159
2-Aug-02	957.55	957.55	935.55	954.75	TURSHRT	-1.99	-99	37,060
23-Aug-02	985.75	996.40	984.70	995.20	ODLNG	-0.41	-20	37,040
30-Aug-02	987.65	1,012.75	986.70	1,010.60	BMFLNG	3.20	160	37,199
20-Sep-02	975.60	975.60	960.70	969.60	TURSHRT	1.12	56	37,256
24-Sep-02	969.95	969.95	960.20	966.20	IDNR4SHRT	-1.10	-55	37,201
21-Oct-02	971.75	976.20	965.65	967.35	TTATSHRT	-0.46	-23	37,178
25-Oct-02	946.80	946.80	929.25	932.20	TURSHRT	9.87	493	37,671
28-Oct-02	932.35	934.90	920.10	922.70	GUTRTSHRT	0.00		37,671
28-Oct-02	932.35	934.90	920.10	922.70	TTATSHRT	5.00	249	37,920
29-Oct-02	922.55	939.70	921.65	936.90	TTAJLNG	5.12	256	38,177
11-Nov-02	957.55	958.55	952.10	954.05	TTATSHRT	-1.29	-64	38,112
15-Nov-02	972.30	992.05	972.30	990.35	BMFLNG	-1.40	-70	38,042
26-Nov-02	1,026.40	1,040.45	1,026.00	1,036.15	FALTURTSHRT	-4.62	-231	37,811
6-Dec-02	1,047.55	1,072.25	1,047.55	1,069.80	BMFLNG	1.30	65	37,876

(Contd . . .)

Table 28.14 (contd.)

Results for All Gap Patterns Combined

Date	Open	High	Low	Close	Pattern	Profit / Loss (Points)	Profit/ Loss (₹)	Cumulative Profit
19-Dec-02	1,077.85	1,079.90	1,070.50	1,076.00	IDNR4SHRT	-3.54	-177	37,699
26-Dec-02	1,085.05	1,100.40	1,085.05	1,094.80	ODLNG	-1.10	-55	37,644
24-Jan-03	1,070.60	1,075.20	1,053.40	1,056.05	TURSHRT	9.20	460	38,104
27-Jan-03	1,057.80	1,059.35	1,030.35	1,037.65	GUTRTSHRT	0.00		38,104
27-Jan-03	1,057.80	1,059.35	1,030.35	1,037.65	TTATSHRT	14.90	743	38,847
28-Jan-03	1,036.35	1,047.95	1,026.75	1,046.20	TTAJLNG	-0.51	-26	38,822
7-Mar-03	1,031.05	1,031.05	1,014.30	1,017.10	TURSHRT	8.79	440	39,261
10-Mar-03	1,017.10	1,021.50	1,004.35	1,006.70	TURSHRT	0.00		39,261
10-Mar-03	1,017.10	1,021.50	1,004.35	1,006.70	TTATSHRT	5.30	266	39,527
17-Mar-03	999.70	1,000.85	982.70	993.00	GUTRTSHRT	0.00		39,527
17-Mar-03	999.70	1,000.85	982.70	993.00	TTATSHRT	1.70	85	39,612
19-Mar-03	993.35	1,011.45	992.90	1,003.90	TTAJLNG	0.62	31	39,643
31-Mar-03	1,000.60	1,000.60	974.10	978.20	TTATSHRT	17.40	870	40,513
1-Apr-03	977.40	992.05	973.50	984.30	TTAJLNG	-2.87	-144	40,369
11-Apr-03	958.90	965.15	935.70	949.80	TURSHRT	4.31	215	40,584
15-Apr-03	951.80	964.20	938.80	951.20	TTAJLNG	-10.12	-506	40,079
17-Apr-03	958.65	958.65	936.70	940.70	IDNR4SHRT	13.16	658	40,736
22-Apr-03	947.10	951.40	937.85	943.50	IDNR4SHRT	-1.14	-57	40,680
25-Apr-03	929.45	931.35	921.10	924.30	TURSHRT	0.50	25	40,705
17-Jun-03	1,052.30	1,083.20	1,052.30	1,081.95	ODLNG	19.13	956	41,661
10-Jul-03	1,146.00	1,163.60	1,146.00	1,162.35	ODLNG	4.89	244	41,906
21-Jul-03	1,140.00	1,146.40	1,112.55	1,115.80	TTATSHRT	18.50	925	42,831
5-Aug-03	1,203.90	1,218.50	1,181.00	1,184.45	FALTURTSHRT	25.47	1,273	44,104
12-Aug-03	1,233.95	1,249.35	1,229.80	1,234.75	FALTURTSHRT	5.37	268	44,373
19-Aug-03	1,286.05	1,307.60	1,268.10	1,277.70	FALTURTSHRT	14.78	739	45,112
9-Sep-03	1,417.80	1,430.70	1,397.65	1,407.05	FALTURTSHRT	17.84	892	46,003
15-Sep-03	1,371.75	1,371.85	1,322.65	1,329.25	TTATSHRT	35.64	1,782	47,786
1-Oct-03	1,416.60	1,430.90	1,407.95	1,420.85	IDNR4SHRT	-11.33	-567	47,219
7-Oct-03	1,478.95	1,498.45	1,467.75	1,477.85	FALTURTSHRT	8.49	425	47,644
14-Oct-03	1,548.70	1,562.85	1,513.75	1,520.80	FALTURTSHRT	35.64	1,782	49,426
15-Oct-03	1,521.45	1,543.85	1,503.00	1,537.00	ODLNG	0.34	17	49,443

(Contd . . .)

Table 28.14 (contd.)
Results for All Gap Patterns Combined

Date	Open	High	Low	Close	Pattern	Profit / Loss (Points)	Profit/ Loss (₹)	Cumulative Profit
31-Oct-03	1,517.10	1,559.75	1,515.55	1,555.90	BMFLNG	8.46	423	49,865
3-Nov-03	1,556.50	1,605.60	1,556.50	1,601.65	BMFLNG	14.02	701	50,566
6-Nov-03	1,610.55	1,630.25	1,605.40	1,612.20	ODLNG	-14.46	-723	49,844
17-Nov-03	1,563.10	1,584.75	1,554.40	1,579.90	TTATSHRT	-24.62	-1,231	48,613
1-Dec-03	1,615.85	1,660.55	1,615.70	1,657.65	BMFLNG	9.48	474	49,087
30-Dec-03	1,878.90	1,914.40	1,858.55	1,873.25	FALTURTSHRT	15.04	752	49,839
6-Jan-04	1,955.10	1,979.05	1,908.75	1,926.70	FALTURTSHRT	38.18	1,909	51,748
19-Jan-04	1,901.90	1,943.10	1,874.95	1,935.35	TTATSHRT	-42.96	-2,148	49,600
23-Jan-04	1,771.10	1,858.50	1,771.10	1,847.55	TTAJLNG	58.74	2,937	52,537
4-Feb-04	1,769.10	1,829.65	1,761.75	1,822.20	TTAJLNG	35.41	1,770	54,308
23-Feb-04	1,853.00	1,867.25	1,800.20	1,808.20	TTATSHRT	35.53	1,777	56,084
26-Feb-04	1,787.45	1,818.60	1,760.55	1,765.80	ODLNG	-39.52	-1976	54,108
19-Mar-04	1,716.30	1,738.60	1,703.55	1,725.10	TURSHRT	-17.38	-869	53,239
12-Apr-04	1,860.30	1,873.75	1,828.95	1,838.20	DOJISHRT	3.50	175	53,414
13-Apr-04	1,838.50	1,885.15	1,819.80	1,878.45	ODLNG	21.57	1,078	54,492
19-Apr-04	1,868.20	1,876.20	1,837.40	1,844.05	IDNR4SHRT	14.81	740	55,233
3-May-04	1,796.10	1,801.45	1,742.80	1,766.70	TTATSHRT	20.42	1,021	56,253
4-May-04	1,769.10	1,803.15	1,768.80	1,793.10	TTAJLNG	6.31	315	56,569
12-May-04	1,699.25	1,721.35	1,689.85	1,711.10	TTAJLNG	-5.14	-257	56,312
14-May-04	1,717.05	1,722.80	1,566.95	1,582.40	DOJISHRT	117.48	5,874	62,186
17-May-04	1,582.50	1,583.80	1,292.20	1,388.75	GUTRTSHRT	177.93	8,896	71,082
24-May-04	1,563.65	1,613.60	1,563.05	1,608.85	BMFLNG	13.93	696	71,778
31-May-04	1,507.05	1,509.05	1,456.20	1,483.60	TTATSHRT	15.91	796	72,574
9-Jun-04	1,550.45	1,561.60	1,541.60	1,548.30	IDNR4SHRT	-5.60	-280	72,294
14-Jun-04	1,508.15	1,509.60	1,474.65	1,481.35	TTATSHRT	19.26	963	73,257
24-Jun-04	1,445.35	1,474.30	1,437.90	1,470.75	TTAJLNG	10.95	547	73,804
1-Jul-04	1,506.65	1,539.15	1,504.55	1,537.20	ODLNG	15.48	774	74,578
20-Jul-04	1,571.70	1,581.05	1,555.55	1,566.10	FALTURTSHRT	13.46	673	75,251
3-Aug-04	1,639.95	1,648.35	1,626.30	1,630.60	FALTURTSHRT	17.55	877	76,129
16-Aug-04	1,597.50	1,603.20	1,582.35	1,599.15	TTATSHRT	-9.64	-482	75,647
17-Aug-04	1,624.00	1,628.45	1,597.45	1,604.35	DOJISHRT	3.41	171	75,818

(Contd . . .)

Table 28.14 (contd.)
Results for All Gap Patterns Combined

Date	Open	High	Low	Close	Pattern	Profit / Loss (Points)	Profit/ Loss (₹)	Cumulative Profit
27-Sep-04	1,722.40	1,726.15	1,707.95	1,717.50	TTATSHRT	-3.71	-186	75,632
5-Oct-04	1,805.85	1,816.55	1,798.60	1,812.45	FALTURTSHRT	2.43	121	75,753
25-Oct-04	1,780.00	1,783.55	1,753.50	1,757.25	TTATSHRT	13.85	692	76,446
8-Dec-04	1,994.15	2,009.70	1,973.15	1,977.95	DOJISHRT	-3.74	-187	76,259
14-Dec-04	1,985.20	2,008.80	1,972.85	2,006.80	IDNR4SHRT	-31.53	-1,576	74,683
13-Jan-05	1,922.50	1,963.40	1,916.95	1,954.55	TTAJLNG	12.83	641	75,324
24-Jan-05	1,925.30	1,932.75	1,902.90	1,909.00	TTATSHRT	6.67	334	75,657
25-Jan-05	1,908.85	1,934.25	1,894.40	1,931.85	TTAJLNG	3.91	196	75,853
27-Jan-05	1,931.90	1,961.75	1,929.00	1,955.00	ODLNG	3.78	189	76,042
28-Jan-05	1,955.25	2,014.25	1,950.85	2,008.30	BMFLNG	13.94	697	76,739
31-Jan-05	2,008.45	2,060.40	2,006.35	2,057.60	BMFLNG	8.98	449	77,188
7-Feb-05	2,097.45	2,098.00	2,049.85	2,055.10	DOJISHRT	21.38	1,069	78,257
21-Feb-05	2,055.15	2,065.75	2,039.90	2,043.20	TTATSHRT	1.67	84	78,341
28-Feb-05	2,061.20	2,106.20	2,047.70	2,103.25	BMFLNG	0.83	41	78,382
8-Mar-05	2,160.65	2,173.85	2,154.00	2,168.95	FALTURTSHRT	2.50	125	78,507
11-Apr-05	2,032.75	2,033.00	2,001.85	2,008.20	TTATSHRT	14.39	719	79,227
15-Apr-05	2,022.50	2,022.50	1,952.75	1,956.30	DOJISHRT	45.98	2,299	81,525
18-Apr-05	1,955.50	1,959.25	1,914.85	1,927.80	TURSHRT	17.92	896	82,421
20-Apr-05	1,908.50	1,941.85	1,902.90	1,929.70	TTAJLNG	2.12	106	82,527
24-May-05	2,016.00	2,031.90	2,009.55	2,028.60	FALTURTSHRT	-2.52	-126	82,401
22-Aug-05	2,383.45	2,403.45	2,355.75	2,367.85	TTATSHRT	3.68	184	82,585
29-Aug-05	2,359.20	2,365.85	2,312.60	2,337.65	DOJISHRT	-2.04	-102	82,483
20-Sep-05	2,567.20	2,582.80	2,546.60	2,578.00	FALTURTSHRT	2.04	102	82,585
26-Sep-05	2,477.85	2,560.85	2,477.85	2,557.35	BMFLNG	29.94	1,497	84,082
10-Oct-05	2,577.10	2,595.15	2,561.00	2,566.85	TTATSHRT	-2.64	-132	83,950
17-Oct-05	2,488.40	2,498.60	2,459.50	2,485.15	TTATSHRT	-9.19	-460	83,491
18-Oct-05	2,485.25	2,517.70	2,452.50	2,468.20	DOJISHRT	-7.80	-390	83,101
21-Oct-05	2,397.85	2,447.85	2,384.05	2,443.75	TTAJLNG	21.92	1,096	84,197
28-Oct-05	2,352.65	2,355.15	2,307.45	2,316.05	TURSHRT	24.84	1,242	85,439
18-Nov-05	2,604.00	2,632.35	2,595.15	2,620.05	ODLNG	-9.99	-499	84,939
5-Dec-05	2,697.60	2,710.65	2,654.35	2,660.50	DOJISHRT	10.12	506	85,445

(Contd . . .)

Table 28.14 (contd.)

Results for All Gap Patterns Combined

Date	Open	High	Low	Close	Pattern	Profit / Loss (Points)	Profit/ Loss (₹)	Cumulative Profit
9-Dec-05	2,706.75	2,761.10	2,698.00	2,756.45	BMFLNG	-4.44	-222	85,224
13-Dec-05	2,776.80	2,815.30	2,764.65	2,812.30	FALTURTSHRT	-21.62	-1,081	84,143
16-Jan-06	2,851.35	2,855.70	2,824.05	2,833.10	TTATSHRT	3.99	200	84,342
17-Feb-06	3,021.65	3,038.80	2,976.70	2,981.50	DOJISHRT	9.93	497	84,839
20-Feb-06	2,982.35	3,010.65	2,955.85	3,005.85	TTATSHRT	-38.41	-1,921	82,919
25-Apr-06	3,548.80	3,552.65	3,433.55	3,462.65	IDNR4SHRT	68.41	3,420	86,339
9-May-06	3,694.65	3,725.40	3,655.65	3,720.55	FALTURTSHRT	-7.43	-371	85,968
10-May-06	3,720.75	3,758.05	3,717.25	3,754.25	ODLNG	-3.71	-185	85,782
15-May-06	3,651.00	3,653.00	3,482.85	3,502.95	TTATSHRT	129.80	6,490	92,272
19-May-06	3,391.85	3,493.05	3,205.25	3,246.90	GUTRTSHRT	111.03	5,552	97,823
22-May-06	3,254.30	3,313.90	2,896.40	3,081.35	GUTRTSHRT	0.00		97,823
22-May-06	3,254.30	3,313.90	2,896.40	3,081.35	TTATSHRT	156.70	7,834	1,05,657
23-May-06	3,068.60	3,221.05	2,997.35	3,199.35	TTAJLNG	100.06	5,003	1,10,661
2-Jun-06	2,961.50	3,099.35	2,940.20	3,091.35	TTAJLNG	-144.70	-7,233	1,03,428
2-Jun-06	2,961.50	3,099.35	2,940.20	3,091.35	TURSHRT	0.00		1,03,428
9-Jun-06	2,721.20	2,875.75	2,707.85	2,866.30	TTAJLNG	117.89	5,894	1,09,322
15-Jun-06	2,634.10	2,814.15	2,634.10	2,798.80	TTAJLNG	138.36	6,918	1,16,240
16-Jun-06	2,799.85	2,960.15	2,799.85	2,890.35	BMFLNG	34.50	1,725	1,17,965
22-Jun-06	2,923.75	3,017.65	2,923.75	2,994.75	ODLNG	41.76	2,088	1,20,053
4-Jul-06	3,151.05	3,177.40	3,130.30	3,138.65	FALTURTSHRT	28.16	1,408	1,21,461
17-Jul-06	3,123.65	3,125.10	2,999.35	3,007.55	TTATSHRT	100.48	5,024	1,26,485
20-Jul-06	2,943.65	3,041.25	2,943.65	3,023.05	ODLNG	49.96	2,498	1,28,983
31-Jul-06	3,131.35	3,179.70	3,110.60	3,143.20	ODLNG	-19.46	-973	1,28,010
29-Aug-06	3,405.05	3,434.95	3,396.10	3,425.70	FALTURTSHRT	-3.62	-181	1,27,829
19-Sep-06	3,493.50	3,514.95	3,438.80	3,457.35	FALTURTSHRT	53.62	2,681	1,30,510
20-Sep-06	3,457.85	3,509.85	3,419.75	3,502.80	ODLNG	10.37	519	1,31,028
26-Sep-06	3,523.70	3,576.75	3,517.15	3,571.75	ODLNG	12.81	641	1,31,669
12-Oct-06	3,562.55	3,626.80	3,545.95	3,621.05	ODLNG	22.87	1,144	1,32,813
23-Oct-06	3,683.40	3,690.85	3,651.20	3,657.30	TTATSHRT	7.68	384	1,33,197
7-Nov-06	3,812.15	3,840.45	3,789.40	3,798.75	FALTURTSHRT	32.46	1,623	1,34,820
14-Nov-06	3,862.00	3,883.00	3,850.75	3,865.90	FALTURTSHRT	15.41	770	1,35,590

(Contd . . .)

Table 28.14 (contd.)
Results for All Gap Patterns Combined

Date	*Open*	*High*	*Low*	*Close*	*Pattern*	*Profit / Loss (Points)*	*Profit/ Loss (₹)*	*Cumulative Profit*
5-Dec-06	4,001.25	4,033.20	4,001.25	4,015.75	FALTURTSHRT	5.51	275	1,35,866
11-Dec-06	3,961.90	3,965.05	3,798.30	3,849.50	TTATSHRT	92.59	4,630	1,40,495
13-Dec-06	3,716.75	3,777.60	3,657.65	3,765.20	TTAJLNG	11.28	564	1,41,059
8-Jan-07	3,983.30	3,987.45	3,913.00	3,933.40	TTATSHRT	29.98	1,499	1,42,559
12-Jan-07	3,944.55	4,059.15	3,944.55	4,052.45	BMFLNG	29.01	1,450	1,44,009
12-Feb-07	4,187.20	4,187.20	4,044.35	4,058.30	TTATSHRT	107.96	5,398	1,49,407
23-Feb-07	4,046.00	4,065.45	3,918.20	3,938.95	GUTRTSHRT	66.59	3,330	1,52,737
26-Feb-07	3,939.10	3,958.90	3,856.70	3,942.00	GUTRTSHRT	0.00		1,52,737
26-Feb-07	3,939.10	3,958.90	3,856.70	3,942.00	TTATSHRT	-22.6	-1,130	1,51,607
28-Feb-07	3,893.40	3,893.40	3,674.85	3,745.30	IDNR4SHRT	128.63	6,432	1,58,039
5-Mar-07	3,726.50	3,726.65	3,554.50	3,576.50	TURSHRT	131.37	6,568	1,64,607
8-Mar-07	3,627.25	3,779.50	3,626.80	3,761.65	ODLNG	98.13	4,906	1,69,513
14-Mar-07	3,768.40	3,768.40	3,623.00	3,641.10	IDNR4SHRT	108.46	5,423	1,74,936
9-Apr-07	3,752.90	3,850.90	3,747.25	3,843.50	BMFLNG	15.54	777	1,75,713
31-May-07	4,250.25	4,306.75	4,250.25	4,295.80	ODLNG	3.05	152	1,75,866
11-Jun-07	4,183.75	4,205.20	4,134.95	4,145.60	TTATSHRT	17.23	862	1,76,727
24-Jul-07	4,620.05	4,647.95	4,609.75	4,620.75	FALTURTSHRT	22.40	1,120	1,77,847
16-Aug-07	4,366.00	4,366.00	4,171.15	4,178.60	DOJISHRT	143.74	7,187	1,85,034
17-Aug-07	4,171.10	4,171.10	4,002.20	4,108.05	TURSHRT	42.19	2,110	1,87,144
30-Aug-07	4,360.35	4,422.30	4,359.75	4,412.30	ODLNG	8.35	417	1,87,561
19-Sep-07	4,550.25	4,739.00	4,550.25	4,732.35	ODLNG	136.60	6,830	1,94,391
8-Oct-07	5,186.25	5,249.30	5,024.75	5,085.10	TTATSHRT	75.22	3,761	1,98,152
15-Oct-07	5,428.35	5,682.65	5,419.90	5,670.40	ODLNG	187.77	9,388	2,07,541
22-Oct-07	5,202.75	5,247.40	5,070.90	5,184.00	TTATSHRT	-7.26	-363	2,07,177
30-Oct-07	5,917.55	5,976.00	5,833.90	5,868.75	FALTURTSHRT	78.39	3,919	2,11,097
8-Nov-07	5,779.30	5,780.80	5,646.75	5,698.75	DOJISHRT	22.76	1,138	2,12,235
12-Nov-07	5,660.60	5,660.60	5,477.50	5,617.10	TTATSHRT	15.20	760	2,12,994
20-Nov-07	5,911.25	5,923.70	5,755.80	5,780.90	DOJISHRT	71.24	3,562	2,16,556
23-Nov-07	5,524.30	5,638.60	5,514.75	5,608.60	TTAJLNG	29.06	1,453	2,18,009
26-Nov-07	5,611.30	5,772.55	5,608.95	5,731.70	BMFLNG	8.17	409	2,18,418
29-Nov-07	5,617.80	5,725.00	5,612.10	5,634.60	ODLNG	-39.38	-1,969	2,16,449

(Contd . . .)

Table 28.14 (contd.)
Results for All Gap Patterns Combined

Date	Open	High	Low	Close	Pattern	Profit / Loss (Points)	Profit/ Loss (₹)	Cumulative Profit
17-Dec-07	6,037.95	6,039.95	5,740.60	5,777.00	TTATSHRT	230.76	11,538	2,27,987
24-Dec-07	5,771.30	6,001.05	5,771.30	5,985.10	BMFLNG	98.37	4,919	2,32,906
15-Jan-08	6,226.35	6,260.45	6,053.30	6,074.25	DOJISHRT	89.84	4,492	2,37,397
21-Jan-08	5,705.00	5,705.00	4,977.10	5,208.80	TURSHRT	0.00		2,37,397
21-Jan-08	5,705.00	5,705.00	4,977.10	5,208.80	TTATSHRT	467.70	23,384	2,60,781
23-Jan-08	4,903.05	5,328.05	4,891.60	5,203.40	TTAJLNG	251.32	12,566	2,73,347
6-Feb-08	5,470.40	5,470.40	5,257.05	5,322.55	IDNR4SHRT	120.50	6,025	2,79,372
11-Feb-08	5,120.55	5,126.40	4,803.60	4,857.00	DOJISHRT	0.00		2,79,372
11-Feb-08	5,120.55	5,126.40	4,803.60	4,857.00	TTATSHRT	237.90	11,897	2,91,269
12-Feb-08	4,877.85	4,949.60	4,820.45	4,838.25	TTAJLNG	-88.38	-4,419	2,86,851
13-Feb-08	4,836.55	4,986.55	4,836.55	4,929.45	TTAJLNG	44.53	2,227	2,89,077
15-Feb-08	5,202.85	5315.40	5,104.75	5,302.90	BMFLNG	-4.01	-200	2,88,877
26-Feb-08	5,200.80	5,281.20	5,200.80	5,270.05	ODLNG	17.24	862	2,89,739
7-Mar-08	4,918.30	4,918.30	4,672.25	4,771.60	IDNR4SHRT	122.11	6,105	2,95,844
10-Mar-08	4,767.80	4,814.95	4,620.50	4,800.40	TURSHRT	-56.44	-2,822	2,93,022
17-Mar-08	4,745.45	4,745.45	4,482.10	4,503.10	IDNR4SHRT	218.62	10,931	3,03,954
9-Apr-08	4,707.05	4,758.25	4,667.50	4,747.05	IDNR4SHRT	-63.54	-3,177	3,00,777
22-Apr-08	5,037.05	5,074.25	4,994.05	5,049.30	FALTURTSHRT	12.94	647	3,01,424
12-May-08	4,981.00	5,021.75	4,913.80	5,012.65	TTATSHRT	-56.55	-2,828	2,98,596
26-May-08	4,953.60	4,953.60	4,858.00	4,875.05	GUTRTSHRT	0.00		2,98,596
26-May-08	4,953.60	4,953.60	4,858.00	4,875.05	TTATSHRT	53.8	2,689	3,01,285
27-May-08	4,877.15	4,932.00	4,846.20	4,859.80	TTAJLNG	-66.12	-3,306	2,97,979
28-May-08	4,862.70	4,926.90	4,835.65	4,918.35	TTAJLNG	7.02	351	2,98,330
2-Jun-08	4,869.25	4,908.80	4,713.00	4,739.60	IDNR4SHRT	105.30	5,265	3,03,595
5-Jun-08	4,586.95	4,690.60	4,536.25	4,676.95	TTAJLNG	44.13	2,207	3,05,802
11-Jun-08	4,469.65	4,541.05	4,468.05	4,523.60	TTAJLNG	9.25	463	3,06,264
13-Jun-08	4,539.50	4,563.35	4,491.35	4,517.10	DOJISHRT	-23.00	-1,150	3,05,115
23-Jun-08	4,351.15	4,351.15	4,225.50	4,266.40	GUTRTSHRT	0.00		3,05,115
23-Jun-08	4,351.15	4,351.15	4,225.50	4,266.40	TTATSHRT	63.00	3,150	3,08,264
25-Jun-08	4,189.60	4,264.55	4,093.20	4,252.65	TTAJLNG	21.15	1,058	3,09,322
30-Jun-08	4,136.25	4,163.00	4,021.70	4,040.55	TURSHRT	75.02	3,751	3,13,073

(Contd . . .)

Table 28.14 (contd.)

Results for All Gap Patterns Combined

Date	Open	High	Low	Close	Pattern	Profit / Loss (Points)	Profit/ Loss (₹)	Cumulative Profit
2-Jul-08	3,895.30	4,107.15	3,848.25	4,093.35	TTAJLNG	159.10	7,955	3,21,028
11-Jul-08	4,166.00	4,215.50	4,014.45	4,049.00	DOJISHRT	75.34	3,767	3,24,795
16-Jul-08	3,861.55	3,920.05	3,790.20	3,816.70	TTAJLNG	-83.47	-4,173	3,20,622
17-Jul-08	3,823.15	3,968.75	3,823.15	3,947.20	TTAJLNG	85.82	4,291	3,24,913
18-Jul-08	3,962.95	4,110.55	3,926.30	4,092.25	BMFLNG	50.04	2,502	3,27,415
12-Aug-08	4,620.95	4,649.85	4,525.75	4,552.25	FALTURTSHRT	91.80	4,590	3,32,005
18-Aug-08	4,430.70	4,447.40	4,379.85	4,393.05	TTATSHRT	15.50	775	3,32,780
10-Sep-08	4,467.50	4,467.50	4,382.35	4,400.25	IDNR4SHRT	44.91	2,246	3,35,025
15-Sep-08	4,231.95	4,237.25	3,955.40	4,072.90	TTATSHRT	137.89	6,895	3,41,920
29-Sep-08	3,990.20	3,997.55	3,777.30	3,850.05	GUTRTSHRT	0.00		3,41,920
29-Sep-08	3,990.20	3,997.55	3,777.30	3,850.05	TTATSHRT	120.20	6,010	3,47,930
30-Sep-08	3,848.70	3,966.85	3,715.05	3,921.20	TTAJLNG	34.01	1,701	3,49,630
6-Oct-08	3,817.30	3,820.85	3,581.60	3,602.35	TURSHRT	195.86	9,793	3,59,424
10-Oct-08	3,502.05	3,502.05	3,198.95	3,279.95	TURSHRT	204.59	10,229	3,69,653
17-Oct-08	3,269.05	3,335.95	3,046.60	3,074.35	TURSHRT	178.35	8,918	3,78,571
20-Oct-08	3,108.20	3,238.40	3,058.95	3,122.80	ODLNG	-45.70	-2,284	3,76,287
20-Oct-08	3,108.20	3,238.40	3,058.95	3,122.80	GUTRTSHRT	0.00		3,76,287
20-Oct-08	3,108.20	3,238.40	3,058.95	3,122.80	TTATSHRT	0.00		3,76,287
24-Oct-08	2,936.25	2,936.25	2,525.05	2,584.00	TURSHRT	337.57	16,878	3,93,165
27-Oct-08	2,583.75	2,585.30	2,252.75	2,524.20	TURSHRT	0.00		3,93,165
27-Oct-08	2,583.75	2,585.30	2,252.75	2,524.20	TTATSHRT	46.60	2,332	3,95,497
28-Oct-08	2,526.20	2,695.95	2,526.20	2,684.60	TTAJLNG	133.14	6,657	4,02,154
10-Nov-08	2,973.30	3,161.25	2,973.30	3,148.25	BMFLNG	0.00		4,02,154
10-Nov-08	2,973.30	3,161.25	2,973.30	3,148.25	ODLNG	145.20	7,261	4,09,414
17-Nov-08	2,813.40	2,835.70	2,694.50	2,799.55	TTATSHRT	-0.22	-11	4,09,404
18-Nov-08	2,802.45	2,802.45	2,664.30	2,683.15	DOJISHRT	91.28	4,564	4,13,967
18-Dec-08	2,955.35	3,072.55	2,922.65	3,060.75	ODLNG	75.85	3,792	4,17,760
29-Dec-08	2,857.15	2,931.80	2,812.90	2,922.20	TTATSHRT	-79.34	-3,967	4,13,793
5-Jan-09	3,058.75	3,131.95	3,056.45	3,121.45	BMFLNG	1.52	76	4,13,869
6-Jan-09	3,121.50	3,141.80	3,056.10	3,112.80	FALTURTSHRT	24.31	1,215	4,15,085
12-Jan-09	2,868.85	2,869.20	2,748.55	2,773.10	TTATSHRT	81.41	4,070	4,19,155

(Contd . . .)

Table 28.14 (contd.)

Results for All Gap Patterns Combined

Date	*Open*	*High*	*Low*	*Close*	*Pattern*	*Profit / Loss (Points)*	*Profit/ Loss (₹)*	*Cumulative Profit*
14-Jan-09	2,748.40	2,853.25	2,748.40	2,835.30	TTAJLNG	59.42	2,971	4,22,126
27-Jan-09	2,686.05	2,777.30	2,685.25	2,771.35	ODLNG	58.44	2,922	4,25,048
20-Feb-09	2,789.30	2,789.30	2,709.30	2,736.45	IDNR4SHRT	38.90	1,945	4,26,993
4-Mar-09	2,611.95	2,655.70	2,611.95	2,645.20	TTAJLNG	7.13	357	4,27,349
6-Mar-09	2,576.75	2,628.10	2,539.45	2,620.15	ODLNG	-69.2	-3,458	4,23,891
6-Mar-09	2,576.75	2,628.10	2,539.45	2,620.15	GUTRTSHRT	0.00		4,23,891
2-Apr-09	3,061.05	3,228.75	3,061.05	3,211.05	ODLNG	119.39	5,969	4,29,860
21-Apr-09	3,376.85	3,414.70	3,309.35	3,365.30	DOJISHRT	-22.22	-1,111	4,28,749
4-May-09	3,478.70	3,664.50	3,478.70	3,654.00	BMFLNG	105.73	5,286	4,34,036
18-May-09	3,673.15	4,384.30	3,673.15	4,323.15	BMFLNG	576.54	28,827	4,62,863
26-May-09	4,239.55	4,256.05	4,092.25	4,116.70	DOJISHRT	80.45	4,023	4,66,885
2-Jun-09	4,530.45	4,586.40	4,451.30	4,525.25	FALTURTSHRT	27.85	1,393	4,68,278
5-Jun-09	4,573.30	4,636.85	4,561.95	4,586.90	ODLNG	-32.13	-1,607	4,66,671
12-Jun-09	4,637.55	4,693.20	4,566.15	4,583.40	IDNR4SHRT	30.96	1,548	4,68,219
15-Jun-09	4,584.65	4,601.05	4,469.60	4,484.00	TTATSHRT	77.73	3,886	4,72,106

Want to see the performance summary when all the gap patterns are combined together. Here it is (Table 28.15):

Table 28.15

Gap Patterns Combined Performance Summary

Total net profit	₹ 472,106		
Gross profit	₹ 559,947	Gross loss	₹ -87,841
Total # of trades	321	Percent profitable	71%
Number of winning trades	228	Number of losing trades	93
Largest winning trade	₹ 28,827	Largest losing trade	₹ -7,233
Largest winning trade %	15.4%	Largest losing trade %	-3.4%
Average winning trade	₹ 2,456	Average losing trade	₹ -945
Average winning trade %	1.8%	Average losing trade %	-0.8%
Ratio avg win/avg loss	2.6		

(Contd . . .)

Table 28.15 (contd.)

Gap Patterns Combined Performance Summary

Ratio avg win/avg loss %	2.1		
Average profit per trade	₹ 1,471		
Average profit per trade %	1.0%		
Max consecutive winners	14	Max consecutive losers	5
Max drawdown	₹ 7,233	Max drawdown %	-3.4%
Profit factor	6.4		
Account size required	₹ 57,537	Return on account	820.5%
Luck factor	15.1		
Recovery factor	65.3		
Pessimistic Rate of Return	740.2%		
Sharpe ratio	1.3		
Accuracy	94%		

Table 28.16 reveals how the year wise break-up of returns would have been with all the gap patterns combined.

Table 28.16

Gap patterns combined Year-Wise Performance

Year	*Profit (₹)*	*NIFTY points Gain/Loss*	*No. of Trades*
2009	58,313	1,166	17
2008	1,80,887	3,618	50
2007	91,846	1,837	29
2006	56,917	1,138	30
2005	9,460	189	28
2004	24,843	497	30
2003	12,195	244	32
2002	2,774	55	29
2001	12,106	242	35
2000	22,765	455	43

Figure 28.1 provides a visual representation of the performance summary.

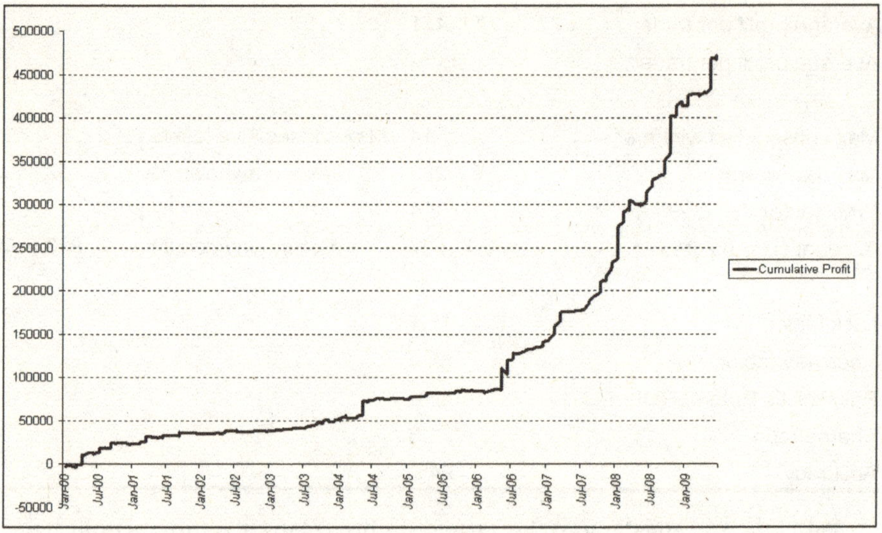

Figure 28.1: **Gap patterns combined equity growth**

Why did I stop at 9,441 points of gain, and not continue till we got closer to the 10,000-point mark? Well, I would leave hitting the 10k mark as an exercise for the reader to add one of my seasonality based pattern, that is to go long one day before Christmas and exit at the 5th trading day's close to make it to more than 10K mark. On a side note I would also caution the aggressive trader not to have too many patterns in the armoury. In real life, if too many patterns are clubbed together, we may be confronted with many conflicts with some patterns suggesting going long and other saying go short simultaneously.

Chapter 29

Walk Forward

When testing any trading strategy, the important point is how well it will perform on price data it has not been optimised on — that is, with out-of-sample data. In short, without out-of-sample testing, it's nothing more than a hope and a prayer to believe that system performance in the future will be anywhere near the optimised past performance. For example, it's possible to take a trading strategy with four independent variables, or parameters, and with hindsight, find the values for each of them that give the best (optimised) results on a specific historical period — say, the last three years (using daily price data). However, these optimised parameter values have, in essence, been cherry-picked for this particular data period, a process known as "curve-fitting", and are unlikely to perform as well on other historical test periods, or in actual trading in the future. It is same as picking the winning lottery numbers for a lottery which announced results yesterday.

However, there are ways to use optimisation effectively. One technique is called "walk-forward optimisation." The best-performing parameters are used to execute the system on a new, historical ("out-of-sample") data period after the sample period. This allows you to find out if the optimised parameters would have improved the results going forward, without cheating by using hindsight. Without further testing on out-of-sample data, there is no way to tell if the system will work in the future.

If the system performs well on the second data set (which represents new, "unseen" price action), the system is considered to have a better chance of working in real trading. The process is referred to as "walk-forward testing" because the system can be progressively applied to new data to see if it continues to perform. So I decided to perform a walk-forward optimisation from 1st of July 2009 to 31st May 2010.

Whenever performing out-of-sample testing, be prepared to expect the performance to be worse than the in-sample tests. This is not a reflection of the quality of the system. It may simply be because the system was developed and optimised on a different data set. Any way, let us put our Pivot Points Combined system through a walk forward test.

Pivot Points Combined

Here are the trade details for all the pivot points combined occurrences during the period 1st July 2009 till 31st October 2010:

Table 29.1
Pivot Points Combined during Walk Forward Period

Date	Gain/loss	Pattern	Profit/Loss	Cumulative Profit
13-Jul-09	137.35	LONGDBAM	6,868	6,868
17-Jul-09	127.30	LONGBM	6,365	13,233
23-Jul-09	44.80	LONGBTHU	2,240	15,473
31-Jul-09	74.95	LONGBM	3,747	19,220
07-Aug-09	43.75	SHORTMM	2,188	21,408
04-Sep-09	102.50	LONGBM	5,125	26,533
29-Oct-09	-38.85	LONGBOS	-1,943	24,590
03-Nov-09	146.90	LONGBOS	7,345	31,935
18-Dec-09	35.10	SHORTMM	1,755	33,690
08-Jan-10	-4.65	SHORTMM	-232	33,458
14-Jan-10	-7.70	LONGBTHU	-385	33,073
22-Jan-10	28.10	SHORTMMM	1,405	34,478
27-Jan-10	14.15	LONGBOS	707	35,185
05-Feb-10	-41.75	SHORTMMM	-2,088	33,098
26-Feb-10	94.70	LONGBM	4,735	37,833
01-Apr-10	77.90	LONGBTHU	3,895	41,728
30-Apr-10	-55.25	LONGBM	-2,763	38,965
06-May-10	-72.80	LONGBOS	-3,640	35,325
07-May-10	-175.55	SHORTMMM	-8,778	26,548
03-Jun-10	25.00	LONGBTHU	1,250	27,798
06-Aug-10	-46.90	SHORTMM	-2,345	25,453
13-Aug-10	-33.80	LONGBM	-1,690	23,763

(Contd . . .)

Table 28.15 (contd.)

Gap Patterns Combined Performance Summary

Ratio avg win/avg loss %	2.1		
Average profit per trade	₹ 1,471		
Average profit per trade %	1.0%		
Max consecutive winners	14	Max consecutive losers	5
Max drawdown	₹ 7,233	Max drawdown %	-3.4%
Profit factor	6.4		
Account size required	₹ 57,537	Return on account	820.5%
Luck factor	15.1		
Recovery factor	65.3		
Pessimistic Rate of Return	740.2%		
Sharpe ratio	1.3		
Accuracy	94%		

Table 28.16 reveals how the year wise break-up of returns would have been with all the gap patterns combined.

Table 28.16

Gap patterns combined Year-Wise Performance

Year	*Profit (₹)*	*NIFTY points Gain/Loss*	*No. of Trades*
2009	58,313	1,166	17
2008	1,80,887	3,618	50
2007	91,846	1,837	29
2006	56,917	1,138	30
2005	9,460	189	28
2004	24,843	497	30
2003	12,195	244	32
2002	2,774	55	29
2001	12,106	242	35
2000	22,765	455	43

Figure 28.1 provides a visual representation of the performance summary.

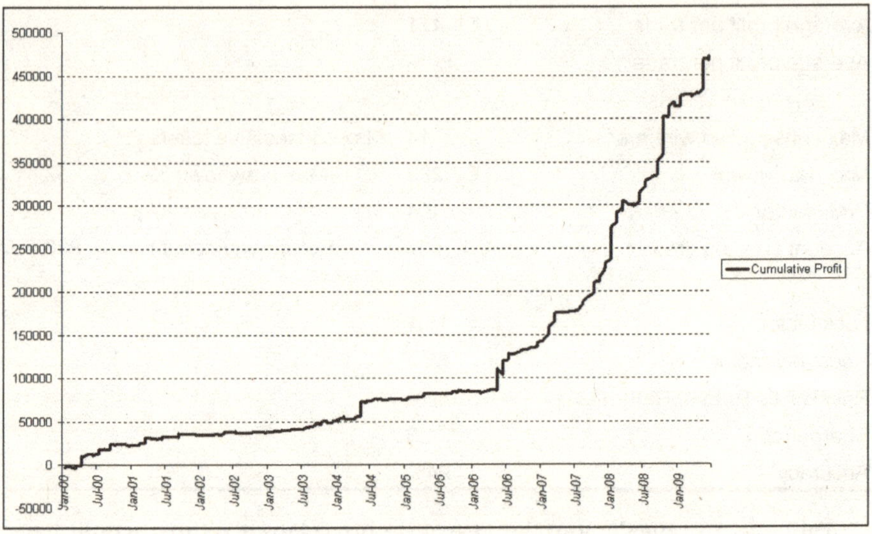

Figure 28.1: **Gap patterns combined equity growth**

Why did I stop at 9,441 points of gain, and not continue till we got closer to the 10,000-point mark? Well, I would leave hitting the 10k mark as an exercise for the reader to add one of my seasonality based pattern, that is to go long one day before Christmas and exit at the 5th trading day's close to make it to more than 10K mark. On a side note I would also caution the aggressive trader not to have too many patterns in the armoury. In real life, if too many patterns are clubbed together, we may be confronted with many conflicts with some patterns suggesting going long and other saying go short simultaneously.

Table: 29.2 (contd.)
Gap Trading Patterns Combined during Walk Forward Period

Date	*Gain/Loss*	*Pattern*	*Profit/Loss*	*Cumulative Profit*
26-Nov-1	23.74	GUTRTSHRT	1,187	25,539
29-Nov-10	-69.00	TURSHRT	-3,450	22,089
06-Dec-10	11.23	TTATSHRT	562	22,651
10-Dec-10	-125.16	TURSHRT	-6,258	16,393
10-Dec-10	38.74	TTAJLNG	1,937	18,330
10-Jan-11	108.94	TTATSHRT	5,447	23,777
11-Jan-11	-71.53	TTAJLNG	-3,576	20,201
12-Jan-11	5.20	TTAJLNG	260	20,460
14-Jan-11	40.03	GUTRTSHRT	2,001	22,462
28-Jan-11	45.71	GUTRTSHRT	2,286	24,747
31-Jan-11	-80.61	TURSHRT	-4,031	20,717
31-Jan-11	-80.61	TTATSHRT	-4,031	16,686
11-Feb-11	-116.45	TURSHRT	-5,823	10,864
11-Feb-11	38.15	TTAJLNG	1,908	12,771
14-Feb-11	62.35	ODLNG	3,117	15,889
28-Feb-11	-103.50	BMFLNG	-5,175	10,714
21-Mar-11	16.96	TTATSHRT	848	11,562
18-Apr-11	66.13	TTATSHRT	3,306	14,868
02-May-11	36.77	TTATSHRT	1,838	16,706
06-May-11	19.02	TTAJLNG	951	17,658
12-May-11	23.96	IDNR4SHRT	1,198	18,856

Well, I know, I know that you the reader would have observed our performance in 2010 in pivot point trading is a loss-making one and an almost zero performance (or broker getting rich performance as my colleagues in my office call) with the gap trading patterns in the 2011 year.

It's important not to over-react a single year with any form of system trading. So I'm not terribly concerned that the performance was subpar. 2010 was marked with a big switch in the Day-of-the-Week performance, that is unlike a Down Friday following with a Down Friday, the Down Friday usually led instead to an Up Monday, and the entire Nifty gains of 2010 could have been captured by playing this Down Friday phenomenon. But alas, how could I or anyone predict such a big switch. Still, I'm not inclined to change my approach due to one bad year. Of course, since all the patterns presented are open with no dubious rules the readers have the option of tweaking any of the patterns in any way they want. Want to know my trading losses in the last one year on Nifty futures trading, they are about 12% from the peak equity that I was managing, and translate into about an upper 8 digit INR. On the other hand, my brother who never was a short-term trader, upon reading and following few patterns in this book (I've asked him several times, but he refuses to divulge which pages those patterns are located) achieved 18% returns in the last one year . . . .

Then comes the June the month of monsoon!

Chapter 30

Sayonara

After you have read this material and studied some of the simple and yet profitable patterns you may be filled with enthusiasm and a belief that you are now ready to conquer the markets. However, before you set out to do that, I want to share with you another important rule. Be patient and do sufficient research instead getting prematurely tempted by low probability or uncertain profitability patterns. Don't artificially "force" trades just because Nifty hasn't formed a tradable pattern in your trading plan. There are enough markets to trade and with calm and patience you will almost always find profitable trading patterns at regular intervals.

I suggest that you take the time to re-read, review and yourself test all the patterns from this book. It is vital that you understand the patterns and their underlying concepts for yourself. Take the time to test the patterns and try multiple combinations of the various patterns discussed in Section 2. You must have confidence in the overall trading plan you develop. If you find a pattern in your trading plan that performs as you think it should, you are on the right track.

The Next Step

Now that you've completed reading this book for the first time, it is time to relax a bit as you have a lot of information to digest. For some readers, this may be an entirely different approach to viewing the market. If you happen to be one such, you may find it useful to go through the book again after some time gap. Then, start developing a trading plan.

Closing this book does not mean having to say good-bye. You may have questions that the book didn't answer. If so, you can always email me korareddy@yahoo.com. I will offer help if I can and if I know the answer.

If I manage to prevent even one new trader from making a costly mistake, then it would have been well worth my time.

You Need This, Too

Active traders have two ways of finding good set-ups: find the patterns on their own, or have someone else do it for them. If you want all the information on patterns discussed in this book, and many others, calculated for you every day and every minute during the trading hours, please visit www.stocksiq.in. This website reviews many patterns and identifies their occurrence during trading hours, thus providing traders that extra edge and intelligence of a detailed historical performance summary.

I wish you success. Trade intelligently!

Afterword: Listening to Amartya Sen

I consider Economics Nobel Laureate Amartya Sen to be one of India's finest intellectuals and if only I had any say in Indian politics, he would be my overwhelming choice to be India's next President. The following extracts are from his book, *The Argumentative Indian*:

> Not only are there persistent recurrences of severe hunger in particular regions (the fact that they don't grow into full-fledged famines does not arrest their local brutality), but there is also a gigantic prevalence of endemic hunger across much of India. Indeed, India does much worse in this respect than even Sub-Saharan Africa. Calculations of general under nourishment — what is sometimes called "protein-energy malnutrition" — is nearly twice as high in India as in Sub-Saharan Africa. [. . .] About half of all Indian children are, it appears, chronically undernourished, and more than half of all adult women suffer from anaemia. In maternal under nourishment as well as the incidence of underweight babies, and also in the frequency of cardiovascular diseases in later life (to which adults are particularly prone if nutritionally deprived in the womb), India's record is among the very worst in the world.

When one of the finest intellectuals said so, I felt I too needed to do something. I have, therefore decided to donate (10 + 3)%* of my earnings from the sales of this book to the Kolkata-based organisation called CINI

* Can't help it as I have this triskaidekaphobia.

(Child In Need Institute). And why to CINI? Because it has the following schemes:

Scheme B
Sponsorship of a month's supply of Nutrimix packets to malnourished children distributed during the Thursday clinics.

Scheme G
Donation towards Corpus Funds — interest accrued thereof will be used for malnutrition prevention and treatment of a child.

As is quite prevalent these days, some people might be tempted to either photocopy this book or buy a pirated copy to save some small amount of money. We are all human and get tempted off and on, so, here is the way to avoid guilt. If you have erred by unlawfully obtaining this book, please send some money to CINI and you will feel great satisfaction and joy.

Initial Protective Stop — An order placed right after a trade is entered in order to help control risk.

Inside Day (ID) — A day whose daily RANGE lies completely within the previous day's range; it's usually also a narrow range day.

Lap Down — A day whose open is below the previous day's CLOSE but not lower than the previous day's low.

Lap Up — A day whose open is higher than the previous day's CLOSE but not higher than the previous day's high.

Last Point of Support — A narrow, low volume price RANGE (possibly 2 Bar NR) that occurs just prior to the commencement of a mark up phase. The market is said to be in equilibrium at such a juncture.

Limit Order — An order to buy or sell at a specified price.

Long — A buy position that seeks to profit in anticipation of the market rising.

Lower High — A high that is lower than the previous day's high.

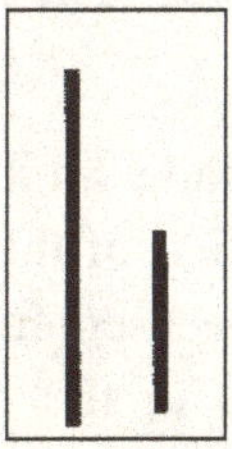

Lower Low — A low that is lower than the previous day's low.

Market — Any organized exchange where buyers and sellers can meet to exchange their goods or services.

Market Order — An order to be executed immediately at the asking price for buys and at the bid price for sales.

Moving Average — The average price of a security over a given period; for instance, a 10-day moving average would be the sum of the previous ten days' prices divided by 10.

Narrow Range (NR) — A smaller daily RANGE relative to that of the previous day.

Non-Trend Day — A day when the first hour's RANGE comprises the full day's range and all subsequent trades occur within the same initial range. Typically, characterized by a narrow daily range and low volume.

NR4 — A day whose RANGE is narrower than the range of each of the previous three days.

NR7 — A day whose range is narrower than the RANGE of each of the previous six days.

Open — The first price registered in the time period under consideration.

Opening Range (OR) — is the first thirty seconds of trading range of each trading day

Opening Range Breakout (ORB) — A trade with entry at a predetermined level above or below the opening range. When the predetermined amount (the STRETCH) is computed, a buy-stop is placed at that amount above the high of the opening range and a sell stop is placed at the same amount below the low of the opening RANGE. The first stop that is traded is the position and an ORB.

ORB Preference (ORBP) — A trade similar to the ORB but the only order entered is the stop in the direction of the entry. The protective stop is entered only after the trade has been entered. The exception to this is if the market trades to the STRETCH in the opposite direction first, then the ORBP is nullified and the resting order is cancelled.

Outside Day (OD) — A day when the high and low prices are, respectively, higher and lower than those of the preceding day.

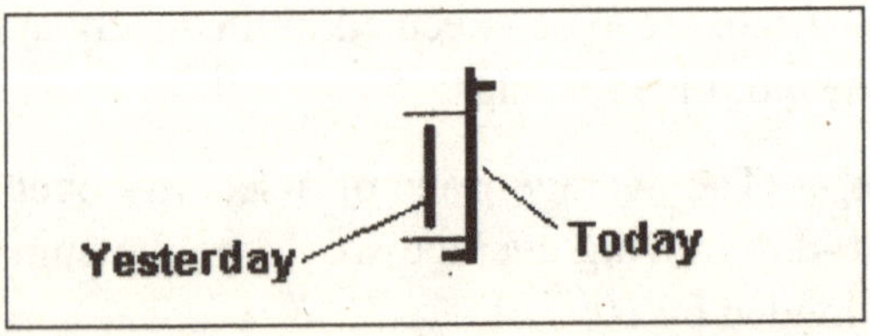

Pivot High — A high flanked by two LOWER HIGHS or two equal highs. In rare cases even three equal highs, flanked by two lower highs.

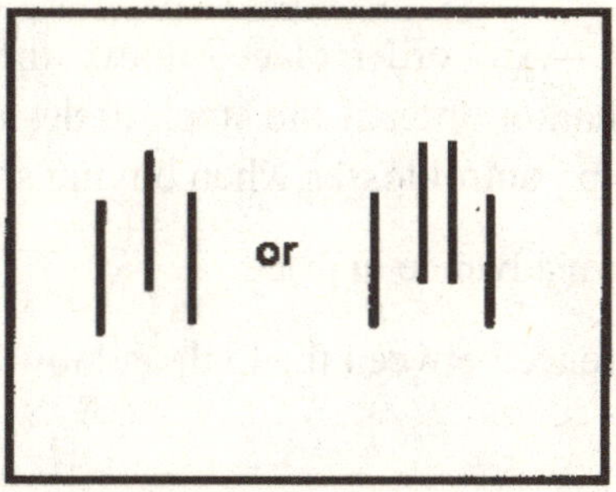

Pivot Low — A low flanked by two HIGHER LOWS or two equal lows; In rare cases, even three equal lows flanked by two higher lows.

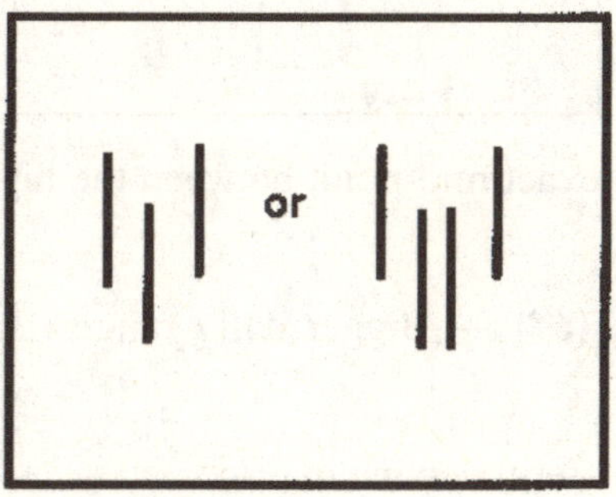

Poor Close — Market closing in the bottom 25% of its RANGE.

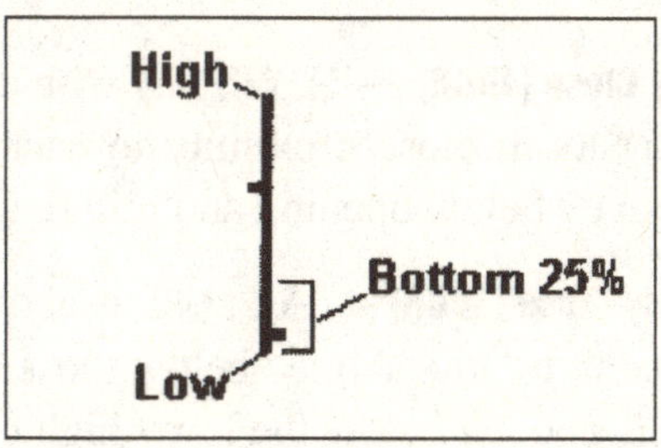

Preliminary Supply —High volume, on a wide spread day that produces a short-lived reaction in a mark up phase. This phase occurs before the buying climax and is the first sign of fresh supply.

Protective Buy Stop — An order placed above the current price of the stock. It becomes a market order if the stock trades at or above the specified price. Used to help control losses when shorting stocks.

Protective Sell Stop —An order placed above the current price of the stock. It becomes a market order if the stock trades at or above the specified price. Used to help control losses when buying stocks.

Rally — A short-term advance in price.

Range — The difference between the high and low of a given day.

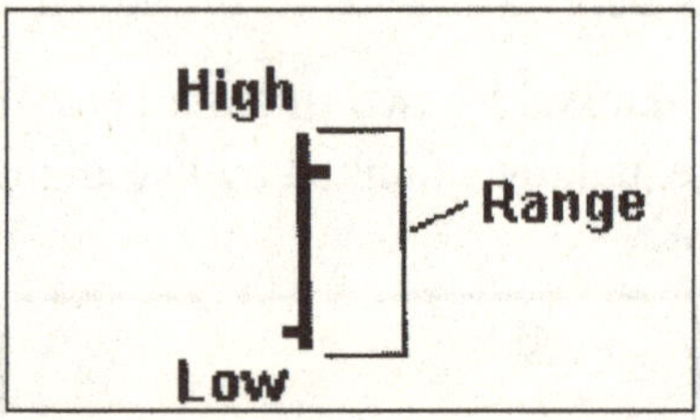

Range, Mid — The exact mid-point between the high and low of a given day.

Range, Wide Spread (WS) — Bigger daily range relative to the previous day.

Reaction — A short-term decline in price.

Resistance — Opposition to advancing prices caused by an increase in available supply.

Reversal — Four Day Close (4DCR) — A WS day with a close above / below the previous four CLOSES in close proximity to each other. Close of the WS day should be above / below opening and mid range.

Reversal — Three Day Close (3DCR) — A CLOSE is above / below the previous three days with its high / low above / below those of the previous three days. The low / high is above / below the low / high of the last three days. The close is above/below the OPEN and MID-RANGE with a (WS) bigger than the average of the last three days.

Reversal — Three Day High (3DHR) — Three NARROW RANGE days are followed by a wide spread day closing above / below the high / low of the three day period. CLOSE must be above the opening and the MID-RANGE for the day.

Shark — Two consecutive INSIDE DAYS.

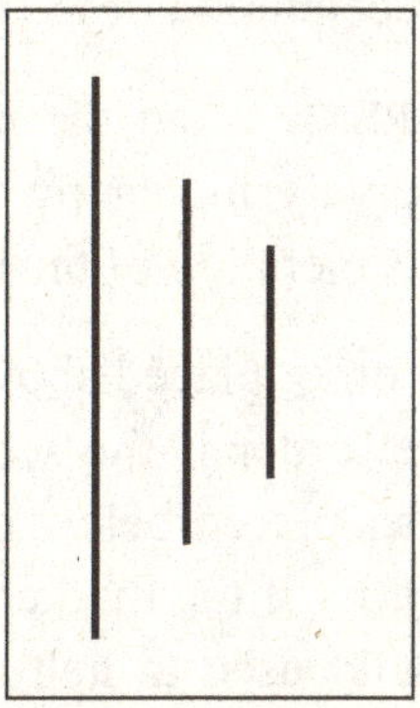

Short — A position that seeks to profit if a market / security drops in value. To sell.

Shakeout — A deliberately forced price reaction with the purpose of stimulating public selling in order to facilitate the accumulation of speculative positions.

Show of Strength (SOS) — A decisive rally after a secondary test of the low, taking the market above the high of the automatic rally, usually accompanied by higher volume than the previous rallies.

Show of Weakness (SOW) — A decisive break after a secondary test of the high, taking the market below the low of the automatic reaction, usually accompanied by higher volume than previous sell offs.

Spring — When price moves below a pivot bottom and a wide spread reversal ensues as follows:

- Two previous CLOSES are reversed;
- CLOSE is above pivot bottom;
- CLOSE is above opening and MID-RANGE;
- Daily RANGE is greater than the previous day's range.

Spring Board — A condition in the price movement of a market that has has been brought to point where it may move into a mark up or mark down period. A springboard can be recognized by the unusually NARROW RANGE relative to the previous day's action.

Stepping Down — In a DOWNTREND when the market holds similar sloping angles of resistance of successively lower pivot tops within the trend, generally, this indicates an acceleration of the existing downtrend.

Stepping Up — In an UPTREND when the market holds similar sloping angles of support of successively higher pivot bottoms within the trend, generally, this indicates an acceleration of the existing trend.

Stop Order — For buys, an order placed above the current price of the security that becomes a market order if the security trades at or above the order price. For sells, an order placed below the current price of the security that becomes a market order if the market trades at or below the order price. Stop orders are normally used to help control risk but can also be used to enter positions.

Stretch — The stretch is calculated by taking the 10 period SMA of the absolute difference between the OPEN and either the High or Low, whichever difference is smaller. .

Strong Close — Market / security closing in the top 25% of its RANGE.

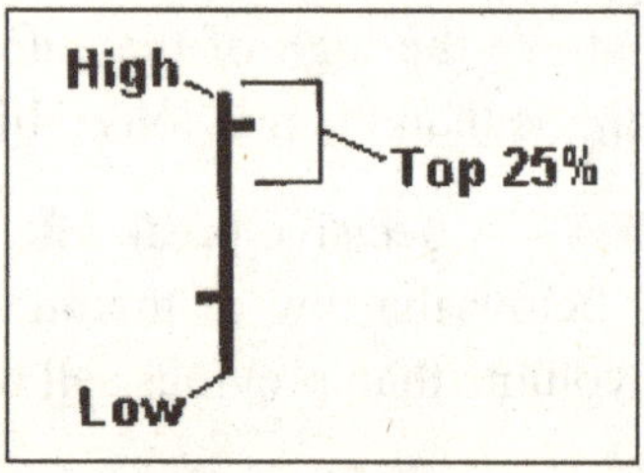

Supply — Securities available for sale in the market.

Support — Opposition to declining prices caused by an increase in available demand.

Tail — A period when the bulk of the trades and the close for the period are at one price extreme with very few trades at the other extreme of the range. Synonymous with spike, tails sometimes form upthrusts / SPRINGS. It is the precursor to most major REVERSALS.

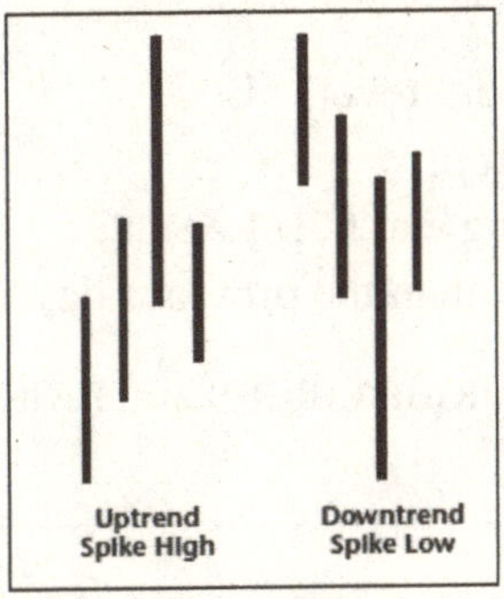

Tail Top or Bottom — Market closing higher / lower for three days in the top / bottom part of the trading range.

Terminal Shakeout — A spring-type action after the formation of a congestion area above and in the vicinity of an important pivot. The result is an extensive area of accumulation with long-term bullish implications.

Terminal Up thrust — A SPRING-type action after the formation of a congestion area above and in the vicinity of an important pivot top. The result is an extensive area of distribution with long-term bearish implications.

Trailing Stop — A stop adjusted higher for LONG positions, or lower for short positions, as the market moves in the trade's favour. Used for locking in profits when the market reverses.

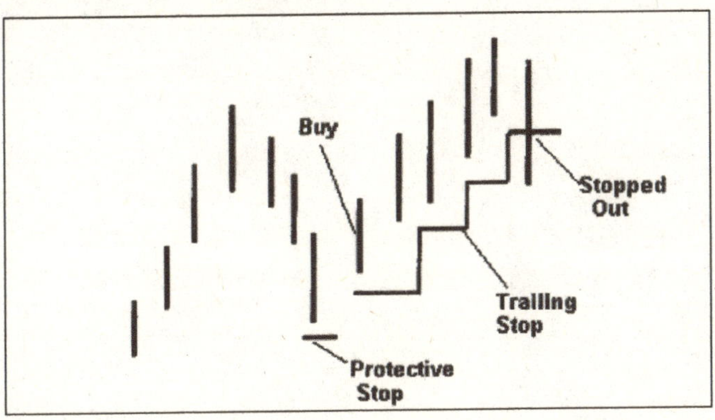

Trend Day — A wide spread day with the open and the close near opposite extremes of the day's RANGE.

Up thrust — An event when price moves above a pivot top and a wide spread REVERSAL ensues as follows:

- Two previous CLOSES are reversed;
- CLOSE is below pivot top;
- CLOSE is below opening and MID-RANGE;
- Daily RANGE is greater than the previous day's range.

Uptrend — A series of HIGHER HIGHS and HIGHER LOWS.

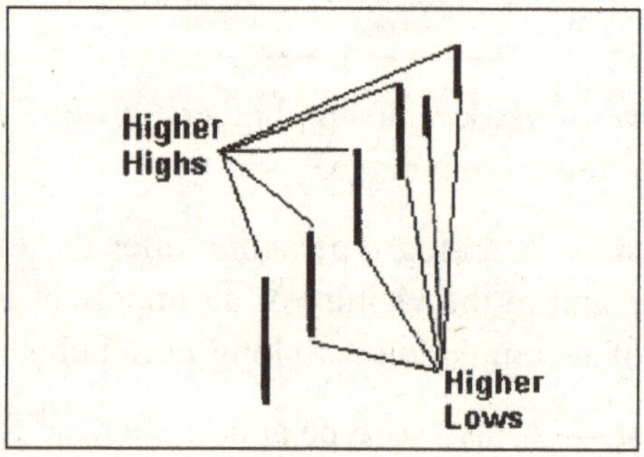

WS4 — A day with a RANGE that is larger than the range of any of the previous three days.

WS7 — A day with a RANGE that is larger than the range of any of the previous six days. It indicates momentum.

References

- Niederhoffer, Victor, *The Education of a Speculator.*[*]
- Niederhoffer, Victor and Laurel Kenner, *Practical Speculation.*[*]
- Crabel, Toby, *Day Trading with Short Term Price Patterns and Opening Range Breakout.*
- Crane, John, *Advanced Swing Trading: Strategies to Predict, Identify, and Trade Future Market Swings.*
- Covel, Michael W., *The Complete Turtle Trader.*
- Farley, Alan, *The Master Swing Trader: Tools and Techniques to Profit from Outstanding Short-Term Trading Opportunities.*
- Goodwin, Andrew, *Trading Secrets of the Inner Circle.*
- Kase, Cynthia, *Trading with the Odds: Using the Power of Statistics to Profit in the Futures Market.*
- Kaufman, Perry, *Trading Systems and Methods.*
- Landry, Dave, *Dave Landry on Swing Trading.*
- Lefèvre, Edwin, *Reminiscences of a Stock Operator.*
- Raschke, Linda Bradford, *Street Smarts: High Probability Short-Term Trading Strategies.*
- Maiello, Michael, *Buy the Rumour, Sell the Fact: 85 Maxims of Investing and What They Really Mean.*
- Nison, Steve, *Japanese Candlestick Charting Techniques.*
- Schwager, Jack, *Market Wizards.*
- Sun-Tzu, *The Art of War.*
- Williams, Larry, *Long-Term Secrets to Short-Term Trading.*

[*] These two books are on top of my reading list and other books are listed in the alphabetical order of author-wise.

Index

4-Year Cycle (Kitchin Wave), 189
54-Year Cycle (Kondratieff Wave), 189
9.2-Year Cycle (Juglar Wave), 189
24 Wild Swings, 159

Average Profit per Trade, 163

Backtesting, 162
Bank of England, 57
Bar Chart, 34-36, 268
Bear Hook, 147
Black Monday, 76
Black Swans (Events), 56
Black Thursday, 76
Bottoms, 38
Buffett, Warren, 19, 21, 55
Bull Hook, 147
Bullish and Bearish Signal Formations, 38
Bullish and Bearish Symmetrical Triangles, 38
Buy and Hold Nifty Strategy Performance Summary, 192
Buy and Hold Strategy, 191
Buying Back, 29

Candlestick Chart, 36
Candlesticks, Elements of, 37
Chart Patterns, 38, 51
Chart Types, 23, 34-39
Compounding, 192
Contract Size, 32
Contraction / Expansion, 91, 268
Crabel, Toby, 13, 57, 97, 148, 279
CRISIL, 31

Dave Landry on Swing Trading, 81, 279
Day of the Week Patterns, 70
– Close-to-Close for Each Day of the Week, 74
– Close-to-Close for Each Weekday if Close is Up, 75
– Close-to-Close for Each Weekday if the Close is Down, 75
– Close-to-Close Relationship for Declines by Weekday (in Percentage), 73
– Close-to-Close Relationship for Declines by Weekday, 72

– Close-to-Close Relationship for Rallies by Weekday (in Percentage), 72
– Close-to-Close Relationship for Rallies by Weekday, 72
– Open- to-Close Relationship for Rallies by Weekday (in Percentage), 71
– Open-to-Close for Each Day of the Week, 74
– Open-to-Close for Each Weekday if Open is Down, 75
– Open-to-Close for Each Weekday if Open is Up, 74
– Open-to-Close Relationship for Declines by Weekday (in Percentage), 71
– Open-to-Close Relationship for Declines by Weekday, 71
– Open-to-Close Relationship for Nifty Rallies by Weekday, 70

Day Trading with Short Term Price Patterns and Opening Range Breakout, 97, 148, 279
Day Trading, 25, 28
Derivative Contract, 30
Doji, 10, 54, 60, 133, 137-138, 148, 236-237, 242
Doji Day, 128-132, 134-136, 236
Doji Patterns, 128
– 1-Point Doji Performance of Nifty, 129
– 10% DBY Doji Open-to-Close Performance of Nifty, 135
– 10% Doji Performance of Nifty, 130
– 10% Doji Yesterday, Close-to-Close Performance of Nifty, 137
– 20% Doji +NR Performance of Nifty, 133
– 20% Doji +WS Performance of Nifty, 134
– 20% Doji Performance of Nifty, 131

Doji, Short Bias, 236
Dōjima Rice Exchange, 9, 30
Donchian, Richard Davoud, 78-79, 225
Double Tops and Bottoms, 38
Dow Jones Industrial Average (DJIA), 55, 76
Drawdown, 149, 158

Elder, Alexander, 49
Elliot Wave Theory (EWT), 47
Elliott Waves, 47
Elliott, Ralph Nelson, 47
Entry Orders,
– Selecting Suitable Entry Order, 41
– Types of, 40-41

Exit,
– Money-Management Exit, 42
– Profit Target Exit, 42
– Selection of, 43
– Strategies, 6, 42-43
– Time-Based Exit, 42
– Trading Exit, 42
– Types of, 92

Expiry Day, 32

Farley, Alan, 189
Fibonacci Numbers, 47

Full Gap Up, 81
Futures Industry Association (FIA), 32
Futures, 23, 31-33, 268, 279
- Origins of, 29-30

Gann Angles, 47-48
Gann Software, 49
Gann, W. D., 47-49, 177, 267
Gap,
- Gap Down, 81, 83-87, 269
- Gap Up, 81-82, 84-86, 226, 229
Gap Patterns, 84
- Buying Mondays and Fridays, 237-240
- Combined, 10, 259-261
- Distribution of Gaps and Laps in Nifty, 84
- Distribution of Nifty Gaps, 85
- Gap Down and a Bottom Range Open on Nifty, 89
- Gap Down and a Top Range Open on Nifty, 89
- Gap Down on Nifty, 86-87
- Gap Patterns Combined, 242
- Gap Up and a Bottom Range Open on Nifty, 89
- Gap Up and a Top Range Open on Nifty, 88
- Gap Up on Nifty, 85, 87
- Inside Day Pattern, 235
- Modified Three Tumbles and a Jump Pattern, 231
- Outside Day Pattern, 233, 272
- Short Bias Doji Pattern, 236
- Three Steps and a Stumble Pattern, 227
- Three Tumbles and a Jump Pattern, 230
- Turtle Short on a Gap Up Pattern, 226
- Turtle Short Pattern, 225
- Two Tumbles and a Jump Pattern, 229
- Two Tumbles, and Another Tumble Pattern, 232
Gap Trading, 81
Gap Trading Secrets, 181, 225
Gaps and Laps, 53, 81, 84, 123
Goodwin, Andrew, 13
Great Depression, 76
Gross Profit, 64

Hedgers, 30
High / Low ORB, 111
High / Low Patterns, *see* New High and New Low Patterns
High as Entry Reference, 124
Hook,
- Bear Hook, 174
- Bull Hook, 174
Hook Days, 147
Hook Observations, 147
Hummer, John, 57

ID, *see* Inside Day
Increased Leverage, 26
India Index Services and Products Ltd. (IISL), 31
Inside Day (ID), 7, 10, 54, 121, 235-236, 242, 271, 275

Inside Day (ID) Patterns, 121
- Close-to-Close Performance — Entry at ID's Close and Exit at the Next Day's Close, 126
- Close-to-Close Performance — Entry One Day After an ID, 126
- ID Open-to-Close; Low as Entry Reference, 125
- ID Open-to-Close Study When Open is in the Bottom Range, 124
- ID Open-to-Close Study, 122
- ID Open-to-Close Study, Open in the Top Range, 123
- ID Performance with Yesterday's High as a Reference Entry, 124
- ID Performance with Yesterday's Low as a Reference Entry, 125

Introduction to Objectivist Epistemology, 148

Jones, Paul Tudor, 179
Juglar, Clemant, 189
Juglar Wave, *see* 9.2-Year Cylce, 189

Kaufman's Formula, 157
Kaufman, Perry, 156, 159
Kitchin, Joseph, 189
Kitchin Wave, *see* 4-Year Cycle, 189
Kondratieff Wave, *see* 54-Year Cycle, 189

Lap Down, 81, 83-84, 271
Lap Up, 81-82, 84, 271
Limit Orders, 41, 42
Line Chart, 34 35
Liquidity, 32
Livermore, Jesse, 20, 22, 44, 181
Long Position, 29
Long-term Secrets to Short-term Trading, 96

Margin, 30, 167
Market Orders, 41
Market Structure, 23, 44
Market Type, 31
Maximum Drawdown, 163, 165
Midday Markets, 186
Minute and Mega Market Clock, 181, 183
Money Management Exit, 42
Monthly Characteristics, 9, 187
Murphy's Law, 52

Narrow Range (NR) Day, 91, 132
Narrow Range Patterns, *see* NR Patterns
NASDAQ, 55
National Index for Trading in Equity, or National Fifty, 31
National Stock Exchange (NSE), 31, 33, 146
New York Cotton Exchange, 174
New York Stock Exchange, 22
New High and New Low Patterns, 78
- 20-Day High and Low on Nifty, 79
- 20-Day Low Action on Nifty on Specific Weekdays, 80
- 20-Day High Action on Nifty on Specific Weekdays, 80

Niederhoffer, Victor, 56-57, 279
Nifty Cash Index, 64

Nifty Futures, 27-29, 31-32, 52, 140, 152, 157, 160, 195, 262
– Futures, Basics of, 31-32
– Futures Contract, 27
– Security Descriptor, 31-32
– Trading Patterns, 17, 196, 199
NR Patterns (Range Expansion and Contraction Patterns), 91
– NR Close-to-Close Observations on Nifty, 92
– NR Open-to-Close Observations on Nifty, 94
– NR4 Close-to-Close Study on Nifty, 99
– NR4 Open-to-Close Study on Nifty, 104
– NR7 Close-to-Close Study on Nifty, 102
– NR7 Open-to-Close Study on Nifty, 106
NR, *see* Narrow Range
NSE, *see* National Stock Exchange

Observing Tri-section, 142
Open and Close Patterns, 55
– Close to Close on Two Successive Days, 58
– Closes from Open When the Market Declined, 60
– Closes from Open When the Market Rallied, 59
– Open to Close in a Single Day, 58
Open and Close Patterns, Multiple Day, 62
– 2-, 3- and 4-Day Close-to-Close Patterns, 65
– 2-, 3- and 4-Day Open-to-Close Patterns, 67
– 5-Day Close-to-Close Patterns, 66
– 5-Day Open-to-Close Patterns, 68
Opening Range as Reference, 123
Opening Range Breakout (ORB), 53, 110, 135, 271, 279
Opening Range Breakout Patterns, 110
– High / Low ORB Patterns, 111
– Open-to-Close Patterns — Entry if Nifty Trades Above the Previous Day's High, 111
– Open-to-Close Patterns — Entry with Reference to the Previous Day's Low, 113
– Pivot Point Based ORB Patterns, 117
– Open-to-Close Patterns with a R1 Level as an Entry Point, 118
– Open-to-Close Patterns with a S1 Level as an Entry Point, 118
– Range ORB Patterns, 116
– Open-to-Close Patterns — Entry at Open Minus Yesterday's Range, 117
– Open-to-Close Patterns — Entry at Open plus Yesterday's Range, 116
– Stretch ORB Patterns, 114
– 2-, 3- and 4-Day Nifty Open-to-Close Patterns — Entry with Open plus Stretch as Reference, 114
– 2-, 3- and 4-Day Open-to-Close Patterns, Entry Reference as Open Minus Stretch, 115

Orders, Types of:
- Limit, 41
- Market, 41

ORB, *see* Opening Range Breakout
ORB Preference, 111, 272
ORB Strategy, 111-117
ORB Stretch, 110, 114-115

P&F Chart, 38, 39
Parekh, Ketan, 55
Partial Gap Up, 81
Pattern Overlap, 169
Payoff Ratio, 165
Penta-Section, 143-145
Perfectly Predicted Nifty Performance (January 2000 till June 2009), 194
Pessimistic Rate of Return, 167
Pessimistic Return on Margin (PROM), 167
Pinero, Sir Arthur Wing, 21
Pivot Patterns Combined, 211-220
Pivot Point Based ORB, 117
Pivot Point, Distributions of Nifty, 140
Pivot Point Trading Secrets, 141, 181, 196
Pivot Points, 110, 139-141, 196, 258
- Calculation of, 139

Pivot Points Combined, 258-259
Pivot Point Patterns, 139
- Buy When There is a Blood on the Street Pattern, 202
- Buy When There is a Blood on the Street (Tuesday) Pattern, 203
- Buy When There is a Blood on the Street (Tuesday — Modified) Pattern, 205
- Buying "Monday" Pattern, 206
- Buying "Thursday" — Modified Pattern, 208
- Buying "Thursday" Pattern, 207
- "Dip Buyer's Advantage" Monday Pattern, 209
- Manic Monday Pattern, 199
- Momentum-Aided Manic Monday Pattern, 201
- Nifty Close Possibilities if Market Traded above S1, S2 & S3, 141
- Nifty Closing Levels when Market Traded above R1, R2 & R3, 141
- Nifty OHLC *vis-à-vis* Pivot-Point Distributions, 140
- Pivot Patterns Combined, 211-220

Point and Figure Charts, 38
Practical Speculation, 57, 279
Price Bands, 32
Price Charts, 19, 38, 170
Price Fields, 37
Price Patterns, 16, 19, 21, 23, 50-53, 64, 97, 148, 279
- Short Term, 51-58

Profit Factor, 164
- Outlier Adjusted, 165

Profit per Trade, 64-65
Profit Target Exits, 42

Range, 51, 53, 88, 89, 91, 110, 116, 117, 121, 123-124, 127, 135, 139, 272, 274-275
Range Expansion and Contraction, 91
Range Expansion and Contraction Patterns, *see* NR Patterns, WS Trading Patterns

Table: 29.2 (contd.)

Gap Trading Patterns Combined during Walk Forward Period

Date	*Gain/Loss*	*Pattern*	*Profit/Loss*	*Cumulative Profit*
10-Aug-09	26.42	TTATSHRT	1,321	12,491
28-Aug-09	-2.93	ODLNG	-147	12,345
07-Sep-09	53.68	ODLNG	2,684	15,028
07-Sep-09	53.68	BMFLNG		15,028
22-Sep-09	-18.21	FALTURTSHRT	-911	14,118
30-Oct-09	-8.11	GUTRTSHRT		
30-Oct-09	-86.91	TTAJLNG	-4,346	9,772
04-Nov-09	97.83	TTAJLNG	4,891	14,663
18-Dec-09	3.88	DOJISHRT	194	14,857
21-Dec-09	6.13	TTATSHRT	307	15,164
29-Dec-09	18.70	FALTURTSHRT	935	16,099
11-Jan-10	-11.92	TTATSHRT	-596	15,503
25-Jan-10	1.48	TURSHRT	74	15,577
25-Jan-10	1.48	TTATSHRT		
28-Jan-10	-44.38	TTAJLNG	-2,219	13,358
03-Feb-10	52.54	ODLNG	2,627	15,985
08-Feb-10	-52.60	GUTRTSHRT	-2,630	13,355
08-Feb-10	-28.83	TTATSHRT		
19-Feb-10	17.96	IDNR4SHRT	898	12,812
05-Apr-10	24.09	BMFLNG	1,204	14,016
19-Apr-10	49.00	TTATSHRT	2,450	16,466
28-Apr-10	66.21	IDNR4SHRT	3,310	19,777
07-May-10	28.89	TURSHRT	1,444	21,221
19-May-10	94.80	DOJISHRT	4,740	25,961
21-May-10	-9.18	IDNR4SHRT	-459	25,502
15-Jun-10	4.96	FALTURTSHRT	248	25,750
23-Jun-10	-33.58	IDNR4SHRT	-1,679	24,071
25-Jun-10	-1.76	DOJISHRT	-88	23,983
09-Jul-10	2.28	BMFLNG	114	24,097
14-Sep-10	-6.45	FALTURTSHRT	-322	23,775
01-Oct-10	52.80	BMFLNG	2,640	26,414
18-Oct-10	6.24	TTATSHRT	312	26,726

(Contd . . .)

Table 29.1 (contd.)
Pivot Points Combined during Walk Forward Period

Date	*Gain/loss*	*Pattern*	*Profit/Loss*	*Cumulative Profit*
01-Oct-10	16.05	LONGBM	803	24,565
08-Oct-10	-32.40	SHORTMM	-1,620	22,945
21-Oct-10	-35.45	LONGBTHU	-1,772	21,173
19-Nov-10	-119.70	SHORTMMM	-5,985	15,188
25-Nov-10	9.25	LONGBOS	463	15,651
09-Dec-10	90.85	LONGBOS	4,543	20,193
30-Dec-10	32.65	LONGBTHU	1,633	21,826
31-Dec-10	23.10	LONGBM	1,155	22,981
11-Jan-11	109.15	LONGBOS	5,457	28,438
28-Jan-11	6.25	SHORTMMMM	313	28,751
31-Jan-11	-88.70	LONGDBAM	-4,435	24,316
01-Feb-11	14.80	LONGBOS	740	25,056
04-Feb-11	-0.25	SHORTMMM	-13	25,043
10-Feb-11	84.20	LONGBOS	4,210	29,253
18-Mar-11	8.95	SHORTMM	447	29,701
03-May-11	-28.10	LONGBOS	-1,405	28,296
04-May-11	-77.30	LONGBOS	-3,865	24,431
05-May-11	91.60	LONGBOS	4,580	29,011
18-May-11	7.50	LONGBOS	375	29,386
27-May-11	-3.00	LONGBM	-150	29,236

Gap Trading Patterns Combined

Here are the trade details for the gap trading united occurrences during 1st July 2009 till 31st October 2010 period.

Table: 29.2
Gap Trading Patterns Combined during Walk Forward Period

Date	*Gain/Loss*	*Pattern*	*Profit/Loss*	*Cumulative Profit*
08-Jul-09	101.94	IDNR4SHRT	5,097	5,097
13-Jul-09	9.33	TURSHRT	467	5,564
20-Jul-09	80.57	BMFLNG	4,029	9,592
28-Jul-09	31.56	FALTURTSHRT	1,578	11,170

(Contd . . .)

Automatic Rally — A technical rebound that occurs just after a selling climax. It is usually very short-lived but sometimes produces large moves.

Bar Chart — Shows the open, high, low and close of a market / stock.

Breakout — A decisive move through an area of resistance or support. Usually characterized by a wide spread day, and CLOSE of the day is typically in the direction of the breakout.

Bulge — A sudden expansion of price or volume; use 20 days as reference when classifying a bulge day.

Climax Buying — A situation characterized by the highest intensity of speculative demand occurring within an uptrend. Usually accompanied by a wide spread day and the highest volume registered within the uptrend. This situation occurs only after the up move has been in effect for some time and marks the approaching end of the ongoing UPTREND.

Climax Selling — A situation characterized by the highest intensity of speculative supply occurring within a downtrend. Usually accompanied by a wide spread day and the highest volume registered within the downtrend. This situation only occurs after the down move has been in effect for some time and marks the approaching end of the ongoing DOWNTREND.

Close — The last trade / price registered in the time period under consideration.

Congestion — A series of trading days with no clear move in either direction. Usually associated with NARROW RANGE days or non-trending days.

Consolidation — A phase where the price doesn't move up or down in any significant manner, typically accompanied by light volume.

Contraction — Market behaviour represented by a congestion or a resting period, whether short-term or long-term, which usually reaches its narrowest phase at the end of the period.

Contraction / Expansion — Market behaviour which suggests that the market is constantly changing from a period of movement to a period of rest — and back to a period of movement. This interchange between the phases of motion and rest, congestion and trend, or trading RANGE and BREAKOUT

Glossary

Some of the following terms are used throughout this book. Even if you are a more advanced trader, you might want to glance through this glossary to see how these terms are defined for the purposes of this book. Some additional terms (price patterns) are also covered here.

1 x 1 Angle — As per Gann, the primary angle moving one unit of price by one unit of time. One unit of time can be as small as five minutes and as large as a month or even a year. One unit of price should approximate fifty dollars and consist of one, two, four or eight minimum price changes (tics such as ¼ cent, .025, etc. . . .). This sometimes appears as a 45-degree slope, but not always. The 1 x 1 Angle is a constant and, therefore, slope can vary on various scaled charts.

2 BAR NR (2BNR) — The narrowest RANGE from high to low of any two-day period relative to any other two-day period in the previous twenty days.

3 BAR NR (3BNR) — The narrowest RANGE from high to low of any three-day period relative to any other three-day period in the previous twenty days.

4 BAR NR (4BNR) — The narrowest RANGE from high to low of any four-day period relative to any other four-day period in the previous thirty days.

8 BAR NR (8BNR) — The narrowest RANGE from high to low of any eight-day period, relative to any other eight-day period, in the previous forty days.

Accumulation — The establishment of an investment or speculative position by professional traders in anticipation of an advance in price.

Real-life Trading, 161
Recovery Factor, 164
Rose, Stu, 57

S&P CNX Nifty (*See also* Nifty), 31-33
S&P Nifty 50 Index, 55
Satyam Scandal, 55
Segal's Law, 169
Seykota, Edward Arthur, 50
Sharpe Ratio, 166, 167, 208, 225, 239
Sharpe, William F., 166
Short-term Price Patterns, 51
Short-term Trading, 96
SMA (Simple Moving Average), 110
Soros, George, 57
Speculators, 30
Standard & Poor's (S&P), 31
Stop Loss, 8, 175
Stop Orders, 40
Stretch ORB, 114
Stretch, 110, 114-115, 276
Support / Resistance Lines, 38

Tax Loss Selling, 188
Taylor Trading (Technique), 46
Taylor, George Douglas, 46
Technical Analysis, 50
Technical Indicator, 45-46, 187, 191
The Education of a Speculator, 57, 279
The Master Swing Trader, 189
The Taylor Trading Technique, 46
Time-Based Exits, 42
Top Range and Bottom Range, 88
Trader, 149, 158, 267, 279
Trading Commissions, 26
Trading Cycle, 31
Trading for a Living, 49
Trading Log, 178
Trading Rules, 149, 170
Trading System, 162-165, 168, 223
Trailing Exits, 42
Tri- and Penta-Section Patterns, 142
– Penta-Section Study after the Open is Down, 145
– Penta-Section Study after the Open is Up, 144
– Tri-Section Study, 143
Triple Tops, 38
Trout, Monroe, 57
Turtle Short, 225-227, 242
Turtle Strategy, 225
Turtle Trading System, 78
Types of Entry Orders, 6, 40

Volume, 45, 52, 119, 146, 268, 271, 273

Watts, Dickson G., 174
Wave Principle, 47
Wave, Kondratieff, 189
Wide Spread Day, *see* WS Day
Wide Spread Patterns, *see* WS Trading Patterns
Williams, Larry, 13, 76, 96, 172
Williams, Michelle Ingrid, 77
Win / Loss Ratio, 64
Wordlock, 97, 98
World Cup Championship of Futures Trading, 76

WS Day, 91, 134
WS Trading Patterns:
– WS Close-to-Close Pattern, 93
– WS Open-to-Close Pattern, 95
– WS4, 53, 97-102, 105-106, 278
– WS4 Close-to-Close Pattern, 100
– WS4 Open-to-Close Pattern, 105
– WS7 Close-to-Close Pattern, 103
– WS7, 53, 97-99, 102-103, 107-108, 234, 269, 278
– WS7 Open-to-Close Pattern, 107
Wyckoff, Richard Demille, 45

Zero Overnight Risk, 26

is a constant feature of the market, with one phase being directly responsible for the occurrence of the next.

Demand — The willingness of traders to buy the a security at a certain price. Assuming all other factors remain constant, the price of the security increases with its demand increases, and *vice versa* in the case of supply.

Distribution — The establishment of an investment or speculative position by professional traders in anticipation of a decline in the security price.

Downtrend — A series of LOWER LOWS and LOWER HIGHS.

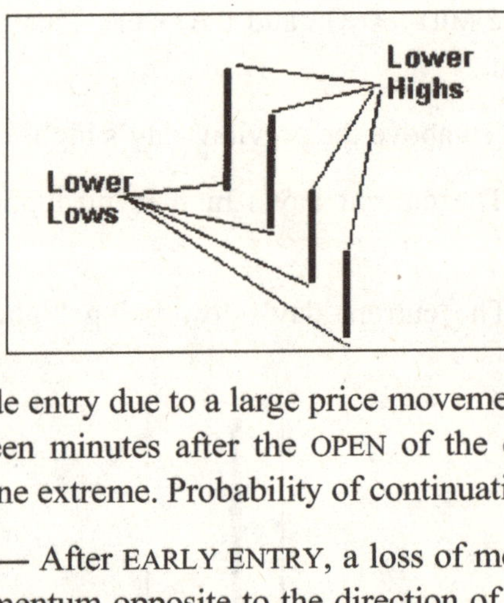

Early Entry — Trade entry due to a large price movement in one direction within the first fifteen minutes after the OPEN of the daily session. The open should act as one extreme. Probability of continuation is 90%.

Early Entry Failure — After EARLY ENTRY, a loss of momentum and subsequent shift in momentum opposite to the direction of the early entry resulting in a move back through the early established extreme.

Expansion — Market action that occurs at the conclusion of contraction and is characterized by wide spread days. Such action usually marks the beginning of a new trend.

Fade — A position taken opposite to the direction of the initial move off the open on a given day. This is usually considered when the initial move off the open is in the opposite direction of the prevailing trend and price pattern studies confirm the trend.

Gap — A break, i.e. gap, between successive prices of a security when it makes a sharp move up or down with no trading occurring in between the successive prices.

Gap Day — A day whose daily RANGE is completely above or below the previous day's range. When viewing intraday charts a GAP may appear on just a higher or lower open without exceeding the previous day's high or low.

Gap Down — An open below the previous day's low.

Gap Reversal — The low of the previous day is completely above the preceding day's action with the CLOSE reversing at least two previous closings; — and above MID-RANGE and the OPEN. This records a very strong change in sentiment.

Gap Up — An open above the previous day's high.

Higher High — The current day's high being higher than the previous day's high.

Higher Low — The current day's low being higher than the previous day's low.

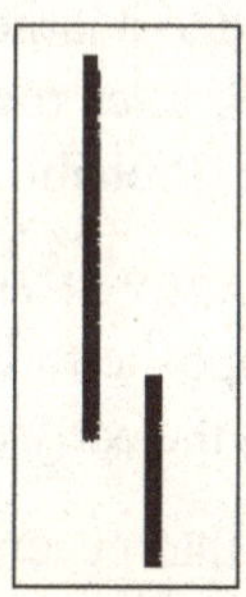

Hook Bear — A day when the open is below the previous day's low and the close is above the previous day's close, with a NARROW RANGE.

Hook Bull — A day when the open is above the previous day's high and the close is below the previous day's close, with a NARROW RANGE.

Hypodermics — A deliberately forced, rapid mark-up in price. The purpose of hypodermics is the stimulation of uninformed buying in order to facilitate distribution.